GREEN WOODWORKING:

A Hands-On Approach

Drew Langsner

Lark Books

Published in 1995 by Lark Books
50 College Street
Asheville, NC 28801
U.S.A.

© 1995, Drew Langsner

Production: Elaine Thompson

Previously published in slightly different format as *Green Woodworking*
by Rodale Press, Emmaus, PA, in 1987.

Library of Congress Cataloging-in-Publication Data
Langsner, Drews.
    Green woodworking : a hands-on approach / by Drew Langsner ;
photos and illustrations by the author. — 2nd ed.
        p.   cm. — (Country workshop handbook)
    Includes bibliographical references and index.
    ISBN 0-937274-82-8
    1. Woodwork—Amateurs' manuals.   2. Lumber—Drying—Amateurs'
manuals.   3. Lumbering—Amateurs' manuals.   I. Title.   II. Series.
TT185.L26   1995
674'.8—dc20   94-42309
                                                         CIP

10 9 8 7 6 5 4 3 2

Every effort has been made to ensure that all information in this book is
accurate. However, due to differing conditions, tools, and individual skills,
the publisher cannot be responsible for any injuries, losses, or other
damages which may result from the use of the information in this book.

ISBN 0-937274-82-8

For information about Country Workshops' hands-on courses and green
woodworking tools, contact Drew Langsner at 90 Mill Creek Road,
Marshall, North Carolina 28753. Phone: 704/656-2280.

Contents

◪.

ACKNOWLEDGEMENTS

While writing the original edition of this book, I benefited from the encouragement and help of many good friends. Woodworking adventures with students at Country Workshops have expanded my knowledge and provided valuable teaching experience. Jam sessions with other woodworkers, at home and while traveling, have also been fruitful.

Once again I would particularly like to thank John Alexander, Bill Coperthwaite, and Gregory Monahan. John, Bill, and Greg carefully reviewed each chapter and contributed many suggestions that were incorporated in the text. I also wish to thank my original editor at Rodale Press, Bill Hylton.

Photos by Drew Langsner and George Bell (pages 10, 81, 83, 84, 85, 86-left, 90, 99, 100, 103, 113, 114-right, 134, 135, 136, 137, and 138), Rick Mastelli (pages 4, 49-bottom), Tad Stamm (pages 26, 52, 65), D. E. Gilbertson and J. F. Richards, Jr.: *A Treasury of Norwegian Folk Art in America* (page 21-left), E. D. Andrews: *Shaker Furniture* (page 22), and H. Stewart: *Cedar* (pages 20, 77).

This book is dedicated to my first woodworking teacher, *Küfermeister* Ruedi Kohler.

Spoons and a bowl carved from freshly cut green wood

An Adventure In Woodworking

This book was originally published in 1987 titled *Green Woodworking*. This new, revised edition brings many details up to date, such as changes in my preferred types of sharpening equipment and the methods used in making tenons. These changes are the result of seven additional years in the workshop.

Although I am not a production craftsman, I do put in many full weeks each year teaching traditional woodworking at Country Workshops. (I also take orders for Windsor and ladderback chairs, in addition to making much of the furnishings and some tableware for our home.) While production work leads to perfecting specialized skills, I find that teaching always presents new challenges as different students come to our courses. As a teacher, I do not work in the generally isolated environment of a production workshop. To explain concepts and to achieve good, quick results, I am constantly innovating and trying new approaches. I'm also faced with questions (and mistakes) that I would probably not deal with in a production situation. In addition, I will gladly acknowledge that my students have often contributed ideas and information that is new and useful to me. The best teaching inevitably includes learning on the part of the instructor.

Throughout this book you will find many uses of two related (and invented) terms, these being "green woodworking" and "green woodworker." Green woodworking is a conceptual bit of nomenclature originally coined by my friend and colleague Baltimore chairmaker and joiner John Alexander. Green woodworking refers to a wide range of traditional woodworking methods that generally involve the craftsperson dealing directly with a log from a freshly felled tree.

A green woodworker often begins a task by *riving* stock using methods similar to splitting firewood. Historically this was done with certain types of wood because riving is fast and (depending on quality of the wood) potentially very economical in that there is little waste. Only a few, simple tools are required. Riving is much easier than rip sawing with hand tools. While some cross cut sawing is generally part of the work, riven stock frees one from dependence on a sawmill and all of the expensive, energy consuming technology that goes along with producing manufactured lumber.

For a green woodworker, riven stock is also often superior to the materials produced by more advanced technology. Riving divides wood fibers, whereas sawing inevitably severs the fibers. A piece of wood with no fiber "runout" along its length is much stronger than a board where fiber runout occurs willy-nilly along its length. Compared to kiln dried lumber, green riven stock is much easier to shape with hand tools. With a properly sharpened drawknife, freshly cut oak seems to shave like slicing butter. Green, rived stock also bends much easier and with far fewer failures than sawed lumber.

But you may be thinking that using green wood will lead to many woodworking disasters. A cabinet made out of (even partially) green wood will inevitably dry, shrink, and fall apart. True. Green woodworkers are well aware that wood changes shape. Most often we see the results of shrinkage as it dries out, but wood can expand also. In fact, we pay far more attention to wood movement than most other woodworkers. We rive, shape, and bend green wood whenever possible; working green wood is easier, more fun, and less likely to fail. But when it comes to assembly and many other tasks that woodworking involves, we pay great attention to the moisture content of wood and even the growth ring orientation of parts in relationship to one another.

This is a book about working green wood, starting with a living tree. I'll show you how to harvest wood from a log and even how to use bark and limbs. We'll hew wood with an axe or split it with wedges into sections called *billets*. We'll use saws, too, but mainly for crosscuts. Then we'll shape the pieces with hand tools. The end result will be objects that are strong, functional, and beautiful.

Your first greenwood projects will probably turn out nicely enough, but it takes practice and alert observation to become skilled with these crafts. After my first ten weeks of apprenticeship with a Swiss cooper, Ruedi Kohler, I could struggle through all the steps of making a simple wooden-hooped container on my own. But Ruedi chuckled to himself for a full day when I asked about making an oval milking bucket with sculpted staves. I've found that just learning the fine points of sharpening hand tools is an unending challenge. As you gain expertise, you'll discover that the subtle refinements of handwork are virtually unlimited.

Most green woodworking crafts and methods were developed before those of mechanization and mass marketing. However, throughout this book, I'll show how technology has also refined, clarified, and occasionally disregarded, some of the woodlore handed down through the generations.

The green woodworker gets to know a piece of wood intimately, because the traditional techniques are dependent on the nature of wood—fiber direction, texture, and relative hardness. When wood grain is ornery, you'll know it, because the work will be a struggle. Using the appropriate species and quality of wood results in a smooth partnership of material and woodworker.

In conventional woodworking, a premium is paid for the stability of kiln-dried lumber. Green-sawn lumber, particularly if one of the hardwoods, is notorious for twisting, bending, cupping, and checking during seasoning. But green woodworkers covet wet wood. It is much easier to work. With sharp tools, even hardwoods such as oak, maple, and hickory are easily worked. Good riving wood splits even more quickly and precisely when green. And green wood bends with a minimum of trouble.

Consider also the unique sight of freshly split or hewed wood, exposed to light and air for the first time. Like freshly picked sweet corn, this special quality can be appreciated only for a few moments, because light and oxidation change the wood immediately, even if a finish has been applied. (Of course, aged, finished, and well-used wood is beautiful too.) In addition, working with green wood involves other temporal experiences, of sound, smell, and touch, as body and tools collaborate to shape a piece of wood. These sensations are amplified because the workshop is an intimate, quiet place, in which power tools are used only for limited purposes, if at all. Through green woodworking, I feel a connection with worldwide craftspeople far back to unknown generations.

My Credentials

If memory serves correctly, my first glimpse of green woodworking as a process was an Eric Sloane drawing of a frontier craftsman sitting at a shaving horse, making something with a drawknife. At the time, I was building playground sculptures (later called "adventure playgrounds") with my friend Jay Beckwith. We were definitely modernists, using power tools, welders, steel, and concrete. I stared at that guy in the illustration. It was another world and one that attracted me.

I began to renew my previous interest in primitive and peasant cultures, with particular regard to their crafting and construction techniques. Vaguely inspired by books on folk architecture, we began to incorporate entire logs and rustic cabins made of bark slabs into our playgrounds.

This was also the time for another rite of passage, my transition from bachelorhood to marriage. And soon after, with a few thousand dollars in wedding gifts and savings, Louise and I bought one-way tickets across the Atlantic. My intention was to travel in rural Europe and Asia and gather information for a book on folk dwellings and the people who lived in them. We were inexperienced travelers, and many of our plans never materialized. But we did learn to accept and appreciate the unexpected, which included some wonderful surprises. I'll tell just one story—how I became an apprentice to a Swiss cooper, a maker of wooden alpine dairy containers.

We were traveling in a VW Beetle and had been tent camping in the Swiss Alps. I was particularly interested in the wonderful log and timber-frame farmhouse-barns, or *Bauernhaüser,* called chalets in English. But to our dismay, we weren't making much progress in getting to know Swiss farmers and their families. On top of that, the weather was depressing—rain every day—and we weren't enthusiastic about another night in the wet tent.

Driving along a secondary highway, we saw a young hitchhiker. Louise suggested that we pick him up on the chance that this fellow might direct us to a dry place to sleep for a night. We didn't know German, but Reas—the German short version of Andrew, which is also my name—spoke English. Reas said he was going to his parents' home in Bern, the Swiss capital, but that if we didn't mind hiking he knew of an Alpine barn where we could stay as long as we wished.

Following a map Reas had drawn for us, we parked at the end of a spur road, packed our rucksacks, and set out. It was early evening in June,

Two of Ruedi Kohler's milking buckets. The smaller one is for goats.

and yet it began to snow. The climb was steep, and we lost the trail several times before finding the cold, empty barn on a high ridge, well above any other habitations. There was one room for the cowherds, with a stone oven and straw strewn in one corner to sleep on. We started a small fire, ate a bit of dinner, and fell asleep.

In the morning we found a six-inch snowfall on the ground, a blue sky, and a beautiful vista. I explored the barn in detail, taking notes and photos and making drawings.

Later we hiked down to the nearest neighbor. This turned out to be an *Alpenhütte,* a special alpine barn where mountain cheese is made. The cheese-maker invited us inside. He was heating milk in a huge copper kettle suspended over an open fire. When the curd formed, he put it into a cheesecloth supported in a wooden hoop of about 16 inches in diameter. The cheese was pressed with stone weights and would be aged for a full year.

The cheesemaker's kitchen, with its walls and ceiling blackened by soot from the open fire, was a fantastic place. For me, the most wonderful things in the *Alpenhütte* were the handcrafted wooden vats and milking buckets. Using improvised "pidgin German," we asked where we could buy a milking bucket. The cheesemaker replied that his were over 100 years old but that there was an aging cooper across the valley who still made them.

The next day, we found Ruedi Kohler at work in his shop. He showed us his wares, including a milk-ing bucket exactly like what I had hoped to find. We bought it. But I didn't want to leave quite yet. Visiting this shop was like being in a dream. *Herr* Kohler was 71 years old but had the energy and enthusiasm of a boy. He did most of his work at a shaving horse, much like the one I had seen in the Eric Sloane drawing. On a wall hung a collection of drawknives, spokeshaves, reamers, augers, and other tools which I couldn't identify.

An inner voice told me that this was a rare opportunity to learn something special about wood-working. With the help of *Herr* Kohler's son-in-law, who spoke French, we asked about the possibility of my learning cooperage. Ruedi Kohler said that the craft was difficult to learn but that he would be willing to try teaching me. Louise and I stayed on that mountain for ten weeks.

I worked Monday through Saturday. On Sundays we visited another traditional cheesemaker, Armin Erb, who also made furniture that combined Swiss traditional forms with his own fantasy.

When we returned to the United States, we decided to locate in a rural area where we could farm and do woodworking. In 1974, we moved to a mountain farmstead in western North Carolina. We chose the area for its climate, water, and wood, and for the subsistence farming methods still practiced there by the older generation.

I continued to investigate traditional woodworking. Many of the older farmers were skilled woodsmen, but there was little traditional woodworking still being done in our community. Our neighbors, Peter and Polly Gott, were the major exception. The Gotts had been homesteading for years and had been exploring greenwood crafts ranging from white oak basketry to log cabin building. Through their generosity, we learned many details about traditional crafts that would have taken a great deal of time to discover on our own. Books were a help, too, including Eliot Wigginton's first edition of *Foxfire* (New York: Doubleday & Company, 1972), Eric Sloane's books on early American woodworking, and books on conventional woodworking, especially R. Bruce Hoadley's excellent *Understanding Wood* (Newtown, Conn.: Taunton Press, 1980). Among the best resources were several English books on traditional woodland crafts.

My first income-producing project was the making of wooden hayforks based on an old Mennonite pattern from Pennsylvania. I learned how to make them from a friend of a friend who was traveling through our area. After a few crude starters, I was making hayforks that were good enough to sell. I eventually made about 200 hayforks and would have continued if I hadn't started writing *Country Woodcraft* (Emmaus, Pa.: Rodale Press, 1978). In recent years, I've done small runs of ladder-back chairs, and I also make Windsors and do cooperage and carved bowls on order.

How to Get Started

Historically, green woodworking was learned through family tradition or an apprentice system. Today, an apprenticeship is generally impractical. It

A Windsor "sackback" armchair made by the author. Collection Robert and Sue Adams.

requires more time than most people have—even if you could find a master craftsperson willing to teach over an extended period. Books and workshop courses can take the place of an apprenticeship, presenting a great deal of material in a short time.

Personal field study can be inspiring and useful, especially at "living history" museums that emphasize the traditions of local folk cultures. The large, well-known museums, like Sturbridge Village and Colonial Williamsburg, are very impressive, but smaller, more personal museums are popping up all over the country. One warning: Some museums tend to romanticize the past.

You can learn a great deal by visiting working craftspeople. Since crafts-workers tend to be busy, you should write in advance. This allows them to refuse gracefully, whereas calling on the phone and asking to visit the same day can put a craftsperson in an uncomfortable position.

This book has been written to guide you by looking over your shoulder and taking your hands through each step of the projects. I don't believe in secrets, but I'm not a living encyclopedia, and a single volume can't contain everything about a subject. I have included a few areas of green woodworking where my own experience is limited. In such cases, I've been careful to credit my sources.

I've omitted commonly practiced hand woodworking skills, such as turning at a lathe, mortise-and-tenon joinery, and plane work. Many good books and magazine articles cover these subjects, and green wood techniques are basically the same as using sawn lumber. The main difference is that green wood is easier to work with than dry wood. But green wood is also somewhat weaker, causing unwanted vibration when thin spindles are turned on a lathe. And *differential shrinkage* (explained in chapter 3) causes green wood to distort as it dries; shaved green cylinders and turned bowls become oval, and special accommodations are needed for mortise-and-tenon joinery. Green wood is not suitable for building conventional cabinets or carcase furniture.

I also have not gone into detail on specialized crafts, such as basketry, log building, cooperage, and chair making. To pursue these crafts, refer to the books and periodicals listed in the bibliography.

Attending a week-long class, such as those we teach at Country Workshops, is often the best way to learn the fundamentals of a craft quite quickly.

Tools

Naturally, you'll need green woodworking tools. You may have a few already, such as a drawknife, an axe, wedges, or a splitting maul. You can make some of the tools yourself. Plans for making a froe and other tools are included throughout this book.

But unless you're a skilled toolmaker, you'll need to purchase a few specialty tools, such as a drawknife, a broad hatchet, and a spokeshave. My advice is to get the best tools that you can afford, picking them up as needed. A good hardware store may have a few of them, and several dependable mail-order companies specialize in selling hand tools. It's also possible to buy excellent used tools, but success here depends on where you live and your woodworking experience, bargaining expertise, and patience.

Warning: Woodworking is Dangerous

Serious accidents can happen when the human body, wood, and sharp tools get together. Ultimately, *you* are responsible for your safety. And when working with instructions, you run the added risk of misinterpreting them. Here are a few guidelines:

1. Do not use tools when you are fatigued or distracted. A study by *Fine Woodworking* magazine revealed that woodworkers are most accident-prone just after eating a filling meal.

2. Follow recommended safety precautions. Wear safety gear (such as eye and hearing protection) when using power saws, grinders, and impact tools (such as when striking steel wedges with a sledgehammer).

3. Chain saws are the most dangerous tools used by green woodworkers. It is especially important to read and follow safety instructions provided by the manufacturer.

Green woodworking often begins by splitting stock from a log. This red oak will be converted into ladder-back chair parts.

PART ONE

An Introduction to Green Woodworking

CHAPTER ONE

What is Green Woodworking?

I originally used the phrase "country woodcraft" to describe my way of working with wood. Louise and I were novice homesteaders, and most of my woodworking related to our rural lifestyle. And the book I was writing at the time was named *Country Woodcraft* (Emmaus, Pa.: Rodale Press, 1978).

One early reader of the book was John Alexander, a Baltimore chair maker who had just written *Make a Chair from a Tree*. (Originally published by The Taunton Press in 1978, a revised edition is now available published by The Astragal Press, Needham, NJ.) John pointed out that the term "country woodcraft" excludes someone like him, working in the basement of an inner-city row house, whereas in fact many crafts that are now considered "country" were also the work of village and even urban craftspeople. "Country woodcraft" also seemed to exclude contemporary evolution or invention. John suggested a substitute term, "green woodworking."

I soon discovered that green woodworking appeals to woodworkers of many backgrounds, age groups, and occupations. It's certainly no secret that city dwellers and suburbanites find handwork to be a satisfying complement to a way of life in which almost everything is manufactured and mass marketed. Green woodworking is also an excellent approach for teaching the use of hand tools to kids of all ages.

John's term crystallized for me one day as I was driving through the heart of West Virginia, en route to visit Rachel Nash Law, the white oak basket maker whom you'll meet later in this book. I was thinking about how to define green woodworking when I rounded a bend and saw the answer right there on the side of the road. Green woodworking, in its most basic form, is a split-rail "worm fence."

Everyone has seen a worm fence, if only in an illustration. They were made by homesteaders back when there was an abundance of easily split, decay-resistant trees like black locust, white oak, chestnut, redwood, cedar, and (this is true) even black walnut. Straight-grained logs were crosscut into lengths about 10 feet long, then split lengthwise into rails. The rails are stacked about 4 feet high, the ends of each stack crisscrossing with the ends of the next. Vertical posts were not required. The name "worm" describes the way these fences zigzag over the landscape.

Green woodworking is a method—actually a bundle of related techniques—of working wood and other material taken straight from a tree.

Like most craftspeople, green woodworkers have their special words, such as *riving, bolts,* and *differential shrinkage.* When they come up, I'll be sure to include a brief explanation.

Our fence maker went directly to the source for his material. The rails were split out, not sawed. Splitting, or *riving,* is the method of choice for dividing wood lengthwise, parallel to the long fibers. This happened to be the fastest and easiest way to do the job; and because the resulting surface follows the fibrous structure of the wood, the rails absorb less moisture and therefore are more resistant to decay.

Green woodworkers use many other methods to shape wood. Logs are hewed with axes or adzes. Curved adzes are used for hollowing large containers and for saddling Windsor chair seats. Knives and gouges of many shapes and sizes are used for roughing out and detail work. Rived wood can be shaped precisely and quickly with a drawknife and then finished with a finely set spokeshave. Bending is extensively used in many greenwood crafts. Bending green wood is probably easier and less technical than you think. Green woodworkers also use a variety of boring tools, including augers, reamers, and nowadays possibly a hand-held electric drill.

Saws are used mainly for cutting across wood fibers. For cutting logs and timbers, the two-man crosscut saw is one of the great inventions; it cuts quickly and easily if properly sharpened. There are many types of hand saws that come into use. In the woods I generally use a chain saw. And I have a bandsaw in the workshop.

Green woodworkers use not only the central trunk, but also tree parts that are usually chipped or neglected. Limbs can be worked—especially a crook or curved shape. Traditional wooden boat builders and timber framers prize the curved limbs of oaks growing in meadows. Naturally bent wood also finds its way into bowed chair backs and curved spoons. The natural bow economizes material, but more importantly, it's much stronger than a curved piece sawed from straight material. Sometimes the tough limb of a conifer can substitute for a true hardwood. An example is cooperage hooping shaved from pine limbs.

Saplings and *withes* (small shoots) have been lashed or woven by many traditional cultures to make dwellings, livestock enclosures, and containers of all sizes. European timber-frame buildings were often in-filled with *wattle and daub*, a framework of withes covered with plaster. Stiff brooms, called *besoms* in England, were made from straight, pliable twigs such as sweet birch. Besoms are still used in some European cities to sweep the public streets. Willow basketry is the most popular surviving craft that uses withes.

Green woodworkers use leatherlike inner-bark, called *bast*, for lashing, pliable weaving strips, and sheeting. Everyone is familiar with the birchbark canoes made by Indians of eastern North America. In Scandinavia, birch bark was traditionally used underneath sod roofing. Indians of the Pacific Northwest turned cedar bark into basketry, clothing, and rope. One of the most durable and attractive seating materials for ladder-back chairs is the inner bark of hickory. In chapter 3, I'll explain how to make a bark container.

Nowadays, roots don't have many woodcraft applications. Harvesting them is hard work, and imbedded grit is rough on edge tools. However, roots are incredibly tough, and root wood often has a very interesting figure. Black walnut roots have always been prized for making beautiful and stable gun stocks. A root maul is practically indestructible; I have a dogwood root maul that has seen over a decade of hard service. Small roots can be woven into baskets. Split spruce root was the favored traditional material for lashing birchbark canoes.

While we're considering materials, I'd like to make a few other observations directly related to the definition of green woodworking.

"Green" refers to the fact that the wood, bark, or root was split or shaped from its natural state, and not sawed out or commercially processed. Whenever possible, wood is rived and shaped green. The main advantage is that wet fibers are tender, pliable, and readily worked with hand tools. You'll be amazed at how easy it is to work green wood.

Ladder-back sidechair designed by Dave Sawyer, made by the author. Red oak with hickory bark seating. Author's collection

Materials are green when collected. But in some applications, green wood should be allowed to dry before use. If an axe head is fitted to a green handle, the handle will shrink and fall out when the wood dries. In cooperage, staves are split and roughly hewed when green, but a tight container requires that the wood be "bone dry" during final shaping and assembly. A similar, although more complex, situation occurs within the joints of wooden furniture. Thin strips of wet wood, such as basket weavers, will bend cold with few problems. But larger stuff, such as a Windsor chair rail, is less likely to fail during bending if the wood is steamed or boiled. You'll find out why in chapter 9.

The worm fence illustrates another characteristic of green woodworking. There was no attempt to

A fine white oak basket from southern Appalachia. (Collection of Louise Langsner)

disguise how the fence was made. It was simple, functional, and complemented the environment.

Although green woodworking is traditional, I don't necessarily use or teach "authentic" or historically correct methods. Historically, some crafts have been very conservative and slow to change; and visitors to my workshop often expect a purity that doesn't exist here. The real world of time restraints and monthly bills affects everyone. Like many craftspeople, I'm open to learning about new tools and techniques that save labor, improve quality, or make my work more competitive in the marketplace. You shouldn't be surprised to find a greenwood chair maker using a band saw to cut ladder-back rungs to length.

Characteristics of Greenwood Crafts

The designs of traditional greenwood crafts tend to be straightforward, functional, and ageless. A fine bowl, spoon, or basket may appear both old and yet modern, simultaneously. For example, a Windsor chair is at home in a contemporary setting as well as in a room of period furniture.

Due to the superior strength of rived materials, greenwood crafts can be low in weight without sacrificing structural integrity. This suited traditional cultures, in which household objects were made to be used for many years.

Often there are detail variations from one example of an item to another. Differences in grain pattern and wood quality mean that a craftsperson

using hand tools must always be alert, adapting techniques to each piece of wood. Because crafts are made one at a time or in small batches, it's easy to make modifications for a particular user. Some craftspeople produce plain and fancy versions of the same item; a special bowl or spoon may be made for a particular occasion.

Most greenwood crafts utilize straightforward, basic construction. Why a joint works, or how it's done, is not always obvious, but joinery is seldom hidden. Understanding wood movement, the result of constant changes in fiber moisture content, is critical to long-lasting construction.

Many traditional crafts withered with the development of production woodworking and commercial marketing. There have been few survivors. Some crafts, like frame and panel furniture, were adapted to machine production. Among the surviving greenwood crafts, basket making is the most visible, probably because it is suited as a home craft, often carried on in isolated locations with low overhead. Although baskets are no longer a necessity, they appear to fill that certain need people have for things handmade. Some other greenwood crafts, such as chair making, log building, and timber framing, almost died, but not quite. We still have some old-time country basket makers, but contemporary chair makers, log builders, and timber framers tend to be newcomers, often from urban backgrounds.

Chairs

The common post-and-rung chair, known also as a ladder-back or slat-back, is a perfect example of an ongoing greenwood craft. The basic design was readily adapted to mass production, but factory-made ladder-backs use sawed stock, and little attention is paid to details such as moisture contents of the components during assembly. The result is generally a clunky chair, short on comfort, grace, and durability.

Godfrey Beaton, a British historian of handcrafts, learned how to make ladder-backs with rived wood and hand tools, and he describes his respect for their simple design in an article, "Thinking About Chairs," in the May/June 1978 issue of a British periodical, *Crafts.*

> A ladder-back chair with a rush seat is a chair reduced to its essentials. It is, quite literally, a stick chair, analogous to a stick man such as a child might draw. It has no superfluous parts, and no excess of materials. Structures of this kind are close to being in what the engineer describes as their "minimum condition." To a

remarkable degree this traditional product embodies a design principle associated with the Bauhaus: that of obtaining the maximum effect from a minimum of material.

Using green woodworking techniques, an entire chair can be made from a small hickory, white oak, or ash log. Red oak can also be used for the frame, although it doesn't provide a seating material. Many ladder-backs are, in fact, made from a combination of different woods.

Until not long ago, there were a few old-timers in southern Appalachia who still made ladder-backs the old way. In the original edition of *Foxfire* (New York: Doubleday & Company, 1972), Lon Reid describes to a group of student reporters from Rabun Gap High School how he makes a chair. It's fascinating to learn that Lon's techniques were actually simpler than those used by his father. Two examples: His father used a "hand turned lathe (possibly a spring pole?) to round his posts and rungs, and he (Lon) uses a shaving horse instead." We also learn that the father bent his back posts by boiling them in water, whereas Lon's chairs were straight backs, or they depended on a natural crook in the split wood.

Baskets

Of all greenwood crafts, basketry has been the great survivor. Ash splint basketry, made by the Shakers and other basket makers, was once common throughout the Northeast. But ash basketry almost died out, probably because of the amount of work required in preparing splints and because the baskets were made in a region that early on was industrialized. The popularity of Shaker crafts is largely responsible for the current revival of interest in ash splint basketry.

Willow basketry is produced and marketed internationally. In central Europe, hazel withes are used by basket makers for stout hauling baskets required by Alpine farmers. A strong point in favor of hazel and willow is that you can easily grow the trees yourself. I'll discuss growing your own materials (called *coppicing*) in chapter 3.

White oak baskets have been made mostly in the southeastern United States. White oak baskets tend to be functional, handsome, and sturdy. Typically, they have a square or round bottom composed of ribs that bend up at the edges to form sides. Rims and handles are lashed in place after the weaving is completed. Melon-shaped baskets are made by starting with a frame consisting of a horizontal rim and a vertical handle loop, secured in place with lashing. Rodlike ribs radiate from the lashing. The form can be bulbous or rectangular, with countless variations.

Rived Crafts

Minimal finish work: Fence posts and rails, sheep and garden hurdles

Rived and joined: Chests, small tables, stools

Rived and lashed: Hoops, kerf-bent boxes, round and oval boxes, sieves

Rived and shaved: Basket hoops, cooperage, hayforks and rakes, ladder-back chairs, scythe snaths, shingles, snowshoes, splint baskets, tool handles, wagon spokes, Windsor spindles

Rived and turned: Many ladder-back chairs, spinning wheels, stretchers, Windsor legs

Log Reduction

Axe and adze: Bee gums; dugout canoes; log containers; shafts (wagons, mills); sled runners (often bent); timbers (log buildings, railroad ties, timber framing); treen-ware (bowls, trenchers, troughs)

Carving: Hardware (handles, hinges, hooks, latches, etc.); miscellaneous (carvings, decoys, pipes, etc.); utensils (scoops, spoons, etc.)

Miscellaneous: Clog shoes, pipes (water), Swiss alp horns

Turned: Bowls, chair parts, lidded containers

Special Materials

Bark: Basketry, canoe skins, lashed containers, rope, seating, sod roof underlay

Roots: Basketry; lashing (canoes, containers, snowshoes, etc.); mauls; pipes (smoking)

Withes: Besoms; enclosures (livestock); hurdles; rod basketry; timber-frame in-fill

Limbs: Boat braces, spoons, clothes hooks, twig furniture

Greenwood Architecture

In the building crafts, two vernacular forms of green woodworking have been revived in recent years—log building and timber framing.

Most Americans associate log work with the frontier cabin, a very basic structure that usually was quickly and cheaply built by the owner. But

A willow basket made in England by David Drew. (Collection of John and Joyce Alexander)

the log building tradition in the Old World, particularly Scandinavia and Alpine and eastern Europe, was a highly developed craft, often the work of specialists.

In central Europe, a single massive timber-frame structure often served all of the shelter needs of a farm. Timber framing, using milled materials, is still commonly used for houses and barns in the Swiss Alps.

Most contemporary log and timber-frame builders now order timbers cut to dimensions from sawmills. Instead of using a traditional in-fill of masonry or plaster, builders often surround frames with energy-efficient stress skin panels. The green woodworking traditions in which these renewed building trades are rooted remain a source of inspiration.

A Green Woodworker's Shop

Often traditional craftspeople worked seated on a sturdy low bench, using their lap and hands for holding wood and working the tools. Many worked outdoors, in a shed, or in front of the family hearth. Basketry is often done sitting on the floor.

The woodworkers whom you'll meet in Part Three work in a variety of settings. A shop can be a shed, a back room at home, or the great outdoors. Since almost all green woodworking equipment and tools are portable, it's relatively easy to change locations with the seasons.

For an indoor shop, 150 to 250 square feet is adequate. Until recently, my shop was 10 by 16 feet, just large enough for a workbench, shaving horse, and lathe.

The most prominent piece of equipment in my shop is the shaving horse, a low bench that you straddle, with a foot-operated swinging clamp. Shaving horses are mostly used for drawknife and spokeshave work. The foot-operated clamp is quicker than a vise, and a small ledge called a "bridge" supports the material being worked on. Another common holding device is a *brake*, used to hold material while it's being split. Most green woodworkers also use a standard workbench with a conventional wood vise.

Green woodworkers don't have to deal with many unhealthful shop problems that threaten other woodworkers. The waste generated by hewing, shaving, and lathe-work makes great kindling. Very little dust from sawing and sanding floats around the shop. There's also no need for toxic materials such as highly volatile solvents or synthetic finishes. And it's quiet!

One real safety hazard is the chain saw, although new ones are considerably safer than those of a few years ago. Band saws, axes, and carving tools can inflict serious injuries, but the potential for danger is less than that of most power machinery. Ear protectors, a dust mask, and safety glasses should be used when called for. Of course, it's important to be careful using any sharp edge tools.

Why Bother?

Green woodworking takes time. And time figures in the "bottom line" of production crafts. If this weren't true, the list of surviving greenwood crafts would be longer. So maybe you're asking, why bother?

When I was making white oak hayforks, I sometimes wondered why they were so popular. I tested my forks against the mass-produced hardware store variety in various circumstances—gathering leaves, turning compost, pitching hay. The handmade forks were inferior. Of course I knew that very few of my forks would ever be put to use in a garden. They were usually bought for display in a den or above a hearth. This disturbed me. I enjoyed making every fork. They were beautiful and appeared functional. But on the job, my hayforks were outperformed by ones that cost half as much.

I talked this over with Daniel O'Hagan, a friend who has also made hayforks. Daniel's reply was philosophical. He said that people have a deep longing for things handmade and for the lifestyle that handmade things represent. In this age of speed and mass production we've almost lost our ability to work with our own hands, as well as in the company of our families and neighbors. Daniel believes that the handmade hayfork is a symbol of an endangered way of life that is still attractive. The hayfork on the den wall serves a function similar to a picture of a thatched cottage in its pastoral setting.

Green woodworking demands a close relationship between woodworker and basic, uncomplicated tools. There is also the challenge of working in harmony with natural properties of a particular wood. You learn by species and sample. You work with wood fiber, gravity, and ever-present fluctuations of moisture content.

The result is the satisfaction of knowing that you've made something yourself, with your own hands and wits. There is a definite contrast to the experience of pushing manufactured lumber through machines that do the actual work.

And sometimes green woodworking is simply better. I'm thinking about the strength and beauty of a green woodworker's chair or a pair of handmade snowshoes, both demonstrably stronger, lighter, and more durable than the factory-made item.

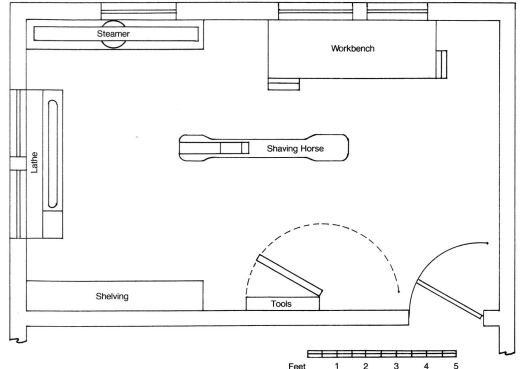

The floor plan of my old workshop, located upstairs in our log house. The shop is 10 feet wide and 16 feet long. I have an overhead shelf above the steamer and the workbench.

CHAPTER TWO

A Cultural Perspective

During the years that I've sat at a shaving horse, I've reflected at odd moments on the role of crafts and technology within various cultures. The subject is sweeping—really beyond the scope of this text. A thorough treatment—which could become a fascinating book—would require an interdisciplinary study including tool making, metallurgy, economics, social systems, etc. This chapter consists of my personal collection of cultural "snapshots," which, as a group, present a generalized perspective of green woodworking.

Nomadic and Hunter-Gatherer Woodworkers

A few examples of nomads and hunter-gatherers who traditionally worked with wood include Scandinavian Lapps, American Indians of the Pacific Northwest coast and the northeast, and natives of Siberia. Because nomads were often on the move, tools and other possessions were generally kept to a minimum. In contrast, village dwellers sometimes acquired many possessions and made large, substantial dwellings. The Indian tribes of the Pacific Northwest valued material wealth, with an unusual twist: the *potlatch* was a ritual display of personal wealth where treasures were given away or sometimes destroyed.

Among northern American Indian cultures, woodworking was highly developed before the introduction of metal tools from Europe. In the Vancouver, Washington, area, excavations have unearthed woodworking tools which were used between 5,000 and 8,000 years ago. Woodworking tools were made from stone, bone, horn, shells, and wood. Common tools included knives, axes, adzes, scrapers, and awls. Controlled burning was used extensively for felling, hollowing, and cutting across logs. Pacific Northwest coast Indians made extensive use of wedges to split planks as large as 4 by 40 feet from giant cedar trees. The same coastal woodworkers were using tools with steel blades at least 500 years ago. Where their metal came from is not known. One source could have been metal attached to driftwood found on the beaches; another possibility is trade across the Aleutian Islands.

Among nomadic and tribal people, woodworking was often done while sitting on the ground. Wood-holding devices were not generally used. Very exacting work and decorative surface carving were common. Woodworking was often combined with other materials, such as bone, hide, and shells. Nomads tended to make and prefer round rather than square shapes. Examples of nomadic crafts using wood include their highly developed means of transportation—kayaks, canoes, sleds, snowshoes. Temporary and transportable dwellings were also usually round. Cylindrical containers (made from bark and wood) were common. In contrast, the village-based hunter-gatherers of the Pacific coast typically built rectilinear dwellings and containers.

Peasant Woodworking Traditions

The woodcraft of peasant cultures probably represents our general notion of traditional green woodworking. The lifestyle of peasants combines subsistence agriculture with a variety of craft skills. Peasant economies are usually based on local needs, trading, and minimal involvement with an official economy.

Peasant woodworkers produced a wide variety of functional crafts. Basketry, carved wooden utensils, and bowls were common household crafts, usually made during winter months when there was slack in farm work. Agricultural implements, such as sleds and harrows, were often made on the side by a local farmer. A homemade wooden plow might require a steel point or other hardware bartered from a local part-time blacksmith.

More specialized peasant crafts included chair making (post-and-rung), cooperage, and making hooped containers (sieves and boxes). These crafts required some special training and were often winter work for farmers. My coopering mentor, Ruedi Kohler, apprenticed as a young man during two successive winters. Until he "retired," Ruedi was a hired Alpine cheesemaker and cowherd most of the year. Cooperage kept him busy with indoor work during the cold Swiss winters.

In some peasant cultures there were also a few full-time specialized craftspeople. Making and repairing carts and wagons required several highly developed skills—there was often a division of labor between woodworkers and blacksmiths. George Sturt's 1923 classic, *The Wheelwright's Shop* (Cambridge: Cambridge University Press, 1923, 1974), is a rare firsthand account of the skills and dedication of the craftspeople who worked in his family's cart and wagon shop.

The wooden folk houses of preindustrial Europe include many exemplary examples of the axeman's art. In wooded, coniferous Scandinavia and the mountainous regions of Europe, axe-hewed log structures were common. Straight, comparatively light conifers are suited to stacking up log walls with crossed, notched corners. Barns and outbuildings could be owner-built, but the best dwellings were generally made by professional carpenters. In areas of deciduous forests—much of England and western Europe—timber framing developed. Heavy, often curved hardwoods were more suitable for making a joined frame, in-filled with masonry. Large log and timber-frame structures were expensive, representing an investment that would pay dividends to several generations into the future.

In peasant cultures, craft skills were transmitted through oral tradition. Craft knowledge is based on what works. Objective tests, or research, are usually unknown. Traditional guidelines can be contradictory from one community to another. A common example of differing "knowledge" are the different rules of when to cut timber by astrological signs and moon phases.

Woodworking and Industrial Culture

Early industrialization was marked by major developments that changed the role of crafts. For various reasons, often not of choice, many peasants left subsistence crafts and agriculture to work full time in cottage industries, factories, and for wealthy landowners. The need for cash was emphasized—to pay taxes and to purchase commercial goods, food, and services.

During the early industrial era, crafts tended to become more specialized. Some specialization probably occurred naturally, but entrepreneurs also had a hand in much of what happened. Crafts such as willow basketry were divided into separate trades,

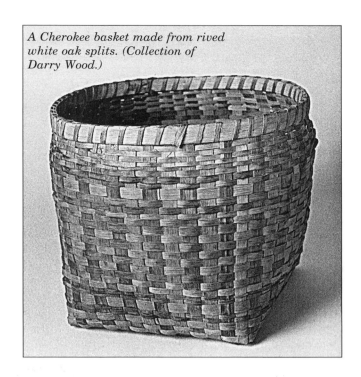

A Cherokee basket made from rived white oak splits. (Collection of Darry Wood.)

such as production of materials (growing and harvesting), processing materials, and the actual weaving (often a cottage industry done on a piecework basis). Finished baskets were marketed by traders with access to distant markets.

The production of Windsor chairs in Great Britain was possibly the earliest example of a production craft that used interchangeable components produced by specialized trades. The origin of the Windsor style is not clearly established, but we know that Windsors were fashionable in the early 1700s. The English and Colonial aristocracy often chose to sit in Windsors when their portraits were painted. By the early 1800s, Windsors were produced and marketed by the thousands. Setting the pattern of commercial development, famous Windsor "chair-makers" were actually businessmen who developed production methods and sold chairs, not the anonymous craftspeople who made them.

Windsor production traditionally required the work of at least three production specialists. Turners produced the legs, stretchers, and spindles. Benchmen sawed and adzed the solid plank seats. Then framers put the chairs together. In larger shops, there was more specialization—such as benders, finishers, and sometimes caners.

Windsor turnings were generally done on a piecework basis by independent craftsmen, known as *bodgers*, who set up shop in the woods. This

Cedar dugout canoe made by Douglas Granum

custom lasted in England until the mid-1900s. J. Geraint Jenkins, one of my favorite authors writing about traditional country crafts, personally knew several bodgers. In *Traditional Country Craftsmen* (London: Routledge and Kegan Paul, 1965), Jenkins described this scene:

> The last of the Chiltern chair bodgers was a short, slim middle-aged man who spoke with the musical "burr" of Buckinghamshire country folk. His father, grandfather and countless generations before him had obtained a living from chair bodging in the solitude of the beech glades. To reach his workshop in Hampden Wood, some six miles from High Wycombe, one passed through a rolling countryside of gentle grassy downland and smooth rounded curves that Huxley thought so suggestive of "mutton and pleasantness."...Soon, one left the road for the thick glades of Buckinghamshire weed (beech), so thick that the rays of the sun failed to penetrate it completely. Here and there young saplings sprouted while everywhere tree stumps marked the progress of some bygone bodger or woodman. Quite suddenly there was a gap in the trees and there in a clearing was the bodger's simple hut, surrounded by felled logs and hedgehog-like groups of drying chair legs and stretchers.

Thanks to the Shakers

During the period of industrialization, the Society of Shakers organized communities with economies based on agriculture and handwork. Except for their brown ash baskets, most Shaker crafts are not examples of green woodworking. Shaker production chairs and oval boxes were made from sawmilled stock. The bottoms of ladder-back chairs were woven with cotton tape, not rush or a locally gathered material. But Shaker designs (and craftsmanship) provided a contrast to the major trends of their time and remain as an inspiration, especially to green woodworkers.

Shaker products emphasized "regularity, harmony, and order." Shaker crafts are known for excellence of quality and integrity of design and construction. The Shakers were against fanciness of any kind, seeing embellishment as "a snare of the devil." They made use of machinery and were not against new inventions. A Shaker-designed duplicating lathe could turn a chair rung in 20 seconds and a post in less than one minute. Other innovations made work easier and safer. Shaker industries represented a distinct contrast with typical commercial factories of "the world," where safety in the work place was a minor consideration.

The Shakers were hard-working people, but their industries, particularly during their peak period (1790 through 1864), were not organized to

A coopered ale pitcher from Norway made in the early 1800s

Bow-back Windsor by Dave Sawyer

compete with capitalism. For instance, the Shakers emphasized the desirability of personal competency in a diversity of skills, aside from having a specialty. Here is an excerpt from the journal of a Shaker artisan, Henry DeWitt, which was reproduced in *Shaker Furniture*, by Edward Demming Andrews (New York: Dover Publications, Inc., 1964):

Dec. 1827 Levi & I began to make a lot of great spinning wheels.

Fri. 21 I made a couple of drawers to put under the vice bench.

Mond. 24 We began to make a small case of drawers with a cupboard at the top of it.

Tues. 25 This day we celebrate in memory of our blessed Lord and Saviour.

Sat. 29 We finished our case of drawers all but staining.

Jan. 1828 Tues. Levi & I began to mend old baskets & chairs.

Sat. 12 Mended 18 baskets & 3 chairs.

Tues. 15 I made a couple of books

Fri. 18 I mended 24 chair bottoms

Mond. 21 I fixed a saw place in a bow & cut new teeth & filed it.

Jan. 31 "My work is so often changed; it is hard to give a true statement of it."

Sometimes a fixing spinning wheels,
At other times to work at reels—
If I should mention all I do,
My time and paper would be few.

Feb 1828 Fri. I cut a walnut tree for basket bails & rims

4 turned 52 reel legs

5 I polished & straightened spindles.

10 I turned about 40 wheels for clock reels.

12 I worked sawing out the cogs to the reel wheels.

The simplicity and honesty of Shaker furniture has inspired many contemporary green woodworkers.

More Recent Developments

The Swiss Alpine coopering that Ruedi Kohler learned in 1920 is known in English as white cooperage. The traditional mountain cooper supplied a variety of specialized containers—tubs, milking buckets, butter churns—used by local, family dairy farmers. This type of coopering could be highly refined. For instance, wooden hooping was retained, and certain containers required special carved handles or sculpted staves.

In the remote Alps the way of life changed slowly; there was definitely a strong measure of pride in a culture that had thrived under severe climatic and geographic conditions. But the developments of the 20th century gradually challenged Alpine economics. Farm sons who traditionally stayed on the land moved to villages and the growing cities. In response to the need for labor, special machinery was developed. New sanitary regulations restricted the use of the old wooden coopered containers to the few surviving mountain herders who produced cheese. Only a few coopers were required to provide new containers and do repairs. There

were no new apprentices since there was no future in the craft. During World War II, rationing of metal provided temporary work for coopers. Then, the postwar plastics industry almost killed the craft.

When I met Ruedi Kohler in 1972, his situation was changing once again. The Swiss were becoming saturated with the products and pace of mass culture. People began to remember and appreciate the special qualities of things made by hand. This led to a revival of interest in the old ways which were generally harder than contemporary existence but often free of the constant stresses of modern life. Once again, customers were coming to Herr Kohler's workshop, keeping the retired farmer and cooper busy. By this time, few herders were left who needed replacement cooperage; the *Kufermeister's* main business was with city folk who wanted family heirlooms repaired or new coopered containers—cooperage which would never contain milk or cream, but be prominently displayed in neat Swiss homes and taverns.

Preserving Craft Skills

Ruedi Kohler's career has spanned most of the twentieth century, linking the peasant tradition with the present revival of interest in handcrafts. The Swiss are aware that Alpine cooperage played a vital role in local culture and that mastery of this complex craft may be lost by future generations.

In Japan, highly skilled master artisans are honored by the government as "living treasures." As I write, there are still a few unofficial living treasures here in North America. These folk-crafters are often hard to locate, because they tend to survive in remote areas where personal make-do is often a way of life. As I've said, among the green woodworking crafts, basketry has survived best. In the North, there are still a few Indians making snowshoes the old way. I recently learned about two families in Arkansas who have been making greenwood ladder-back chairs for generations.

Researchers are now recording how various crafts were done "the old way." Eliot Wigginton's Foxfire Project links young people of southern Appalachia with the traditions of their heritage. Henri Vaillancourt, well known for his birchbark canoes, has established the Trust for Native American Cultures and Crafts. The Trust has made videotapes of Native Americans making snowshoes, building an Algonquian birchbark canoe, and tanning leather. The Yurt Foundation (located in Buck's Harbor, Maine) has also done field research of native crafts.

Recording these skills is a slow process. It begins with developing a personal relationship with people who may meet few outsiders. Cameras and tape recorders can make them uncomfortable. Even when a folk-crafter is willing to share skills, the research may go slowly because these methods have never before been presented to a stranger. Another problem is that legitimate researchers sometimes follow the trail of entrepreneurs who took financial advantage of craftspeople.

Green Woodworking Today

Most green woodworkers that I know approach their craft somewhat differently than the old-timers did. Today there is a receptiveness to new methods, materials, and tools—including a slow but worthwhile trickle down from mainstream wood technology research. We now know more about bending wood and why a well-made ladder-back chair holds together.

I made this high chair for my daughter, Naomi.

From my perspective, the future of green woodworking looks promising. Customers are learning to appreciate genuine crafts. No one would buy a handmade Windsor chair that copies the ones sold by Sears; and no factory—not even the best—can compete with those made by my friend Dave Sawyer, whom you'll meet in Part Three. A handcrafted ladder-back chair may sell for ten times the price of one at a discount store; but when you buy the real thing, you have something of beauty and comfort that will last for generations of daily use. Also, only an individual craftsperson or a very small shop can build a chair to meet a particular customer's requirements.

Possibly for the first time ever, baskets are selling for prices that can support a modest livelihood. Skilled basket makers working in white oak and ash are now selling all the baskets they can make. This is particularly impressive since the international basket market includes extremely cheap basketry from Third World countries. Customers are willing to pay for baskets crafted with indigenous materials in the local tradition.

I was never able to keep up with orders for white oak hayforks. It may seem that making dozens of hayforks would be boring and repetitious. But because each piece of wood was different and I was working with hand tools only, each fork was a challenge.

Finally, I should point out that contemporary green woodworking is not restricted to traditionalism but is evolving. Several chair makers have developed the theme of the traditional ladder-back. For example, John Alexander's refinement of the common ladder-back involves research on why a wet/dry joint holds together. Dave Sawyer's design for a firewood tote, which is the bending project in chapter 9, is an example of an excellent new design.

Of all green woodworkers, perhaps basket makers have been the most prone to experiment. Rachel Nash Law, whose work is shown in Part Three, has been developing her own variations of traditional white oak basketry. Other basket makers are using their craft as an art medium, with less interest in function and tradition. Personally, I prefer baskets that are meant for use. But this doesn't mean that the techniques of green woodworking should remain the property of traditionalists. Please feel free to use the information from this book in any direction that you care to take it.

During the first day of a ladder-back chairmaking course at Country Workshops, students rive posts and rungs from a clear, straight-grain oak log.

Boring rung mortises for a ladder-back

PART TWO

Working Green Wood

Limbs from a gnarly old apple tree make excellent spoon wood.

CHAPTER THREE

Materials

Getting wood, bark, or a specially curved limb is an integral part of green woodworking. It's an adventure, generally an enjoyable one. Green woodworkers don't purchase standard materials from a lumber dealer. Instead, they search woodlands and field edges for materials in a ritual that is as old as mankind's involvement with making things.

While materials for green woodworking are a renewable resource, they're not unlimited in supply. In one year I cut all the premium white oaks from our hardwood forest to make hayforks. These were trees about 80 years old, and there were about eight of them.

We do have a number of small white oaks in our woods the right size for basket making, but none is good enough to make fine splits.

I also believe that developing a conscientious responsibility for land stewardship is an important consideration in collecting materials. It's important to leave high quality seed trees throughout an area. Careless logging can also cause serious erosion and stream sedimentation.

The challenge of working wood species with differing characteristics is one of the nice things about green woodworking. But when materials are mediocre, or worse, the amount of time consumed is seldom worth the effort, except as a learning experience. The best materials are often difficult to locate, so we may be required to use wood that leaves a little to be desired. One traditional solution, called *coppicing*, is to plant and maintain groves of a single species for a specific craft use.

Which Wood for What?

Each greenwood craft has its own requirements, often combining several wood characteristics. Occasionally, only one kind of wood is suitable for a particular craft, but usually several species are suitable, each with slightly different characteristics. Individual woodworkers often have different favorites for the same craft. Your location and local availability will make the difference. If you can't get the material that I suggest for a project, try what's available. Refer to the tables in this chapter.

Experiment.

Green woodworkers often use straight-grained hardwood, such as white oak, hickory, and ash. This is not to say that I don't appreciate figured woods like hard curly maple or wild cherry. Both are wonderful woods and I do use them, but usually in small amounts for special uses, such as knife handles or wooden hardware. Figured wood won't split predictably, if at all. It's difficult to shape and impossible to bend.

Whenever possible, I use freshly cut wood or wood stored to maintain moisture content and to discourage decay. I'll explain how to store wood later in this chapter. For rived woodcrafts, such as chair making and basketry, choose a wood with coarse, long fibers that splits easily and predictably. Short-grained wood is preferable for carving or hewing, techniques that require working across the fiber and often with fine detailing. Other desirable characteristics may include pliability, toughness, lack of taste, and decay resistance.

Tree species are divided into two groups, both of which contain a wide range of characteristics that affect woodworking. *Deciduous* trees, generally called "hardwoods," have broad leaves which are usually shed after a year's growth. *Coniferous* trees, the "softwoods," have needlelike leaves that are dropped by rotation—new needles develop before the old needles fall off. The conifers are sometimes called "evergreens."

But these terms are misleading; nature has provided plentiful exceptions to the general characteristics of each group. There are, for instance, deciduous trees that retain leaves around the year, including holly, eucalyptus, and the shrublike rhododendron. In tropical zones, most broadleafed trees keep leaves around the year. Citrus trees are a well-known example. And for further confusion, the larch is a conifer that loses its needles each winter.

Not all deciduous "hardwood" trees have hard wood. Linden, poplar, and alder are as soft as most conifers. Among the conifers, eastern red cedar and southern yellow pine are harder than some hardwoods.

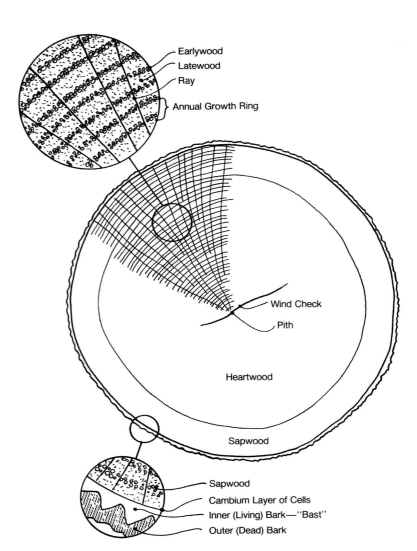

Earlywood
Latewood
Ray
Annual Growth Ring

Wind Check
Pith

Heartwood

Sapwood

Sapwood
Cambium Layer of Cells
Inner (Living) Bark—"Bast"
Outer (Dead) Bark

Cross section of a ring-porous hardwood. The prominent rays are typical of the oaks. The wind check is a minor crack found in many logs.

Structurally, wood cells consist of hollow fibers, not unlike a bundle of straws. The cell walls are almost entirely made of cellulose, a type of carbohydrate. When you work wood, it's often much easier to divide fibers lengthwise than to cut across them. When you split wood, the force is perpendicular to the lengthwise axis; the fibers separate easily.

Hardwoods contain two types of large, sap-conducting cells, *rays* and *pores* (or *vessels*), and are sometimes called *porous* woods. Softwoods are referred to as *nonporous*. These terms refer to cell type, not to actual porosity.

Ray cells are arranged in wide, flat flakes that radiate out from the center of the tree, crossing the growth rings. Rays are usually prominent in some hardwoods, particularly oak, locust, hackberry, beech, sycamore, and cherry.

Hardwoods are divided into three porosity types. *Ring-porous* hardwoods are distinguished by comparatively large earlywood (spring growth) pores and much smaller latewood pores. Examples include oak, ash, hickory, osage orange, catalpa, mulberry, and elm. For a chairmaker who rives and shaves posts and rungs, these woods are excellent materials because they split easily and predictably at the plane where the large-pored cells and the small-pored cells meet. In *diffuse-porous* hardwoods, earlywood and latewood have pores of approximately the same size. These hardwoods include cherry, maple, beech, birch, dogwood, and sycamore. In between the well-defined extremes are the *semiring-porous* hardwoods, such as black walnut, butternut, and black locust. The pore structure of these woods can vary considerably from specimen to specimen. Some resemble diffuse-porous

This split log shows how branches (and knots) originate at the pith. Note the distorted grain surrounding the knot.

woods, but others resemble ring-porous species.

The ray cells and the prominent earlywood vessels of the ring-porous hardwoods form distinct planes of weakness. This is an advantage to the green woodworker, because these woods rive and shave easily. An exception is elm, which is almost impossible to split and difficult to shave. All of the ring-porous hardwoods bend well, including elm.

All wood is *hygroscopic*, a fancy word meaning that the fibers continuously absorb and lose moisture according to environmental conditions. In *The New Science of Strong Materials* (New York: Walker and Company, 1968), author J. E. Gordon coined the term "swellulose" to describe the effect of water on cellulose. Water can literally be squeezed from green wood. Try it, using a clamp or vise. When you imagine a bundle of fibers absorbing moisture, you can appreciate that wood swells in thickness, not in length. Lengthwise movement is minimal, usually about one-tenth of 1 percent, while fibers can swell or shrink in width as much as 12 percent. Moisture also affects strength. Thoroughly wet wood may have just one-third the strength of the same wood when dry.

Wood moisture content (m.c.) is stated in terms of a percentage that compares the weight of a particular sample to that same piece after drying in a kiln. For example, a wood with 75 percent m.c. weighs 75 percent more than a thoroughly dried sample. Some really juicy green woods have 100 percent m.c. or more. This can be confusing since a piece of wood obviously cannot be all water; remember that moisture content is a ratio, expressed as a percentage, of wet to dry weight.

Freshly cut green wood contains two types of moisture. Moisture inside the cells is called *free water*. Moisture in the cell walls is *bound water*. As wood dries, it first loses free water, down to about 30 percent m.c. This is the *fiber saturation point*, at which the cell cavities are empty. The cell walls are still saturated. Until drying wood comes down to the fiber saturation point, it remains stable; it doesn't shrink, check, or warp. Wood begins to "move" when it loses bound water.

In the eastern United States, air-drying in a drafty shed can bring wood to a m.c. between 15 and 20 percent. Moisture content will continue to drop in a heated house to 5 to 10 percent m.c. In the arid west, wood air-dries to below 10 percent m.c. Kiln-drying lowers wood to about 5 percent m.c.

Because wood is hygroscopic, moisture content can also go up. If hardwood flooring is removed from a kiln, taken to a building site or lumberyard, then left unwrapped during a period of humid weather, it will eventually reach the same moisture content as a piece that has been only air dried.

All of a tree's growth takes place in the cambium, the narrow ring of cells that forms the boundary between bark and wood. As the cambium cells

The fast-growing red oak on the left is significantly stronger than the slower-growing sample on the right.

grow and divide, the inner cells develop into wood and the outer cells become bark.

Look at a cross section of a log, and you'll often see a distinct transition between *sapwood* on the outside and *heartwood* on the inside. In a living tree, the sapwood cells conduct nutrients to and from the leaves and the roots. The inner circle of heartwood acts as a structural skeleton for the tree.

As heartwood develops, chemicals called *extractives* impregnate the cells. These extractives give many types of heartwood a distinctive color. The function of extractives is to make the heartwood decay resistant and sometimes unpalatable to insects. All sapwood, including that of species known for decay resistance, will rot quickly when exposed to conditions which cause decay.

There is no relationship between hardness and decay resistance. Hickory, one of the hardest common woods, rates very low in decay resistance. Black locust, another very hard wood, is famous for longevity in contact with soil and is prized for fence posts. White oak heartwood is resistant to decay partially because the heartwood pores are filled with globular obstructions that block air and moisture. Red oak, which decays quickly, has large open pores which conduct and hold moisture. Among the conifers, there are many species that have excellent decay resistance. Cedar, cypress, and redwood are among the best.

Knots are the remains of limbs. When you begin splitting out materials, you'll observe that all sig-nificant knots originate at the pith. Knots are often unworkable with hand tools. The wood surrounding a knot is distorted on both sides. A common structural engineering guideline is that a knot, and the surrounding distorted grain, should be considered as a hole or void in a piece of wood. Green woodworkers generally avoid all but the very smallest knots. The exception is log and timber work where knots are not loved but tolerated.

Growth rate determines wood quality. Trees growing in shaded forest put on height more quickly than those growing in open sun. They also shed lower limbs as the crown limbs render them redundant. The result is that forest-grown trees tend to have a straighter grain and fewer knots than trees grown in the open. As might be expected, trees in the open face less competition for sunlight and nutrients and therefore tend to develop girth rather than height. Large bent limbs reaching out to sunlight are common.

Growth rate also affects the strength of wood—particularly the thickness and weight of cellular structure. Curiously, among deciduous ring-porous species, fast growth results in stronger wood. Here's why. In late spring and early summer, the cambium of deciduous trees quickly develops large, weak pores. Smaller, stronger cells are developed later in the season. When the environment is conducive to growth, the proportion of smaller late-growth cells to larger early-growth cells is greater than under

Avoid using reaction wood from leaning trees. The stressed cellular structure often splits, shrinks, or distorts unpredictably.

less-favorable conditions. Among conifers, however, fast growth results in weaker wood.

Troublesome wood is produced in the lower trunks of trees growing on steep slopes. Distorted cells called *reaction wood* serve to straighten out or support the tree and direct the crown growth upward. Among conifers, compressive reaction wood develops on the convex side of the tree, pushing the tree so that it is vertical. With hardwoods, reaction wood in tension develops on the concave side of the pith, straightening the tree by pulling it upward. In most wood, longitudinal shrinkage is generally a negligible factor, but it can be ten times greater than normal in reaction wood. Since the stress is uneven, the effect is unpredictable. The zone of reaction wood generally extends well beyond the obvious curve on a log. Reaction wood may undergo unexpected splitting, fracture, and distortion during shaping and drying.

Note Regarding Tables

The tables on the following pages were compiled to help you select materials. Resources included publications of the United States Department of Agriculture (USDA) Forest Products Laboratory (FPL), library research, my experience, and commentaries from other woodworkers. Do not assume that the lists are complete.

Many species are known by various names in different locations. Characteristics often vary within a species from area to area. Basswood (also known as "lime" in England) is listed as linden. Eastern white pine, which is not listed, can be substituted for northern white pine. Chestnut, a once widely used wood that is now virtually extinct due to the chestnut blight, is included for comparison and historical interest.

Comparative Hardness and Softness

Hardness is the property that makes a surface difficult to dent, scratch, or cut. Softness refers to woods that work easily with hand tools and have a soft, uniform texture. From Forest Products Laboratory tables, plus author's additions marked with an asterisk (*).

Hard	Intermediate	Soft
Apple*	Alder*	Aspen*
Ash, all	Chestnut	Birch, gray
Beech	Cypress	Buckeye*
Birch, white	Fir, Douglas	Butternut
Birch, yellow	Gum, red	Catalpa*
Cedar, eastern red	Hemlock, all	Cedar, northern white
Cherry, wild	Mulberry*	Cedar, southern white
Dogwood	Redwood	Cedar, western
Elm, all	Sassafras*	Cherry, pin leaf*
Gum, black	Spruce, all	Cottonwood
Hackberry		Fir, true
Hawthorn*		Linden
Hickory		Magnolia
Holly*		Maple, silver
Hornbeam, American		Maple, striped
Ironwood*		Pine, northern white
Larch, western		Pine, ponderosa
Lilac*		Pine, sugar
Locust, black		Pine, western white
Locust, honey		Poplar, yellow
Maple, red		Tupelo, water
Maple, sugar		Willow*
Mesquite*		
Oak, all		
Olive*		
Osage orange*		
Pear*		
Pecan*		
Persimmon*		
Pine, southern yellow		
Sycamore		
Walnut		
Yew, Pacific*		

Comparative Bendability

Species with good bendability will readily bend into a curved form. This is not to be confused with "bending strength," which refers to load-carrying capacity of a horizontal member. Within a species there can be great variations in bendability from one tree to another. Author's list compiled from Forest Products Laboratory tests, personal experience, and library research. Author's additions to tests marked with an asterisk (*). Among "good" bending woods, the highest-ranking are hackberry, white oak, red oak, and hickory; ash is lowest. Many poor bending woods are not listed.

Good	Fair	Poor
Ash	Alder	Butternut
Beech	Cedar, Atlantic white	Conifers, most
Birch, all	Cedar, northern white	Cottonwood
Cedar, western	Cherry	Dogwood
Elm, soft	Chestnut	Gum, black
Filbert*	Fir, Douglas*	Linden
Gum, sweet	Gum, black	Oak, live
Hackberry	Gum, red	Poplar, yellow
Hickory	Locust, black	Sycamore
Madrone	Maple, red	
Magnolia	Pine, southern yellow	
Maple, sugar	Redwood*	
Mulberry		
Oak, red		
Oak, white		
Osage orange*		
Pecan		
Walnut		
Willow		
Yew		

Comparative Toughness

Toughness is the capacity to withstand suddenly applied loads. From Forest Products Laboratory table, plus author's additions marked with an asterisk (*).

High	Intermediate	Low
Ash, all	Apple*	Cedar, northern white
Beech	Cedar, eastern red	Cedar, southern white
Birch, yellow	Cherry	Cedar, western
Dogwood	Chestnut	Fir, balsam
Elm, all	Cottonwood	Fir, white
Hackberry	Cypress	Linden
Hawthorn*	Fir, Douglas	Maple, silver
Hickory	Gum, red	Mulberry*
Hornbeam, American	Hemlock, all	Pine, northern white
Ironwood*	Holly*	Pine, ponderosa
Locust, black	Larch, western	Pine, sugar
Locust, honey	Pear*	Poplar, yellow
Maple, sugar	Pine, southern yellow	Spruce, Englemann
Oak, all	Pine, western white	
Osage orange*	Redwood	
Pecan*	Spruce, eastern	
Persimmon*	Spruce, Sitka	
Walnut	Sycamore	
	Tupelo	

Comparative Decay Resistance (Heartwood)

Yellow pine shows such variance that it's hard to determine where the "average" specimen would fall; at its best, yellow pine rates "high." From Forest Products Laboratory table, plus author's additions marked with an asterisk (*).

High	Intermediate	Low
Catalpa	Elm, all	Alder
Cedar, all	Fir, all true	Ash
Cherry	Fir, Douglas	Aspen*
Chestnut	Gum, red	Beech
Cypress	Hemlock	Birch, all
Ironwood*	Hornbeam	Buckeye
Juniper, all	Larch, western	Butternut
Locust, black	Locust, honey	Cottonwood
Mesquite	Oak, red	Gum, sweet
Mulberry*	Oak, swamp	Hackberry
Oak, white	Pine, northern white	Hickory
Osage orange*	Pine, yellow	Linden
Redwood	Tamarack	Magnolia
Sassafras*		Maple, all
Walnut		Pecan*
Yew*		Persimmon*
		Poplar, true
		Poplar, yellow
		Spruce, all
		Sycamore
		Tupelo
		Willow*

A ladder-back chair can be made using any of the wood species in the High category of the listings for Comparative Toughness.

Comparative Freedom from Odor and Taste When Dry

From Forest Products Laboratory table, plus author's additions marked with an asterisk (*).

Excellent	Acceptable	Undesirable
Apple*	Cottonwood	Cedar, all
Ash	Cypress	Fir, Douglas
Beech	Locust, black	Larch, western
Birch	Locust, honey	Pine, all
Buckeye*	Oak, all*	
Butternut*		
Catalpa*		
Cherry		
Chestnut		
Dogwood*		
Elm		
Fir, balsam		
Fir, white		
Gum, black		
Hackberry		
Hemlock, all		
Hickory*		
Holly*		
Linden		
Maple, all		
Pear		
Poplar, yellow		
Rhododendron		
Spruce, all		
Sycamore		
Tamarack*		
Tupelo, water		
Walnut*		
Willow*		

Comparative Riving Quality (Clear Samples)

Good to Excellent	Fair	Poor
Ash	Alder	Elm
Butternut	Apple	Eucalyptus
Cedar, northern white	Beech	Gum, black
Cedar, western	Birch	Gum, blue
Chestnut	Buckeye	Hornbeam
Cypress	Catalpa	Oak, swamp
Hackberry	Cedar, eastern red	Persimmon
Hemlock, all	Cherry	
Hickory	Cottonwood	
Larch	Dogwood	
Locust, black	Fir, Douglas	
Locust, honey	Hawthorn	
Oak, red	Holly	
Oak, white	Linden	
Osage orange	Magnolia	
Pecan	Maple, all	
Pine, eastern white	Mulberry	
Redwood	Oak, live	
Spruce	Pear	
Walnut	Pine, southern yellow	
Willow	Poplar, yellow	
	Sumac (alanthus)	
	Sycamore	

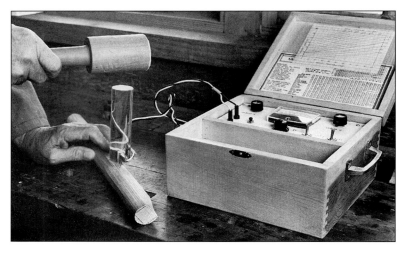

A moisture meter works by measuring electrical resistance between two probes.

Getting Your Materials

There are several possible approaches to getting materials for green woodworking. The method you use will depend on where you live; available equipment, help, and time; your physical condition; your budget; and other factors. Various methods of obtaining green wood are discussed in the following pages.

It's often easy to collect more wood than you can use. Since a priority is to work *green* wood, you'll have to store extra wood to prevent drying or work with wood that is drier (and harder) than desirable.

My recommendation is to collect only as much wood as you guess you can use in half a year. This takes some calculation. For example, a quality oak log, 10 inches in diameter and 8 feet long, should yield enough wood to make four ladder-back chairs. One summer I felled a 24-inch diameter red oak that was mostly clear for over thirty feet. This one tree supplied material for three chairmaking workshops and my own use—about 35 chairs. A very nice 6-inch-diameter white oak sapling, 6 feet long, might make six to eight firewood totes or a dozen medium-sized baskets.

Selecting a Log

Quality is important. Poor logs yield a low proportion of usable wood—you may be lucky to get anything. Sorry wood is much harder to work than good wood.

Start out by knowing the species and log size you're looking for. For most uses, an ideal log is perfectly straight and round. Any variation will show up during splitting as curved or distorted wood. Bowed logs often contain reaction wood.

Knots mean trouble. They originate at the pith, and wood on either side will be distorted. Limbs that fell off during early growth are often covered with scar tissue that is reflected by lumps on the surface of the bark. Bark furrows are good indicators of grain direction. If vertical bark crevices spiral up the trunk, the wood will twist as it splits.

The flared buttress of a log often contains distorted, wavy grain, especially in hardwoods over 12 inches in diameter, and the lower two or three feet may not be usable for green woodworking. (Log buttresses make great chopping stumps, though.)

As explained earlier, growth rate correlates with strength. Look for fast-growing hardwoods and slow-growing softwoods: At a sawmill, you can easily compare the spacing of growth rings on logs;

Spiral bark furrows indicate twisted wood.

in the woods, you can get an idea of growth by chopping or sawing a small notch out of a tree before felling it. You can take a complete core sample with an increment borer, but this tool costs about $75.

If you're buying from a sawmill, find out when the logs were cut. The sapwood of some species deteriorates very quickly during summer. When you check end grain, also look for signs of decay. For a good view of a dirty log, you may have to saw an inch or so off one end. Bluish stains often indicate hidden rot or imbedded metal. A gapping split may lower the value of a log for lumber but not necessarily for green woodworking.

Logging Basics

Doing your own logging is probably the most satisfying, challenging, and interesting way to get green wood. Small-scale logging is an adventure. Felling a tree is dramatic.

Small and medium-sized timber can be felled with a chain saw in only a few minutes. But felling is a skill that's not quickly mastered. *Logging is dangerous.* Felling small trees, though not as dangerous as felling larger ones, can still be lethal; saplings growing in a dense stand of young growth often lodge among other trees on the way down or bind between standing trees, turning a small pole into a wicked, loaded spring.

Woods lore is filled with rules on when to cut timber. There are rules based on whether or not sap is rising, moon phases, constellations, wind direction, and more. Often, the rules contradict each other. The following basic guidelines have been substantiated.

Quality timber can be cut any time of year. The movement of sap varies from season to season and from species to species, but the effect is only a slight change of moisture content.

Don't cut timber if it's windy—you won't have control over the falling tree. Trees cut in fall and winter will be less prone to damage from insects, decay, and checking, but be sure to remove your timber from the woods before the return of warm weather. Timber cut during spring and summer should be removed from the woods as soon as possible.

Hickory cut for peeling bast (inner bark) for chair seating should be felled during the period of active cambium growth. This is usually late spring through early summer. In other seasons and in dry years, peeling bark can be difficult if not impossible.

The rudiments of felling a tree are fairly simple. In this chapter I'll explain how to fell a small or medium-sized tree. For details on specific situations, I suggest a specialized text, such as D. Douglas Dent's *Professional Timber Falling* (Beaverton, Oreg.: D. Douglas Dent, 1974), which is available from the author at P.O. Box 905, Beaverton, OR 97005.

You need only a few tools. The absolute minimum piece of equipment is a sharp axe for felling, bucking, and limbing. However, felling and bucking with an axe is impractical for most of us. Good axe work is a skill acquired through a great deal of practice. Felling and bucking with an axe also generates considerably more waste than sawing.

For cutting small saplings and limbs, I often use a basic pruning saw. To cut logs thicker than 3–4 inches, use a one- or two-man crosscut saw or a small chain saw. A logger's crosscut saw is much safer than a chain saw, and if properly sharpened, it works quite easily. (For information on sharpening

and maintaining a crosscut saw, refer to Warren Miller's *Crosscut Saw Manual*, available from the Government Printing Office, Documents Department, Washington, DC 20402-9235. Stock number 001-001-00434-1.)

If you prefer a chain saw, I suggest buying a lightweight model with a small engine (2 to 3 cubic inches), fitted with a 14- to 16-inch bar. New chain saws have excellent chain brakes and anti-vibration handles. Get a quality brand that can be serviced locally. Be sure to study the owner's manual, especially the sections on sharpening and safety.

You'll also need a polled axe or a hatchet for driving wedges. Thin felling wedges are used to prevent saw-blade pinching and sometimes to correct felling direction. Chain saw wedges are plastic, to prevent damage to the chain's teeth. In the woods, I carry a 2-foot-long piece of string with a large washer on one end as a plumb line to check tree lean. If you're using a chain saw, take along a T-wrench to adjust chain tension.

In the woods, you should wear stout boots with rough soles. Clothing should be close fitting, so it won't snag on limbs. Wear a hardhat for protection from widow makers—dead limbs that come down unexpectedly. Chain saw shops sell hardhats with attached eye and ear protection. Special loggers safety pants are highly recommended. These will slow and stop a chain saw chain that goes out of control.

When you go into the woods, work with a buddy. Don't allow children or dogs to be nearby.

Before dropping a tree, examine it for lean and obviously dead limbs. Deep leaners cause felling problems; they can split unexpectedly. To check the lean of an apparently straight tree, retreat about 50 feet and compare the trunk to your piece of weighted string. If there's any question, check the tree again at a right angle to the first sighting line.

Next, clear out a work area so you can move around easily without tripping or getting clothes snagged. Locate an escape route to take when the tree begins to fall. It should be roughly back and to one side of the felling direction. Examine nearby trees in the felling direction. You want to avoid lodging the tree you're cutting in standing timber.

Well-balanced trees that stand almost plumb can be felled in any direction. Slight leaners, and those with unbalanced limbs, are felled to the favored side; in such cases, you can control the felling angle within an arc of about 45°.

Felling consists of two cutting sequences: removing a wedge, sometimes called the face cut, in the felling direction; and making a back cut to release the tree. A hinge of unsevered wood divides the face cut from the back cut.

The face cut, or notch, consists of two cuts. First, define the top of the stump with a level cut. Then make a sloped cut coming down to the first—level—cut. The notch depth should be one-third of the tree diameter. The inside line of the face cut where the level cut and the sloped cut intersect must be perpendicular to the felling direction.

The back cut, or felling cut, is also level and at least 2 inches above the level cut of the wedge. This creates a step, which helps to prevent the falling tree from slipping backward. *Be sure not to saw through the hinge area.*

When felling a tree thicker than 10 inches, you can insert a felling wedge in the back cut right behind the saw blade or chain bar. This will prevent pinching if the tree should begin to lean backward.

When the tree begins to fall, remove the saw and head along the escape route. (If you're using a chain saw, kill the motor.)

Ideally, the tree falls as planned. When it does, I experience a feeling of relief. Complications are experienced by everyone who has cut any timber. If the tree begins to lean backward, 180° from the felling direction, you may be able to send it in the right direction by pounding on the wedge. If this doesn't work, or if the tree becomes lodged, leave the immediate area and get experienced help. Lodged trees and back leaners are dangerous, even for experts. In recent years, two professional loggers in my community were killed while attempting to free lodged trees.

Once it's down, the tree is crosscut, or *bucked,* into logs of suitable lengths. In many instances green woodworkers use only the lower, straightest section of a tree, below the limbs and the bark scars, which cover hidden knots. The remainder of the tree can be cut into firewood; limbs can also be neatly stacked as erosion control or left for wildlife shelter.

You may also be able to harvest saw logs if the remaining log is more than 12 inches in diameter at the fat end and at least 8 inches at the tip end. Of course you face the job of hauling the log to a sawmill or milling on site with a chain saw mill or portable band mill.

Bucking and limbing can be tricky. Logs roll over suddenly or slide downhill. Always work from the uphill side, with secure footing. Before beginning to buck a log, survey the situation. If a felled

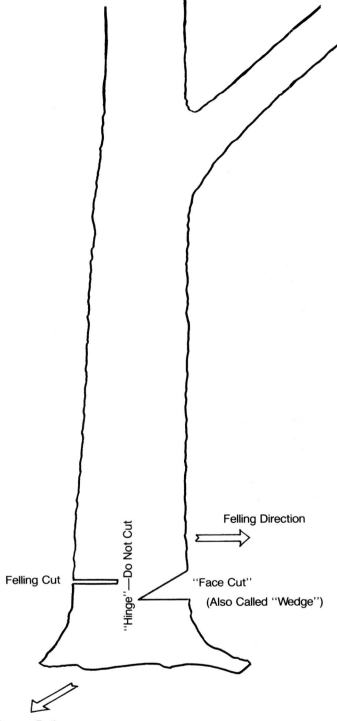

Felling. 1. Determine felling direction and escape path. 2. Clean up the work area. 3. Saw the face cut. 4. Saw the felling cut at least 2 inches above the base of the face cut. 5. Do not saw through the hinge wood. The escape path is angled back and to one side of the felling direction. The recommended escape distance is 20 feet.

tree is supported by other logs or uneven terrain, the trunk and limbs will be stressed. When a log is supported between two points, the upper half is in compression and the lower half is in tension; if you saw straight down, your saw will bind before you get through. Instead, make a shallow cut on the top, then saw through the log working from the bottom up. This type of cut is possible only with a chainsaw.

If a section of a felled tree is cantilevered into space, the lower half of the trunk will be in compression and the upper half will be in tension. First cut about one-fourth of the way through the bottom, then complete the cut from above.

Logs lying perpendicular to steep slopes tend to slide downhill as you cut through them. To keep the saw from being pinched, insert a wedge into the cut as soon as possible.

When limbing, check for branches that support the tree or are sprung on obstacles. Think ahead about what will happen when you saw through them; like the trunk, limbs under load have stresses of compression and tension.

Green woodworking stock can often be hauled or dragged out of the woods without too much trouble. If you've cut something that's too heavy, split it into sections that you can deal with. Or, get help from someone with a tractor.

Buying Logs

I enjoy doing some occasional logging. But I often purchase cut logs from a woodlot owner or a local sawmill if they can supply wood that I either don't have or want to hold on to for future use. It's quicker and safer to buy logs than to do the logging yourself.

And it's not expensive. The hypothetical chair log I mentioned earlier, measuring 8 feet long, with an average diameter of 10 inches, potentially contains 32 board feet of lumber. At $3 per board foot, a typical 1994 price for high grades of red or white oak, first rate material for one ladderback chair might be $24. The percentage of usable material in a log goes up quickly as diameter increases, and you may find a seller will ask only the price for ungraded timber.

Your challenge is to locate the seller and explain what you're looking for. Keep in mind that the average sawmill operator or woodlot owner has other things to do than deal with a woodworker out to buy a single log. Explain that you require the best quality, and be clear that you're willing to pay a premium price.

You may have to choose a larger log than needed. Sawmills in our area deal with logs that are commonly 12 feet long. A large-diameter log may suit you better, because smaller ones are usually from the upper end of a tree where there are knots and branches. The butt log will be clearer.

The seller may be willing to buck a log to your required lengths. If you have a truck, ask to have the log loaded by forklift. If you don't have a truck, the seller may be able to arrange delivery.

Finally, a note about quality. Even with careful selection, there's always a possibility that a log will not meet your expectations. This is a chance that you take whether you purchase a log or do your own logging.

Green Wood for City-Based Woodworkers

If you live in or near a rural area, especially east of the Mississippi, you should be able to get suitable wood for just about any type of green woodworking without much trouble. Urbanites and westerners will have a greater challenge. But having lived in a San Francisco suburb, I suggest that anyone can find materials, although you may have to work at it.

Green woodworkers in many western states have a great selection of conifers to work with, but finding suitable hardwoods is a challenge, especially strong, straight-grained wood that rives and shaves well. Walnut and pecan may be available, and there are natural pockets of hardwoods such as Oregon ash, Oregon white oak, and paper birch.

Always ask permission before taking any wood, dead or alive, off private or public property. Usually, the answer will be positive, especially when you explain what you want the wood for. Use your intuition on offering to pay or to haul brush or cut up firewood in exchange. You might even barter with your finished craftwork.

Check out new real estate developments; you may be able to get good stuff before the bulldozers move in. Orchards are excellent places to find woods such as apple, pear, walnut, olive, persimmon, pecan, and filbert. Wood becomes available during annual pruning and when older trees are removed to make room for young stock. Home yards can also be a source for ornamentals, fruit, and nut trees, including exotics that don't naturally grow in your area. You might also check with park and highway departments and forest services. Companies that do tree surgery and maintain power line right-of-ways may be willing to tell you where they'll be working so that you can pick up wood before it's cut into firewood or ground into chips.

If you're willing to do some long distance driving, you can visit an area where the wood you need grows naturally. Maps showing the natural habitats of trees are included in many tree identification books. When you get to an area, ask at local stores or the forest service about nearby sawmills. Small quantities of wood for basketry, carving, or cooperage can be carried in a car. If you need a larger quantity but don't have a truck, consider renting or buying a small trailer.

Another possibility is *coppicing*—growing your own materials. In a coppice the established root systems of felled trees are allowed to put out new aboveground growth. An advantage is that these trees will grow much more quickly than freshly planted seedlings. Coppices should be located in specially selected and prepared ground to further speed growth. Willows, for example, are planted in wet, rich earth. In England, beeches and alders were traditionally coppiced, and willows are today. We coppice willows and filberts, and both yield basketry materials just two or three years after planting.

Western Woods for Green Woodworking

Conifers	Deciduous	Exotics (Introduced)
Cedar, western	Alder	Apple
Cypress, Arizona	Ash, Oregon	Cherry
Fir, Douglas	Aspen	Eucalyptus
Fir, true	Birch, paper	Filbert
Hemlock, western	Buck Buckeye	Holly
Juniper, western	Cottonwood, black	Horse chestnut
Larch, western	Dogwood, Pacific	Mulberry
Pine (various)	Elder, box	Olive
Redwood	Hackberry, western	Pear
Spruce, western	Madrone	Pecan
Yew, Pacific	Maple, big leaf	Persimmon
	Mesquite	Walnut, English
	Myrtle (California laurel)	
	Oak, Oregon white	
	Walnut, black	
	Willow	

Storing Wood

Conventional woodworkers store their lumber in a dry, sheltered space. But the green woodworker ideally wants an ongoing supply of fresh, wet wood. Wood begins to dry out as soon as a tree is cut. Even

The knobby bark of this straight red oak indicates concealed knots surrounded by distorted grain.

if left intact, a tree felled during the growing season loses moisture by transpiration through its leaves. When it's bucked into logs or firewood, moisture escapes through the porous end grain much more quickly than through the bark. Moisture within the cells is lost first. As moisture bound in the cell walls evaporates, the drying wood shrinks. Checks develop to accommodate the stresses, and as drying continues, the log cracks.

The objective of seasoning lumber is to lower moisture content evenly, so that internal moisture migrates toward the surfaces and end grain without causing stresses that result in cracks and checking.

There are a number of ways to minimize checking and cracking. Pressure can be relieved by sawing a log into boards or splitting it into *billets* (the English country term for split sections of a log). Another method, often combined with sawing or splitting, is to coat the end grain of each piece in order to slow down the loss of moisture. End grain sealers include a beeswax and paraffin mixture, latex paint, aluminum paint, and roofing asphalt. Proprietary end grain sealants are also available.

To keep a log or large timber from checking, you can saw a kerf down the entire length of one side. This will relieve pressure, preventing splits from developing on the other sides. To be effective, the kerf should be sawed all the way to the pith.

Unless steps are taken, wet wood continues to lose moisture content until it stabilizes at the *equilibrium moisture content*, which is determined by local atmospheric humidity.

During the loss of bound water, wood distorts in cross section. The shrinkage tangent to the growth rings is approximately twice that of shrinkage at the perpendicular *ray plane*. This is known as *differential shrinkage*.

Differential shrinkage causes boards to cup and warp. Tangential shrinkage on flat-sawed lumber causes boards to cup away from the pith. Quartersawed boards are comparatively stable because tangential stress is minimal and evenly distributed. A beam "boxed" around the heart of a log tends to retain its shape as it dries. But it will check. A beam taken from one side of the pith dis-

torts into a rectangle or diamond shape in cross section. Differential shrinkage also causes green cylinders shaped outside the pith area to dry into an oval section. Pith wood is avoided, because it commonly checks or splits.

There's no point in fighting shrinkage. But when you understand it, you can put this force to work. We'll be dealing with differential shrinkage as we work on the projects in the following chapters.

In some applications, green woodworkers require very dry materials. Three examples are wheelwrighting, chair making, and cooperage; wheels, chairs, and barrels fall apart if spokes, rungs, and staves shrink after assembly. But for most greenwood crafts, the ideal is to maintain a high moisture content, so that wood is rived to final size and shaped while still green, soft, pliable, and easy to work.

Wood can be kept wet longer, for ease of working and to minimize checks and distortion, by several methods. End grain coatings slow down the loss of moisture and help to prevent rot. I use two coats of a paraffin-based end-grain sealant. Latex paint and white or yellow glue will also work. Trough carvers and bowl turners can prevent cracks from ruining a turning by burying finished work in a pile of shavings. Pieces are taken out of the pile for only about an hour each day so the wood will dry at a slow rate.

Wood can be stored under water. Our small pond generally contains a variety of sunken hardwood. Ladderback chairmaker John Alexander uses an old skiff filled with water. A 55-gallon drum or a plastic garbage can will also work. Submerged wood will not rot unless the water or wood contains a fair amount of air. Oak will stain with a bluish mold but usually only on the surface; this can easily be shaved away. Wood stored under water may also become coated with algae, but I haven't found this to be a problem.

Green wood can be sealed in plastic bags from which most of the air is removed just before closing with tie strips. (Plastic bags are also useful for keeping dry wood from regaining moisture.) For controlled slow drying, turn the bag inside out daily, and put the wood back inside.

Green wood is vulnerable to the threat of staining and decay caused by fungi that use carbohydrates within wood cells for food. Decay fungi physically break down the cell walls by secreting enzymes. Advanced decay of wood into a powder is often called dry rot. But this damage is caused by moisture, not dryness.

Decay-causing fungi thrive in an environment very similar to conditions that we tend to live in, especially in the eastern United States during summer. By changing just one condition on the following list, you can prevent wood decay.

1. *Temperature.* Optimal temperatures for decay range between 75° and 90°F. Growth stops below 40° and above 105°F.

2. *Oxygen.* Decay fungi require oxygen.

3. *Moisture.* Wood moisture content of about 30 percent is ideal for decay. Decay stops below 20 percent m.c.

4. *Food.* Carbohydrates in sapwood are preferred. Heartwood decays more slowly because it naturally contains fungi-resistant substances. Sapwood is popularly considered weaker than heartwood, but in fact there is little difference in strength between the two. The reason for this misconception is that sapwood decays quickly, resulting in dramatic loss of strength.

You can delay decay by the same processes used to slow evaporation. End grain coatings keep decay organisms from entering wood. For this reason, it's important to coat end grain immediately, before micro-checks develop. Green wet wood stored in plastic bags is safe because the moisture content is too high. If the air is removed just before sealing, the fungi will be deprived of oxygen.

Underwater storage is also effective in discouraging decay. Bacteria and certain soft rot fungi can attack submerged wood, but the resulting damage is usually very slow. The oldest known examples of woodworking have been preserved at sites that are either very dry or waterlogged. Submerged ruins of the Swiss Lake Dwellers have resisted decay for centuries. Woodenware made by Northwest Coast Indians 2,900 years ago was found under water near Vancouver, Washington. Preserved hulls of several Viking ships have been found in swamps.

Winter temperatures may keep fungi from invading. Furthermore, frozen wood retains moisture. A shed or the shady north side of a building makes a good storage location in winter. Small quantities of green wood can even be stored in a home freezer.

Decay and drying proceed much faster in summer. Store logs in the shade, and elevate them from the ground on cross pieces. Plastic tarps can discourage decay if the moisture level is already too high for the organisms. But if a log is partially dry, plastic can retain moisture at a level conducive to decay. What's more, in warm weather a tarp can raise temperatures by retaining interior heat. In some cases, removal of bark is helpful.

Insects can also be a problem. The sapwood of summer-felled hardwoods is commonly invaded by ambrosia beetles. They bore pinhead-sized holes in damp wood, opening it to invasion by fungi, which subsequently feed the beetles. Although nearly invisible, the fungi weaken the wood. Powder post beetles attack both freshly cut and seasoned timber; hickory and the oaks are liable to severe injury. The larvae of roundheaded pine borers chew tunnels that enlarge as the grubs grow. Tunnels can be 2 feet long and 1/2 inch in diameter by the time the mature beetles emerge.

Wood stored on or near the ground is particularly susceptible to attack. You can discourage an invasion by removing bark and sapwood from logs. Fall and winter cutting sometimes prevents insect damage.

For certain projects you'll need dry wood as well as green. Stack wood to be dried with inch-square "stickers" separating each layer. This air space around each piece of wood promotes transpiration of moisture so that wood dries before fungi become established. The weight of the stack helps to keep wood from warping, and you can place heavy weights on top. A drafty shed is a perfect location for drying wood.

Moisture content can be lowered to an m.c. that approaches kiln-drying by bringing wood indoors, particularly during winter when homes and shops are heated. Wood should first be partially dried in a shed, because very quick drying is likely to warp wood or cause interior "honeycombing." Use stickers for indoor drying. When wood is dry, it can be dead-stacked without stickers. Small quantities of wood can be dried to less than 10 percent m.c. by suspending the wood on a rack above a wood stove or furnace. Directions for making a simple kiln, consisting of an oil drum and a radiant heat lamp, are given in chapter 10.

Special Materials

Greenwood crafts traditionally use many tree materials in addition to wood from the trunk. Saplings, limbs, and shoots are used for baskets, livestock enclosures, and wattle-and-daub in-fill for timber-frame structures. The inner bark—known as *bast*—of certain trees can make strong, durable sheeting, strips, rope, and lashing. Rootlets, especially of spruce and cedar, are excellent for lashing. A knotty root node can be made into a very tough maul.

TRADITIONAL CRAFT USES FOR NON-LUMBER PRODUCING PARTS OF TREES

Bark (used in sheets and strips)

Canoes: Birch, elm (second choice, after others), western cedar

Containers: Birch, elm, linden, magnolia, western cedar, yellow poplar

Roofing: Birch (sod underlay in pre-industrial Scandinavia), linden (shingles in eastern Europe)

Rope: Elm, linden, smooth willow, western cedar

Seating and basketry (bast strips): Elm, hemlock, hickory, linden, paper birch, pecan, smooth willow, western cedar, yellow poplar

Saplings (tree stems under 6 inches in diameter)

Basketry (splits): Ash, hickory, northern white cedar, pecan, soft maple, white oak

Hooping (cooperage): Ash, beech, hickory, hard maple, white oak, red oak

Spoons (rived billets): Birch (Scandinavia), dogwood, hard maple (Switzerland), sycamore (England)

Limbs

Hooping (cooperage): Pine

Lathing (wattle-and-daub, timber-frame in-fill, livestock enclosures): Ash, birch, elm, filbert, willow

Mauls: Beech, hickory, hornbeam, persimmon

Spoons: Apple, birch, hard maple, rhododendron

Shoots, Rods

Basketry: Filbert, willow

Hooping (cooperage): Filbert, willow

Rustic furniture: Willow

Withes (Twigs)

Basketry: Western cedar

Besoms: Birch

Rope: Western cedar

Roots

Basketry: Western cedar, spruce

Carving: Birch, maple, walnut

Lashing: Cedar, pine, spruce

Mauls: Dogwood, hickory

Contemporary green woodworkers have found some of these materials to be superior to factory-made products. Saplings, limbs, bark, and roots are not only beautiful, but have individual character that is impossible to produce with machinery. There is no comparison between a willow or splint basket and one made from commercially manufactured materials. One of the most beautiful and durable seating materials for ladder-back chairs is hickory bast. If it's kept indoors, hickory bast appears to be as durable as rawhide. I've examined a century-old ladder-back that is said to have its original bark seat. The birchbark canoes that Henri Vaillancourt makes are a delight to look at in addition to being strong and durable. The paper birch sheeting is lashed to the frame with split spruce roots.

Project: A Bark Container

As a tribute to Native American crafts, for our first project I've selected two cylindrical bark containers made by Native Americans. The Cherokee "berry box" can be made quickly. The bottom isn't flat, but this container is meant to be carried by a shoulder strap or hung on a wall hook. The other bark container, which is still made by Cree Indians in northern Quebec, has a flat bottom. Small versions are carried, and larger ones serve as storage containers (they make beautiful wastebaskets). The Cree baskets often have a tightly fitted lid.

These folded and lashed containers could be improvised on the spot as needed or made with a great deal of care. Here in southern Appalachia, descendants of white settlers made similar bark "huckleberry boxes" probably as late as the 1950s.

Tools. You need a knife, brace and bit, chalk, awl, and spring clamps.

Materials. The bark from several hardwoods and conifers peels easily, in large pliable sheets. Tulip poplar, which was generally used to make the Cherokee bark containers, peels early in the growing season—usually late May through June. The duration of the peeling period seems to correlate to seasonal rainfall. Paper birch also peels during early summer. I've used magnolia with some success, but it's brittle. Other peeling barks include elm, linden, smooth willow, and western cedar.

The bark from one small tree will yield material for several containers. In selecting a sapling, keep in mind that the diameter of your bark container will be almost twice that of the tree that you cut; to make a container 6 inches in diameter, select a 4-inch sapling. Cherokee carrying baskets are

Containers made from tulip poplar bark. The "berry box" on the left is a Cherokee pattern. The square bottom container is a traditional Cree design.

usually about two-thirds taller than the diameter. Flat-bottom Cree baskets are generally squatter, about one-third taller than the bottom dimension. The sapling should be straight, with a slight taper and few limbs or imperfections. With tulip poplar, sealed bark scars over areas where knots exist will peel easily, and they can add an interesting touch to the container's appearance.

Freshly cut bark is fragile. To protect the bark, the sapling should be carried or dragged with only a tip end contacting the ground.

You can work with a full-length sapling, but it's awkward. If you don't need a long pole, crosscut your sapling into sections. To determine the length, add the distance across the bottom and the heights of two sides. If you're using poplar bark, you can allow small branch holes in the sides of the container, but not in the bottom or the area near the seams. Discard bark sections with holes larger than 1/2 inch across.

Examine your length of pole to determine the best place for the seams. Mark out and cut the two ends by girdling around the sapling with a knife. Then make a lengthwise slit through the bark from one end to the other. Often, the bark will easily slip loose from the cambium. If the bark resists, insert your fingers under the bark and lift upward. Grabbing and pulling a corner will damage the moist, fragile bark. When the bark comes loose, leave it wrapped around the sapling.

To make the Cherokee basket, use the pattern with the eye-shaped bottom (see illustration on page 46). With the bark on the pole, draw the centerline around the circumference onto the bark (chalk is a good marking material). At opposing points 180° from the lengthwise slit, make two marks indicating the width of the bottom. These are equidistant from the centerline. Example: For a 6-inch bottom, each mark is 3 inches from the centerline. Next draw an eye shape with arcing lines that

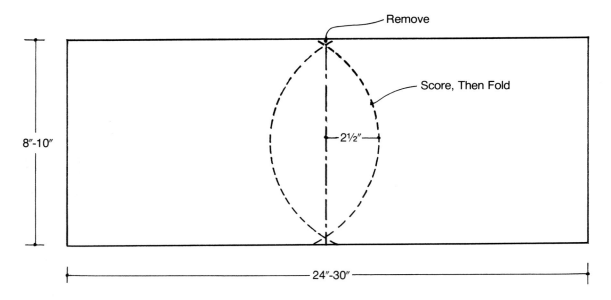

Schematic for making a Native American berry box. Score on the broken line. Cut away the bark in the shaded area.

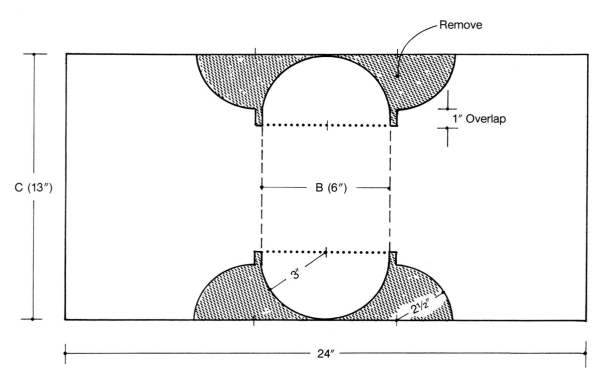

Typical dimensions of a bark container with a flat bottom. Score on the vertical broken line. Fold (but do not score) on the dotted line. Cut away the shaded area.

connect at the slit. The ends of both arcs should just cross the centerline, making a small X in each corner. Using a knife, carefully cut halfway through the bark along the eye outlines.

Remove the bark from the sapling. To fold the sides, hold down both eye corners with one hand while lifting one end with the other hand. Then lift the other end. Adjust the overlap at the sides to pleasing proportions. Small spring clamps are useful for holding the sides in place for boring holes and lashing.

Use chalk to locate the lashing holes. The stitching pattern can be crossed diagonals or slashes, or the stitches can run straight across with diagonals on the inside. Holes are 1/8 inch to 3/8 inch in diameter, depending on the lacing material. Holes can be punched with a reamer or a pocketknife or drilled. I use a brace with an auger bit. Some barks, like poplar, tear very easily when wet, so be careful.

Hickory bast is one of the best lacing materials. Cedar bast is excellent, and linden, elm, and willow can also be used. The Cree baskets are traditionally laced with spruce roots, and tanned leather strips will also work. Other lacing materials include wild bramble (also called blasphemy vine), very thin white oak splits, and twine.

After lacing the sides, lash on a sturdy inner rim to reinforce and hold the round shape as the bark dries. The rim can be a thin branch or split of white oak, ash, hickory, or any other good riving wood.

The Cree bark basket has a flat, square bottom. Our neighbor, Peter Gott, has worked out a simple formula for determining the dimensions of the bottom based on the circumference of the pole. (I doubt that any Indians used a formula, but it will eliminate trial and error experiments.) The distance across the bottom edges equals the circumference of the sapling minus 1 inch, divided by 2. The 1-inch measurement is for the stitched overlap.

With the bark still on the pole, use chalk to draw the bottom outline at the center of the piece (see illustration on facing page). The base overlaps approximate half-circles. Note the smaller 1-inch overlap area at the bottom corners of the sides. Use a knife to cut out the pattern. Then score halfway through the baseline of the two sides. The baseline of the large half-circle overlaps is not scored.

A lidded Cree box made from paper birch bark (Collection of Henri Vaillancourt)

The flat-bottom basket is assembled like the eye-shaped Cherokee basket. To make a lid, flatten a piece of bark and cut out a round shape, 1 inch larger than the outside diameter of the assembled container. The inner rim is a wood split lashed to the bottom of the lid.

CHAPTER FOUR
Knife-Work

Many contemporary woodworkers have little use for knives. Whittlers still use knives, but many wood-carvers now depend on high-speed power tools that cut through wood by grinding, like a dentist's drill. For some woodworkers, a knife is a scribing tool used to lay out joints.

But not long ago, knives and axes were the basic tools available to many woodworkers. Axes were used for splitting and shaping wood when a large amount of material had to be removed. Knives were for detail work.

In greenwood crafts, knife-work often takes a prominent place. A sharp knife is the essential tool for carving spoons, dippers, and wooden hardware, such as door latches, wall hooks, and handles. When I make a ladder-back chair, I may use a knife to detail rung tenons and the knobs of front and back posts. Knives are essential for basket making and other greenwood crafts that utilize bark, roots, and withes.

I first began to appreciate the possibilities of knife-work during my apprenticeship with Ruedi Kohler. Swiss coopers use knives for a wide range of tasks that most woodworkers would assign to other tools. Prior to hooping a staved container, small locating dowels are fitted between the staves to hold them in place during assembly. These dowels are carved from short, rived blanks of boxwood, a hard, slow-growing conifer. To rive the dowel blanks, a knife is placed across the end grain of a 1-inch-long piece of boxwood, then struck with a hammer. The blanks are carefully whittled, then fitted into holes bored in the sides of each stave. Once the staves are hooped together, a larger knife is used to carve away a narrow wedge-shaped section from the inside of both rims. The result, which looks like lathe-work, makes the staves appear much thinner than they really are. A small pointed knife is used to carve the male and female interlocking tabs for the wooden hooping. And a knife is used even to cut the hand-hold into an extended stave on a milking bucket. (See photo, page 7.) Finally, a Swiss cooper is expected to be a skilled chip carver. The hooping on special milking buckets—given as prizes at traditional Alpine athletic events—is often decorated with geometric carvings and an incised inscription.

I learned through Swedish woodworker Wille Sundqvist that knife-work is still held in high regard throughout Scandinavia. Carving woodenware was a traditional pastime during the long northern winters. Learning to work with one's hands is considered to be an integral part of elementary education. A Lapp-style sheath knife is the Scandinavian equivalent of our pocketknife.

After spending a few days with Wille Sundqvist in 1977, I invited him to our farm to teach a group of American woodworkers for a week. Wille agreed, and the result was the first of our Country Workshops. For projects, Wille has students make spoons and large wooden bowls. In doing this, they not only learn how to carve spoons, but they learn too about the nature of wood and about tools, including tool sharpening. Many students also make their own knives. Most of my knowledge about knife-work (and the hewed bowl project in chapter 5) comes from Wille and his son Jogge, who has also taught at Country Workshops.

Carving Materials

All but the most ornery of hardwoods are suitable for working with a knife. Knots, burls, and curly grain are usually avoided. Wooden kitchen utensils are made from hard wood with short, dense fibers. Kitchenware must be carved from woods that don't impart taste or odor. Wooden hardware—latches, knobs, and hinges—can be carved from any hard wood, including coarse-grained woods such as oak.

Carvings that aren't subjected to wear or stress can be crafted from much softer woods. Linden is a common favorite; the fiber is very soft, in addition to being fine and tight, so it takes crisp details. Other soft carving woods include yellow poplar, buckeye, and willow.

Carving Knives

In the Scandinavian tradition a general-purpose wood-carving knife has a narrow, pointed blade about 3 inches long. The bevels should be clearly defined and of even width from the handle to the

After a coopered container is put together, I taper the interior rim to make the staves appear thinner. The knife is skewed so that it takes a slicing cut. At this stage the staves are held in place with white glue.

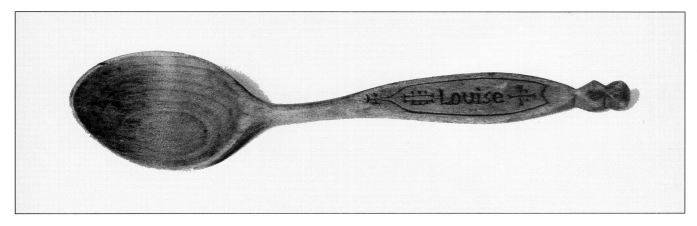

Wille Sundqvist made this "yogurt spoon" for Louise Langsner.

knife point. The blade is narrow for scooping cuts, such as at the neck of a spoon where the bowl joins the stem. The blade should be long enough for taking a slicing cut and yet not cumbersome when carving details. The point can be used for incision work, such as surface decorations. The handle must be large enough for a comfortable grip. It should be narrow and smooth where it joins the blade, and without a guard, since you may need to grasp the flat sides of the blade between thumb and index finger.

Few knives meet all these requirements. A very small sheath knife may be suitable, and some wood-carvers prefer a good-quality pocketknife. But all too often, the cross section of the blade is not really suitable for use as a woodworking tool, and the steel is too soft to hold a sharp edge.

In Sweden, many woodworkers use *sloyd* (or handcraft) knives made by firms that specialize in carving tools. The best-known brand is Erik Frost, located in Mora, but there are others located throughout Scandinavia. Frost knives have a good laminated steel blade, a plain birch handle, and a very reasonable price tag—about $9 as this is written. In the United States, Frost knives are sold by mail order through several woodworking tool suppliers.

The laminated blade of a Frost sloyd knife sandwiches a thin wafer of hard, high carbon steel between two thicker slabs of much softer steel. As on most knives, the blade is beveled on both sides. The hard center lamination holds a sharp cutting edge much better than softer steel does. But hard steel is brittle. You can bend a razor blade, which is also hard steel, just so far and it will suddenly snap in half. The soft steel sides strengthen the knife. You can actually put the blade in a vise, bend it at a 45° angle, and then straighten it. In addition to holding an edge, hard steel resists sharpening. The soft steel sides make sharpening easier, since you only have to remove a narrow band of hard steel.

Of course, it's nice to have several carving knives. Frost offers knives with 3- to 5-inch blades. You may need a larger knife for quickly removing large shavings. You'll also want a smaller knife for incision work, such as cutting bark and carving decorations. Here even a 3-inch blade becomes cumbersome. I don't know of a really nice, general-purpose, short-bladed carving knife on the market. However, it's not difficult to make your own by modifying a Frost blade. The sidebar on page 54, "Making a Carving Knife," shows how.

Sharpening

In woodworking, tool sharpening is divided into two broad divisions: edge tools and everything else. Edge tools include plane blades, chisels, gouges, drawknives, spokeshaves, hewing axes, and knives. Saws and boring tools are examples of "everything else." Sharpening is a complex subject; I'll introduce some of the basics in this chapter and give further details when we sharpen the tools used in succeeding chapters.

A knife is sharpened much like any other edge tool, except that most knife blades are beveled on two sides rather than leaving one side flat (such as chisel and plane blades).

The sharpening process can be divided into three stages: shaping, honing (also called whetting), and polishing. Each process removes the grooves created by the abrasives used in the previous stage.

Shaping is required if a blade is nicked or if the bevel or profile must be altered. Shaping can be done on an electric bench grinder, but because knife blades are very thin the heat generated by a grinder is likely to result in a loss of temper. Instead, use a grinder that turns in water or a very coarse bench stone. These abrasives cut slowly, so there's no chance of overheating.

Once the blade is in good shape, it's honed and polished with bench stones. First you hone a sharp edge as fast as possible by using a quick-cutting, medium-grit abrasive. Polishing is removing the scratch marks left by the honing stone.

For sharpening knives, bench stones should be at least 2 inches wide and 4 inches long. The most versatile size for a general purpose bench stone is twice that length.

The size of abrasive particles in bench stones ranges from 1 micron—about 1/50 the thickness of a human hair—to over 150 microns. Coarse abrasives sharpen quickly, but they leave deeply grooved tracks that must be removed with a succession of finer abrasives; the bevel of a really sharp blade will shine like a mirror.

Bench stones are made in a bewildering variety of materials.

Until recently, most of the coarser bench stones available to American and European woodworkers were made from aluminum oxide or silicon carbide. The finer polishing stones were quarried noviculite, known as Arkansas Stones. All of these stones were supposed to be lubricated with thin oil during use.

In the 1980s Japanese "water stones" were introduced to western woodworkers. Water stones

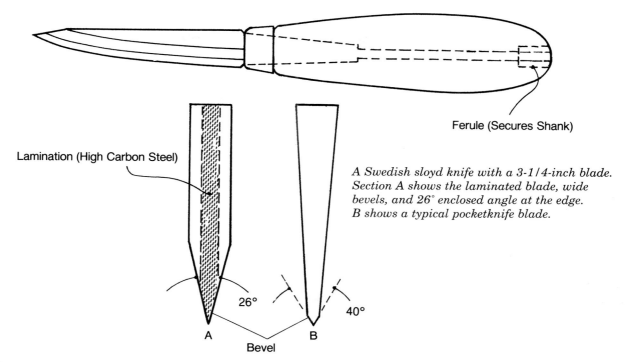

Lamination (High Carbon Steel)

Ferule (Secures Shank)

26°

Bevel

40°

A

B

A Swedish sloyd knife with a 3-1/4-inch blade. Section A shows the laminated blade, wide bevels, and 26° enclosed angle at the edge. B shows a typical pocketknife blade.

literally use water to create a paste on the stones' surface during honing and polishing. The less expensive water stones are synthesized from certain muds and other materials. The more expensive ones are quarried.

Japanese water stones cut much faster than any western oil stones. The finer polishing stones polish considerably finer (and faster) than the best hard, black Arkansas stones. Water stones are even messier to use than oil stones. Because they are soft, they must be resurfaced quite often. (But this is not difficult. I'll explain how on page 54.)

Ceramic and diamond stones are also now available. Ceramic stones are made for fine honing and polishing. The ones that I've used are incredibly slow. Also, only the finest high polish ceramic stones meet basic criteria for flatness. The others are warped from the firing process during manufacturing.

Synthetic diamond stones consist of fine particles bonded to a steel or plastic matrix. Diamond stones cut even faster than Japanese water stones. But they are not available in fine polishing grits. And they gradually wear away as the diamonds fracture during use.

Here's what I currently use:

For coarse shaping work I use several types of electric equipment. For tools that require a hollow grind I use a slow speed, 80 grit aluminum oxide wheel that runs in a water bath. For large, curved tools, such as an inshave, I like to use small, inexpensive drum sanders that attach to an electric drill. The tool being ground is held in a vise and the sander is run over the blade. For initial flattening, a small belt sander is hard to beat. (I mount a hand-held type belt sander upside-down to the surface of my sharpening bench.) For the finer type of shaping work I use coarse or medium diamond stones. I have not been impressed with the coarse water stones, which wear away extremely quickly.

Whetting in my shop is now done with diamond stones and water stones. The diamond stones are used dry. I start with a medium (270 grit) diamond stone, followed by fine (600) or super-fine (1200). Then I use a 1000 or 1200 grit water stone. I'm not sure why, but with the harder tool steels these water stones leave a considerably finer surface than the 1200 grit diamond stone.

For polishing, I use 4000 to 8000 grit water stones. These stones are available in a range of shapes and sizes, including various slips and cones. To polish the bevels of gouges and turning tools I use a very hard felt buffing wheel and white "stainless steel" buffing compound.

The old oil stones have been put into storage, as have the ceramic stones that were purchased for testing purposes.

Sharpening a sloyd knife. Fingers of the left hand press down on the knife bevel. The blade is rubbed back and forth diagonally at one end of the bench stone.

Sharpening stones can be fitted to wooden holders so they can be secured in a vise or to a bench top. Some stones come glued into fragile little boxes; for a sturdy holder, you can mortise a rectangular cavity in a block of wood. To mount a wedge-shaped slip stone, mortise a cavity with a sloped bottom.

Most stone holders are about 1 inch in height. But if you plan to use the stones for sharpening a drawknife, make your holders about 6 inches tall. The extra height allows clearance between the angled drawknife handles above the workbench surface.

Recently, I've made several Japanese-style holders which secure stones with end blocks and small wedges. The mortise doesn't have sides. Also, the bottom of the mortise doesn't become loaded up with metal dust, stone residue, and oil.

Now let's sharpen a knife. You may find these sharpening directions to be a departure from other methods. This system combines methods used by Western and Japanese woodworkers. With practice, you should be able to produce and maintain very sharp, highly polished blades for all edge tools.

First, examine your knife blade. Ideally, the blade has flat, well-defined bevels. The flat bevels act as a registration plane so that you can control your depth of cut. But the blades of most knives—including some made for woodworking—are manufactured without distinctly beveled edges. Usually, the cross section resembles a long, thin wedge, with very narrow bevels at the edge. If your knife lacks well-defined bevels, I suggest getting one that has them. Reshaping a conventional wedge-sectioned blade is very difficult.

The *enclosed angle* of a blade is crucial to its performance. This is the angle formed by the two bevels at the cutting edge (see illustration on page 51). The angle of a kitchen knife is about 40–45°. The enclosed angle of a knife used for woodworking should be 26–30°. To check the angle, use a protractor, or cut a 26–30° V in a thin piece of metal or cardboard.

If your knife blade is close to 26–30°, sharpen it at the factory-made angle and try it out. If the enclosed angle is off by more than 2 or 3°, correct the blade by reshaping with a coarse or medium diamond bench stone.

To make the enclosed angle *narrower,* begin shaping at the heel of the bevel, and gradually cut toward the edge. Stop when a wire edge (or burr) forms on the opposite side of the edge. To *widen* the angle, start at the edge and cut inward. In either case, do half of the necessary correction, then turn the knife around and shape the bevel on the other side of the blade. When the bevel angle is correct, you're ready to proceed to the next step—honing.

In describing how to hold a knife for sharpening, I'll assume that you're right-handed. Grasp the knife handle with the lower finger pads of your right hand. The blade should point to your left with the edge facing away from you. Place the fingertips of your left hand along the bevel. Your left thumb should contact the back of the blade, in opposition to your index finger.

Lower the bevel to the surface of the stone, and rock the blade back and forth slightly to discover the exact point where the bevel lies flat on the stone. Press the knife bevel against the stone, and rub the blade back and forth, at an angle of 13–15° to the axis of the blade. In effect, you are making minute abrasive scratches along the entire bevel. Using the weight of your upper body, be sure to maintain hard, even pressure on the bevel so that it remains in full contact with the stone. Beginners often fail to get a good edge because they apply too little force. Another reason, which is much harder to correct, is that the blade often isn't held at a steady angle. It helps here to avoid extra body motions.

After about 30 passes, examine the blade. If the knife is sharp, you won't be able to see the actual edge even with a magnifying glass. Also, you'll feel a burr, called wire edge, indicating that the abrasive stone has begun to push a small amount of metal over the edge. To check for the burr, pass your fingertips along the bevel while angling away the edge. As soon as you can feel a burr, you've honed as far as possible with the abrasive that you're using.

Unless your knife was quite sharp to begin with, the chances are that you haven't got a burr yet. When you go back to the stone, rotate the knife 180°, and hone the other beveled edge. (You

Using Your Body Efficiently

During the past few years, I've been learning about *body mechanics* from Carl Swensson, a Baltimore woodworker who was formerly a tennis pro. Body mechanics is concerned with ways of applying balance, use of leverage, and the force of gravity. In sports, or any physical work, your body movements should be under maximum control. The body mechanics for sharpening are similar to those for doing other woodworking. For precise sharpening—or knife-work, or hewing—you should develop a body position that is stable, with as little extraneous movement as possible. First, create a steady base for your body by spreading your feet about 18 inches apart. Hold your arms close to your ribs, so they can't flop about. Ideally, only two joints in each arm will move during any sharpening process. If more body parts become involved, your "machine" will begin to wobble and lose control in addition to wasting energy. When you're in a balanced position, most of your body can relax. Facial grimacing is a waste of energy.

wouldn't do this with a tool having a single bevel, like a chisel.) The position for your right hand is basically the same, only tilted a little to accommodate the bevel angle for the other side of the blade. Your left thumb presses down on the bevel, while the other fingers steady the back edge.

Find the exact bevel angle, and rub the blade back and forth as before. This time, after about 30 passes, begin to arc the handle away from your body in order to whet the curve of the blade toward the point. On a sloyd-type knife, the entire length of the bevel, from handle to the pointed tip, is ground to the same width. On many other knives, however, the bevel narrows as it approaches the tip; this requires that you lift the knife in order to sharpen toward the point. As you lift, the enclosed cutting angle widens. The wider angle isn't good. Lifting also results in a smaller contact patch on the stone. This is one reason why knife blades tend to wear a groove into sharpening stones. To minimize this effect, use different places on the stone from one time to the next. Also, stay within 1 inch of the end of the bench stone to counter the hollow created in the middle by other tools.

Again, after about 30–40 strokes, stop to examine the blade, checking for the telltale burr.

Bench-Stone Maintenance

As you use a bench stone, the surface becomes irregular. It's important to keep your stones flat. One reason is that it's very difficult to hold a tool at a steady rubbing angle if the stone surface is shaped like a wave or a dish. In addition, the nonbeveled side of tools with a single bevel should be kept very, very flat, and this isn't possible if your stones aren't flat also.

The easiest way to flatten a bench stone is to rub it on a piece of wet/dry sandpaper backed by a slab of plate glass. The glass should be about 5 by 12 inches and at least 3/8 inch thick. Flatten coarse shaping stones with 80x paper. Use 120x paper for honing stones and 180x or 220x for polishing stones. Sprinkle some lubricant—oil or water, depending on the type of stone being dressed—onto the glass. Tear a piece of sandpaper in half and center it on the glass. Then sprinkle oil or water onto the sandpaper. Rub the stone, bearing down on the abrasive paper, for about half a minute. Observe the surface of the stone, and you'll see a flat border where the stone makes contact with the paper and a concave inner area that you still have to wear down to. Also, sight across the surface of the stone with a straightedge held lengthwise and then cross-wise. Continue dressing until the entire surface checks out flat.

Japanese water stones flatten much more quickly than Western oil stones but may require dressing several times for each hour of use. Oil stones can usually be kept flat with once-a-year maintenance.

All bench stones should be stored under a dust cover or in a closed box or drawer. Dust will clog the pores, making the surface virtually useless. Dirty oil stones can be cleansed by heating in an oven.

Synthetic water stones (800–1200 grit) can be stored submerged in water in lidded plastic boxes made for refrigerated foods. Polishing water stones (4000–8000) should be stored dry.

Continue from bevel to bevel until you can feel a slight burr along the full length of the edge. If you don't have a wire edge within two or three minutes, use a stone with a coarser grit until you get a burr, then return to the previous stone, treating both bevels.

The final step, polishing, repeats the above rubbing procedure. Use your finest-grit bench stone. Again, be sure to get a burr along the full length of the edge. Then flip the blade and form a burr from the other side. Rub with less pressure to remove the burr.

When are you done? Look at the difference in finish and light reflectance between this stone and the one used before. When the surface finish stops changing, you've gone as far as possible with that particular abrasive. With experience, you'll feel when the blade is as sharp as it can get with a particular stone. Until you get the hang of this, you might use a magnifying glass to check your progress.

Woodworkers have all sorts of ways of checking for sharpness. You can shave some wrist hair, but coarse hair shaves much more easily than fine hair. You can also balance the edge on a fingernail, then angle the nail toward vertical to see how long the blade holds. Actual use is the best test.

To maintain this wonderful edge, do touch-up polishing often. Ideally, you should be able to produce a minute wire edge after rubbing on your polishing stone only 15 or 20 times. Then remove the burr with some light pressure, and get back to work. If you can't form a wire edge quickly, go back to a coarser grit stone and work up to the polishing stage once again.

Knife-Work Techniques

Wille and Jogge Sundqvist teach several knife techniques called *grasps*. Some grasps are for making quick, massive cuts, while others are used for detail work. These grasps are based on a few common principles.

You must be convinced that knives and all other blade tools cut wood (and flesh) *much* more easily with a slicing action (tangential to an object) than at right angles. In workshops, I demonstrate this by pushing the edge of a sharp knife against the tips of my fingers, with the comment that I'd be unwilling to pull the knife across my fingers even lightly.

All grasps include a safety factor. The way you hold a knife must involve a way to stop the blade so you *can't* get cut.

For effective control, only one or two joints of either arm should move when making a cut. You should be in a stable position, with the wood or your arms braced against your body.

Use the knife bevel to control depth of cut.

Jogge Sundqvist demonstrating the most basic grasp, used for large shavings. Be sure to slice across the blade as you push outward.

Like other hand tools, a knife cuts easily along straight grain or across wood fibers, but not against the grain. It's often necessary to alter wood or holding positions in combination with the various grasps.

Taking many shallow, but smooth, cuts is always preferable to cutting deeply and leaving a rough surface.

The most common grasp, used by whittlers everywhere, is useful for taking large shavings off the end of a piece of wood. The knife is gripped palm down, with the blade pointed left and its edge directed away from your body. Your thumb can be wrapped around the handle or pressed against the back of the blade. Your left hand holds the wood, and the back of the hand should be braced against your left thigh. The cutting action is a diagonal slice down and to the right. Slice away from your legs and into space, or position your right leg as a stop for your right hand.

Using the same grasp, small and detailed cuts can be made by holding the wood close to your chest.

By rotating the knife 180°, you can make several useful shaping and detail cuts. Brace the wood against your chest, or pull your left elbow against your side. When carving the neck of a spoon, the blade points up toward your left shoulder, and you

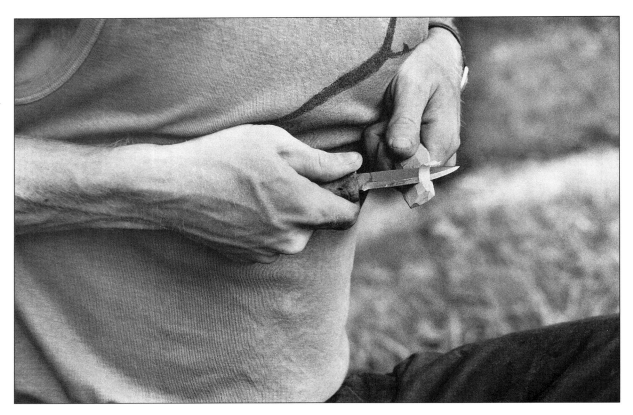

With this grasp, slice outward by rolling the base of your fist on your chest.

Pull the blade simultaneously toward your body and downward.

Using this two-handed grasp, the right thumb acts as a pivot finger. Fingers of the left hand provide additional force.

pull downward. To carve toward the end of a piece of wood, place your thumb against the end or wrap it around the opposite side. Use your thumb as a pivot. Slice upward by rotating your wrist.

A powerful but controlled cut can be made by placing the base of your fists, knuckles up, against your chest, with both elbows pointing outward. Hold the knife between your thumb and index finger, with the blade directed toward your left elbow. Hold the wood in your left hand in a similar manner, forming a mirror image of the right hand. A slicing cut is made by pivoting outward with both hands. The base of your fists, which remain positioned against your chest, acts as a fulcrum. Pull your large, upper arm muscles backward toward your body, and roll your fists outward, across your chest.

Another effective method is the dagger grasp, in which the knife is held as if you were about to stab something. Although it feels awkward at first, this grasp permits short strokes that combine power with accuracy. To take large shavings, hold the far end of the wood with your extended left arm, resting the back of your hand against your left thigh. Pull the knife toward your chest, holding it at an angle so that your right arm will be stopped against your stomach. Using this grasp, you can also make small, highly controlled cuts by arcing your wrist so that the blade moves parallel to your forearm.

You can also use both hands to guide the blade. With these grasps, the right hand acts as a fulcrum, while the fingers or thumb of the left hand apply additional force against the back of the blade.

Making a Carving Knife

In Scandinavia, woodworkers often make their own carving knifes. If you're so inclined, you can start from scratch by forging a blade from a high carbon steel rod. Another option is to fabricate a blade from tool steel bar stock. Both of these approaches require skill and knowledge of annealing, hardening, and tempering steel. A much simpler approach is to use a ready-made blade, modifying it if necessary to your needs.

Excellent laminated knife blades are available inexpensively from cutlery specialists and woodworking tool suppliers. I've made several knives using Frost blades. You can buy an unmounted blade, or you can split the blade out of a knife handle you don't mind sacrificing. Wrap tape around the blade so that you can't get cut. Then ask someone to hold the knife by the blade on a worktable so you can crack off the handle with a chisel and hammer.

Here's how to reshape the profile of a laminated blade. Because the center lamination is harder than a hacksaw blade, you can't saw through it. (You could grind it, but this risks overheating and losing the temper.) Draw a straight line on both sides of the blade where you want it cut off. Clamp the blade flat to a tabletop. Use a hacksaw or a three-cornered file to cut a groove through the soft side lamination. Stop when you run into the hard center. Turn the blade over, clamp again, and cut the opposite groove. You can now easily snap off the end of the blade. Hold the blade in a vise, and snap it off. Wear safety goggles.

Use a bench grinder to shape the new profile of the blade. With a grinder, you have to keep the blade cool so that it doesn't lose its temper. Stop grinding often to cool the blade in water. A better method is to have someone continually spray water on the blade as you grind. An inexpensive hand sprayer works fine.

Shaping the bevel is more difficult than grinding the profile. I recommend using a coarse diamond bench stone, unless you're very good at freehand grinding. The bevels should be an even width, running parallel with the cutting edge. Note that the bevel line runs into the top edge of the blade instead of coming into the point. Finally, the tang should be shortened to about 2 inches long.

For the handle, use hard wood with short, dense grain, such as hard maple, cherry, beech, birch, or apple. Highly figured or burled wood makes a beautiful, tough handle, but it will have to be shaped with rasps.

You can split the handle blank from a log or saw it from a board. Green wood is much easier to carve than dry wood. But if you use green wood, you should wait for it to dry before mounting the blade to the handle or the wood may crack as it dries and shrinks around the tang. The handle can be from 3/4 to 7/8 inch in thickness and 1 to 1-1/4 inches high. A typical length for the handle of a wood-carving knife is 4 or 5 inches.

Boring the tang hole: with a pencil, draw centerlines down all four sides of the handle blank and across both ends. Position the handle vertically in a vise. (Or if you have a drill press, use it for this step.) Use a small try square to check for plumb from two perpendicular directions. Drill a row of 3/32-inch holes along the centerline of the end that is to receive the tang. Bradpoint bits are easy to position accurately. If you use a high-speed twist bit, first dimple a row of centering holes with an awl or nail. Bore to the depth of the tang.

Wrap the blade with tape so that you won't cut yourself. Clean the sides of the mortise so that you can get the tang into it. Don't be too fussy with this. I use a very thin 3/8-inch sculptor's chisel. You could also run a hand-held electric drill in and out of the hole, slanting it at different angles. Stop as soon as you can insert the tang all the way.

The next step is to design the handle. Leaving the tang in place, outline the handle shape on sides, top, and bottom. The side view can take any shape that is comfortable and provides a good grip. The top view should be symmetrical. The end that joins the blade should be narrow, so you can comfortably "choke up" on the handle, with your thumb and first finger against the sides of the blade.

If the handle shape includes a negative curve, saw a kerf at the deepest point to act as a knife stop so that you won't remove too much wood. Your knife strokes can run with or across the grain but not into it. Stop often to observe your work from different angles. Since this is a knife handle, continually test it for feel in various grasps. You can work with the blade in or out of the handle. When you get the shape just right, sand the handle smooth.

The blade is permanently secured with ordinary two-part epoxy. If the fit is loose, locate the blade in the exact position that you want with two miniature wedges. Don't try to put a large blob of epoxy into the hole at once—air will become trapped, and you won't get the hole filled. Fill the hole gradually, pushing the epoxy in with a toothpick. If the mortise is wide and unsightly, you can color the last bit of epoxy by mixing in a little sanding dust from the handle wood. Finally, finish the handle with oil (I like tung oil), remove the tape from the blade, sharpen your knife, and begin a spoon.

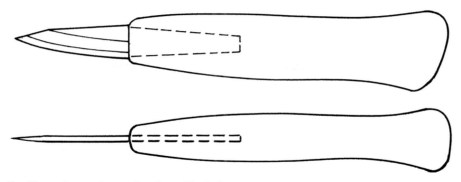

Profile and top views of a short-bladed carving knife that I made. The blade was made from a standard sloyd blade. The blade tang is secured in the hardwood handle with epoxy. After 10 years use, it hasn't loosened.

Carving knives that I've made using Swedish sloyd blades

A few of my serving spoons, made from apple wood.

Project: Carving a Spoon

Spoon making is an excellent exercise in carving techniques. You'll learn how to look at objects very carefully from various angles of view and how visual aesthetics relates to the function of an object. Attractive proportions and balance can transform a spoon into a small piece of sculpture.

You can make mixing spoons, ladles, servers, soup spoons, porridge spoons, salad servers, butter spreaders, and rice paddles. Serving spoons are often made with an attractive angled stem. An end hook is a nice feature, especially for dippers.

Tools. Only a few tools are required—you can take your spoon-making "kit" along when traveling or work in the living room while visiting with friends. Hand-carved spoons make prized gifts.

A spoon-making tool kit includes a good, all-around carving knife and one or two gouges for hollowing out the bowl. The carving blank can be roughed out with a light hatchet or a small bow saw with a blade that can be rotated at any angle. (A coping saw will also work.) A small vise or clamp is necessary if you're going to saw out the blanks. You'll also need sandpaper in several grits.

Visualization of possible spoons within a crooked limb. Note the smaller bowl of the upper spoon. Be sure to avoid the pith wood.

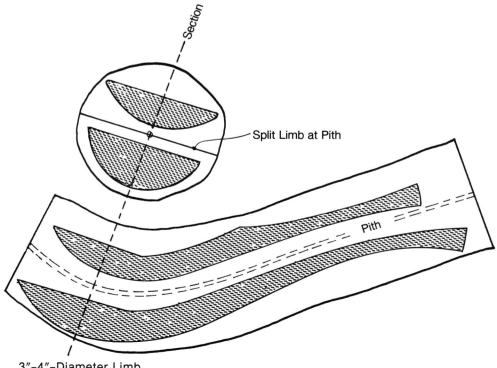

Materials. You can use almost any kind of wood that has short, dense fibers and is tasteless and odorless. My spoons are usually apple or dogwood and are always crafted green. Ruedi Kohler uses hard maple to carve cream skimmers. English spoon carvers prefer sycamore. Swedish spoon makers usually carve birch and sometimes birch root. Other suitable woods include beech, holly, pear, and persimmon. In southern Appalachia, slow-growing, convoluted rhododendron used to be called "spoonwood." Crooked limbs may provide wood in the approximate shape of the spoon. The advantage of using something with a natural crook is greater strength, since carving severs fewer fibers, especially around the bowl.

Countless generations of spoon carvers have evolved classic shapes that are hard to improve on. I advise beginners to copy existing designs before trying personal ideas. If your first spoons are copies, you'll have a chance to practice knife grasps and hollowing the bowl without the distraction of trying to be creative. You'll also be more likely to make nice spoons from the start, sparing yourself frustration. Feel free to copy the pattern in the illustration on page 60 and the spoons in the photograph.

Well-designed spoons share certain characteristics. They tend to be lightweight and well balanced, and they do the intended job comfortably. A really fine spoon will be pleasing to observe from any angle. Note that the spoons in the photographs are very three-dimensional; they're not flat but offer interesting angles when seen from any angle.

For strength, the leading edge of the bowl, which is end grain, should be comparatively thick. The bottom of the bowl can be very thin. The bowl of an eating spoon should be fairly shallow. It won't feel comfortable in your mouth if it's deep. The area where the bowl joins the stem should have adequate strength. The stem must feel comfortable in all positions in which the spoon will be used.

For wood, select a trunk section, sapling, or limb, called a *bole*, from any of the trees mentioned above. The minimum size is about 3 inches in diameter. Anything larger is fine. The piece can be straight or bent. (Wille and Jogge prefer the bent ones.) You may want to begin by making a practice spoon from a soft wood, such as white pine. The sawed length of the limb or trunk should be no longer than the spoon you're about to make.

The easiest way to reduce the bole into a spoon blank is by splitting it. Split 2- to 3-inch-diameter boles in halves to make two spoons, one from either half. Larger boles can be split into a number of radial sections. I like radial splits because the uniform grain is easier to carve. However, you then sacrifice the advantage of using a crook. It's a trade-off.

The most accurate method for splitting spoon blanks—and other smallish boles—is to use an axe for a wedge, hitting the blade's flat head (or *poll*) with a wooden club. (You can read how to make the club in chapter 6.) Stand the bole upright on a log stump. Position the blade of the axe so that it passes across the pith, then strike the axe poll with the club. If you're making radial blanks, the second split should be positioned to make quarter sections. For visual reasons, I seldom combine contrasting heart and sapwood in the same spoon. Discard the heartwood or sapwood, whichever is smaller. It's important to remove all of the pith, or the spoon will certainly split during drying.

The next step is drawing the outline of the top view of the spoon. You can draw on wet wood with a soft pencil or a marking pen. (My favorite greenwood marker is an Eberhard Faber Blu-Blak pencil, number 740, available from a stationery store.) Use a straightedge to draw a centerline down the middle of the blank, then draw the outline about 1/8 inch oversize.

The blank can be roughed out with a light hand axe or a bow saw. Hewing with an axe is a greater challenge and more adaptable once the skill is developed. Hewing is also considerably more difficult than sawing. An advantage of sawing the top outline is that the kerf yields vertical sides on which you can easily draw the side profile. I recommend that you saw out your first spoons. I'll introduce hewing methods in chapter 5.

A European style bow saw, with knobs that rotate the blade, works especially nicely. You can make one quite easily or buy one from a woodworking tool supplier. You can also use an ordinary coping saw or a band saw.

Bow saws work best cutting on a pull stroke, with the teeth angled toward your body. Take light strokes, without putting much pressure on the blade. Let the saw do the cutting. As you enter a curve, gradually saw back and forth while advancing only slightly. If necessary, rotate the knobs so that the saw frame doesn't bump into the stock. When you adjust the knobs, make sure both are set

Making a Bow Saw Blade

The blades that I've purchased with factory-made bow saws are not particularly effective. I replace them with lengths of ordinary band-saw blade. I use a 1/4-inch blade with eight teeth per inch. Before you can use a band-saw blade, you need to drill a small hole in each end to accept the holding pins. Since band-saw steel is hardened, it must be annealed (softened) before you can drill through it. Here's how. Heat the last inch of the blade red hot over a propane torch or kitchen gas stove. Then remove the blade to one side of the flame and allow it to cool slowly. Finally, dimple the end with a center punch and drill the required hole with an ordinary twist bit. Then do the other end.

in the same plane so that the blade isn't twisted. Reposition the blank in the vise as necessary for easy cutting, and keep the saw perpendicular to the face of the blank. If you have a hard time sawing on the pull stroke, try reversing position and sawing with the push stroke. Some people do much better pushing.

Once the top view of the spoon is cut out, draw the profile view on the sides and saw it out.

Now you'll get to practice some knife grasps. Start by taking the edges off the sharp corners, particularly at the bottom of the bowl. Use the knife bevel as a guide to take long shallow shavings.

Stop often to examine where you're going. My colleague Carl Swensson says to make small mistakes, not large ones that will get you into big trouble. Compare your spoon with the model that you're copying. Learn to analyze the shape in terms of the overall configuration, which is gradually refined. Look at your spoon from various angles, and hold it by the stem in the position in which it will be used. A common problem among beginners is making the neck too skinny. Also, leave the bowl oversized for now, so that it's large enough to hold by hand when you hollow it. Carefully flatten the lip of the bowl so that it describes a flat plane.

When your spoon is blocked to approximate shape, it's time to carve the bowl cavity with a gouge. The method that I learned from Wille Sundqvist is unusual because it doesn't require holding the spoon in a vise. This method uses one or two conventional gouges. Special bent spoon-carvers knives can also be used.

Gouges are sold in different widths, measured in millimeters and different *sweeps* or curvatures, ranging from #1, which is almost flat, to #11, a U-shaped *veiner*. *Spoon* gouges and *bent* gouges are nice to have, but they're not used for spoon carving. I recommend starting with a #8 sweep 18mm gouge and possibly a #3 sweep 18mm gouge.

Before starting to hollow the spoon bowl, draw an outline of the inner edge of the rim. The gouge grasp for hollowing may seem awkward at first. With practice, you'll find that it's fast, efficient, and safe. Start with the #8 sweep gouge. Grasp the gouge blade with your right palm facing upward. Fold your index finger around the stem of the blade. Extend your thumb toward the butt of the handle. The blade should point to your left. (This is also the grasp for using a crooked knife.)

With your left hand also palm up, grasp the spoon around the neck. The bowl should point away from your body; the handle end should point toward your stomach.

Extend your left thumb across the top of the bowl. Press the heel of your right hand against the end of your left thumb. The gouge cutting edge is somewhere between 12 and 3 o'clock on the spoon bowl.

Lower the blade to the wood. Use the end of your left thumb as a fulcrum to take a cut, starting at the rim and scooping toward the center. Be sure to maintain contact between the heel of your right hand and your extended left thumb. This is your safety provision. Take long, shallow cuts, rather than digging down and then stopping. After some practice, grasp further down the stem of the spoon so that you can gouge the bowl between 3 and 6 o'clock. The front of the bowl should have a shallow slope; the back can be steeper.

Reverse the spoon in your left hand so that the handle points away from your body. Hollow the bowl between 7 and 11 o'clock as seen from the original spoon position. This area is harder to carve than the first side, especially on a small spoon. Be sure to keep your left thumb in the safety position. Return to the original holding position whenever necessary. It's O.K. to modify your hand positions, but the safety stop and the basic grasp with both hands are always required.

When the bowl reaches the desired depth, smooth it out with very shallow cuts. This is where the #3 sweep gouge is used. Smooth gouge-work means less sanding later.

After the bowl is hollowed, return to the knife-work. Trim around the edge of the bowl. View the

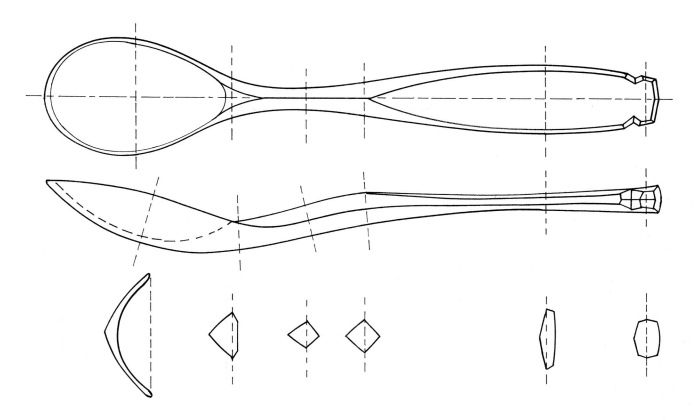

Top view, profile, and sections of a spoon made by the author. The length is 8 inches.

profile of the spoon, sighting for irregularities in the bowl rim and incongruous bumps in the handle. Examine the spoon from above to see if it's symmetrical. Check the bowl thickness by feeling the inner and outer surfaces between your thumb and index finger. If it's too thick, you can carve more off the exterior or deepen the bowl and then lower the rim.

Perhaps the most challenging part of finishing a spoon is detailing the end of the stem. You have to cut across the grain, and the final result should be symmetrical. Be sure to slice with the knife, either away from or into the cut. A simple, eye-pleasing finial at the tip is a traditional Scandinavian touch.

If you don't finish your spoon in one day, you can keep the wood wet by storing it in a plastic bag or in damp sawdust.

Your spoon must be dried before it can be sanded. Because they're so thin, spoons usually dry without checking. To be sure, you can partially seal the pores by rubbing the wood with a boiled potato. This slows down surface transpiration. Then put your spoon in a warm place to dry—for instance, above a heater or wood stove. You can tell when

wood is dry by holding it against your cheek or clapping it against another piece of dry wood and listening. The sound should be musical, not mushy.

Before sanding the tool marks off your spoon, you may decide to do some more knife- or gouge-work. The dry wood is harder to work, but it cuts more cleanly and crisply. Don't sand and then go back to using an edge tool, because traces of abrasive grit will dull your knife.

Start sanding with a small piece of 80-grit paper, about 1-1/2 by 5 inches and folded into thirds. Be careful not to sand the rim of the bowl too thin. Sand off all the rough tool marks. Then sand the abrasive marks off with 120-grit paper, followed by smoothing with 180- or 220-grit. When the spoon is smooth, quickly dip it in hot water to raise the surface fibers. When it dries, resand the fuzzy areas. For a finish, I suggest using walnut oil (purchased at a health food store). Use a day-long soak, or rub in the oil with a clean, white rag. Rubbing vigorously produces heat which aids penetration. Allow the oil to dry for a few weeks before putting the spoon to use.

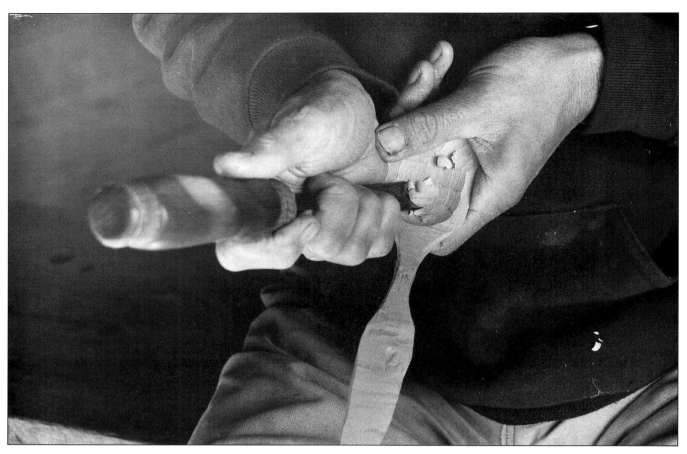

Hollowing a spoon with a straight gouge. The left thumb acts as a fulcrum and a safety stop for the gouge.

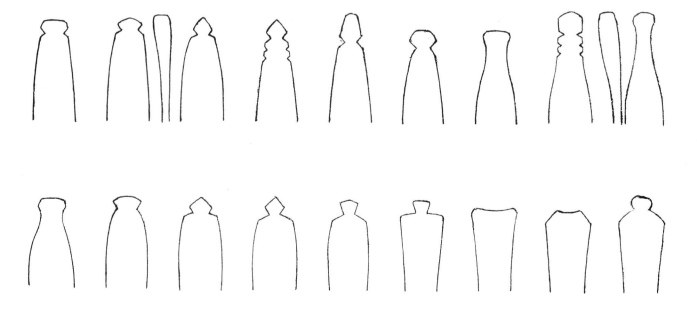

Spoon finials

Variationer på ändavslutningar för skedskaft

spoonhandels

1992. 11. 01

Wille Sundqvist

Sharpening Gouges

Learning how to sharpen a gouge isn't that difficult if you've done well with knife sharpening. The main difference is that a gouge has only one bevel, on the convex side. The inside of the blade flute is straight.

Sharpening the bevel of a gouge. Rotate the blade (don't roll it) so that the exterior bevel rubs on the bench stone.

When you get a new gouge, examine the bevel carefully to see that it is flat. The base of the bevel, where it joins the back of the blade, should be rounded. This creates the clearance needed at the back of the blade for gouging out a cavity. If your gouge has a micro-bevel, a small, secondary bevel near the cutting edge, you'll need to remove it by reshaping with a coarse bench stone. Otherwise, proceed with honing.

Secure an appropriate stone to the bench top (in a holder). With the handle pointing to your right, grasp the upper end of the blade with the fingertips of your right hand. Place the tips of your left index, middle, and ring fingers on the near edge of the blade flute.

Lower the gouge bevel to the stone, with the handle lifted about 25° from horizontal. Rub the blade forward and backward on the stone over a distance of about 3 inches. At the same time, rotate the blade away from your body on the forward rub and toward your body on the back rub so that the entire surface of the bevel is abraded. Press down fairly hard on the stone.

After about 30 rubs, check for a wire burr along the flute. If you've got a burr, proceed with the polishing stone. If you don't have a burr, try the same stone for 30 more rubs. If you still don't get a burr, drop back to a coarser stone until you do. Then work up again through the finer stones.

Use a fine-grit slip stone to remove the minute polishing burr on the inside of the flute. Place the slip stone flat inside the flute of the gouge. Being sure to grip well back on the sides of the slip so you can't get cut, rub the stone back and forth while rotating the gouge blade to insure contact within the full arc of the flute. *Be sure to keep the slip stone flat in the flute;* lifting it will alter the enclosed angle of the edge. Stop when the burr is removed. If you've created a slight burr on the outside of the bevel, return to the polishing bench stone and very lightly remove it. A final polish can be achieved with a hard felt buffing wheel.

CHAPTER FIVE

Hewing

Most readers of this book will have some experience using an axe, but you may not be familiar with its older relative, the adze. In use, these tools overlap, with each having certain specialties. The main difference is that the blade of an adze is perpendicular to the handle, like that of a garden hoe.

When you swing an axe, the blade describes a flat plane. A wedge-shaped blade striking end grain will split wood. A blade shaped more like a knife or a chisel can be used to shape wood by severing wood fibers. This is known as hewing.

The arc of an adze describes a scooping action similar to that of a mattock. In profile, adze blades are curved to suit that arc. The cutting edge may be straight or cupped. Adzes with a straight cutting edge are used to hew flat or slightly curved surfaces. Examples include building timbers and some wooden boat framing. "Lipped" adze blades have an upturned radius at each corner to prevent grain tear-out.

The cupped blade of a hollowing adze resembles a very large, bent gouge. Uses include scooping out wooden bowls, saddling the thick plank seats of Windsor chairs, and crafting dugout canoes.

Traditional axes and adzes were made in a very wide range of weights and shapes. A skilled blacksmith could easily modify a design to suit the needs of a particular craftsperson or make special patterns suitable for different trades. With the development of industrial technology, new tools and machinery displaced most of these specialized hand tools.

The common hardware store axe, which has an enclosed blade angle of about 45°, is a basic splitting tool. The blade must be thick enough so that it can work as a wedge, pushing bundles of fibers apart. (Splitting techniques are discussed in chapter 6.) Hewing is usually limited to chopping limbs or occasionally felling small trees. The *poll*, which is the flat head opposite the blade on a single-bit axe, can be used to drive wooden or plastic felling wedges.

Double-bit axes tend to be thinner. One bit can be kept sharp for felling or limbing, while the other blade is ground at a wider angle for splitting. This is probably the ultimate woodsman's axe. But since most timber cutting is done with saws, double-bit axes are seldom needed, and the second cutting edge can cause serious injuries when the axe is swung or carried.

Types of hewing axes differ mainly in blade cross section and handle length. The cross section of a hewing axe blade can be either symmetrical (with bevels on both sides of the cutting edge) or asymmetric (with one flat side and one bevel, like a chisel). Thus, the four general axe types are: 1. the single-bevel, short-handled axe; 2. the single-bevel, long-handled axe; 3. the double-bevel, short-handled axe; and 4. the double-bevel, long-handled axe. The short-handled axes are usually called hatchets.

In shop nomenclature, hatchets are known as *bench axes*. They are distinguished from ordinary camping hatchets by a thinner blade and often a single bevel.

Large, single-bevel axes used to hew logs and beams are known as *broad axes*. The head of a broad axe used to hew an American log cabin weighs from 6 to 10 pounds and has a cutting edge 8 to 14 inches long. Smaller broad hatchets, weighing 2 to 4 pounds, are used in the shop and for carpentry.

To hew with a double-bevel axe, you must tilt either the blade or the material so that the inner bevel can make a slicing cut in line with the wood being hewed. The single-bevel broad axe can be used with an easy, plumb action—that is, straight up and down. The disadvantage of a broad axe is that it's limited to hewing flat and slightly convex planes.

Thin-section, double-bevel axes and hatchets can be used for hewing flat planes, V-notches, and concave shapes. If the enclosed blade angle is too wide—shaped for splitting—you can modify it by regrinding the bevel closest to your body, creating an asymmetric double-bevel section. Refer to the illustration on the facing page.

Handle length is determined by the use an axe is put to. Full-length handles help you to deliver the force needed to split end grain. But for hewing I often find that hatchet and axe handles are longer than necessary. Hewing calls for exacting control; often

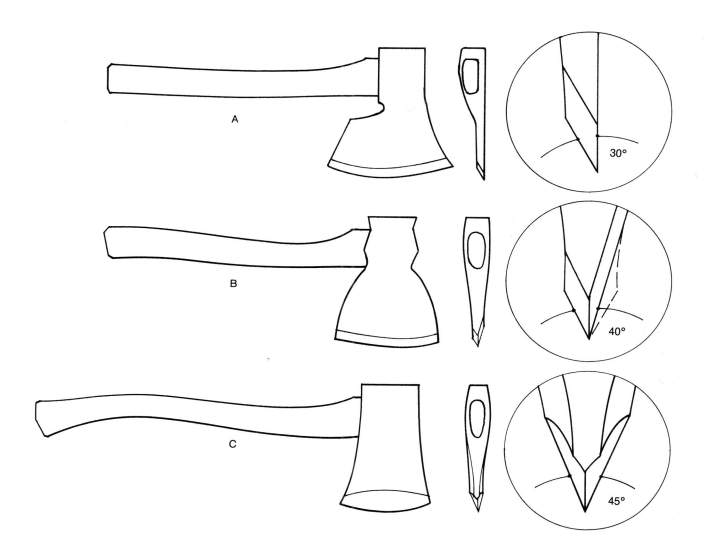

Hatchets. A. A German single-bevel bench axe. B. An English double-bevel Kent axe. The bevel angle on one side has been made steeper. The broken line indicates the original bevel. C. A double-bevel camp hatchet, useful for splitting but not hewing.

you need to grip the handle closer to the head than you would for splitting. Heavy axe heads require the shorter handles. The handle of a heavy bench axe should be just long enough to give you something to hold on to. You can saw a long handle down to a reasonable length or make a replacement.

In selecting a hewing axe of any type, first consider the blade; the handle can be replaced. Hewing requires a thinner blade than you'd use for splitting wood, with an enclosed blade angle of about 30°. For balance, hewing axes generally have a low profile. A tall head makes the axe difficult to control because it tends to wobble as you swing. The corners of the blade must be prominent if it is to be useful for cut-

ting. Edge bevels should be crisply defined, with a consistent bevel angle from corner to corner. A curved blade cuts better than a straight blade because it slices more easily.

Like knives, some of the best axes are made with laminated blades. The laminated edge of a single-bevel axe consists of a thin slab of high carbon steel, forge-welded to the inner side. You can often see the lamination by examining the ends or inner side of the blade or the bevel. Laminated double-bevel axes are scarce. The carbon-steel lamination is sandwiched between the two sides of the blade.

If you're buying a used axe, reject anything with deep pitting near the cutting edge. Superficial rust

Bench axes. The axe at the top is a cooper's broad hatchet, made in Germany just before World War II. It has a single bevel and a laminated blade. The middle axe is a Japanese carpenter's hatchet. The lower hatchet is a reproduction of a 10th-century Viking axe from Sweden. The blade is double beveled.

is easily removed using sandpaper lubricated with sharpening oil. You can test the cutting edge for hardness with a new mill file. To get a feeling for hardness, first try out the file on some steel of known hardness; the shank of a screwdriver is about the same hardness as a good axe blade. The file must bite, but it shouldn't remove large filings. If the edge feels very soft against the file, there's a good chance that the axe has lost its temper in a fire or that the original laminated edge has been ground off. If the file slides across the edge, as if over glass, the edge is very hard and brittle. This can be acceptable, but sharpening will be tedious, and you'll have to watch out for chipping.

In selecting a single-bevel axe, be sure that the flat side of the blade looks straight when examined vertically. Horizontally, the inner side should take a slight convex bow, so that the blade corners won't dig into the wood being hewed. The curve can rise 1/16 to 3/16 inch, depending on the length of the blade. The edge, when viewing the profile of the blade, should also appear curved, rising 1/4 to 3/4 inch from the center to the corners. Occasionally, the eye is offset from the plane of the blade. This helps to create knuckle clearance when hewing flat surfaces. Usually the handle of a broad axe bends away from the blade at the required angle.

Adzes are also made with long and short handles and with different bevels. The handle of a *foot adze* is about 30 inches long, and the tool is used while straddling or standing on the wood being hewed. The shorter *hand adze* is used for smaller-scale work, such as notching logs or scooping bowls. Tightly curved adzes require a short, stubby handle. Adze blades generally have a single bevel. The flat bevel of a foot adze is on the inner side of the blade, while the gougelike blade of a scooping adze requires an exterior bevel.

Sharpening

Sharpening an axe or adze involves the same steps—shaping, honing, and polishing—as knife sharpening. Axe and adze blades are larger, and they are often made from softer steel. You may find yourself restoring an antique or modifying something that's available.

Shaping often includes defining new bevels and removing nicks and rust pits. The straight inner side of a broad axe may require flattening—not an easy project.

Minor shaping can often be done with a mill file. But serious refurbishing may call for using abrasive machines, such as a bench grinder or a belt sander. Always carefully study the configuration of a tool before grinding—it's sometimes tempting to start grinding before being sure what to do. Understand *why* a tool is configured as it is before you change the shape.

When you use power abrasives, be sure to follow the recommended safety procedures. Eye protection is a necessity.

Power grinding carries the risk of overheating metal, causing a loss of temper. A typical woodworking tool blade is tempered between 375° and 400°F. That's not very hot; higher temperatures are easily created by grinding friction and will drastically soften tool steel. Temperatures can get out of hand unnoticed. At 500°F, tool steel turns blue and loses temper. Anyone who uses a bench grinder has experienced this. When an edge turns blue, the only remedy, short of rehardening and retempering, is to grind off the entire area.

Heat always moves toward cold. When you grind, heat migrates away from the area being abraded. Hot spots tend to occur as an edge gets thinner and in corners where heat is trapped.

Coarse abrasives cut more quickly and coolly than finer abrasives. Glazed grinding wheels and abrasive belts contain fine metallic debris between the abrasive particles. They cut slowly and generate excessive heat. Grinding wheels should be dressed frequently. White or green wheels of vitrified aluminum oxide cut more coolly than the more common gray silicon carbide wheels. White and green wheels cost more and wear more quickly, but are worth the investment.

Heat buildup can be minimized by slowing down the speed of the abrasive. On belt-driven equipment, you can generally change pulley sizes. Belt sanders run considerably more coolly than powered grinding wheels. Hand-cranked grinders with a 22-to-1 gear ratio are excellent for delicate work but lack the power required for substantial shaping.

An alternative to grinding with a stationary machine is to secure the tool in a vise and go at it with a hand-held off-set grinder or a mini-belt sander. Small power tools are usually powered with a universal (AC-DC) brush-type motor, which can be slowed down with a device called a speed control. This method gives you better visibility of the tool blade. A disadvantage is that you aren't shielded from sparks, so wear eye protection.

Always set safety shields and tool guides carefully, and make sure that all adjustment nuts are tight. Before I turn on a grinder, I go through a dry run to make sure that the blade can be accurately positioned as it's moved across the abrasive. Once you start grinding, keep the blade moving at all times. If you don't, the metal is sure to overheat and lose temper.

Machinists commonly use a fine water mist as a continuous coolant during grinding. A mist system isn't expensive, but it requires an air compressor for

A flat-bladed hand adze (left) and a foot adze (top, center) have single bevels on the inner side of the blades. Hollowing hand adzes (right and bottom) should have an exterior bevel.

power. You can accomplish the same cooling effect by getting a helper to spray water with a hand-mister of the sort used for spraying houseplants. Another method is to immerse the tool in a bucket of water as soon as it begins to get hot. Use your fingers as a temperature gauge by holding the blade as close to the grinding edge as is safe.

If a blade requires a new edge profile, define it before shaping the bevel by grinding straight across the edge. This is called *jointing*. Use light, even pressure.

Files must have handles to protect your palm from the file tang and from the edge of the tool being sharpened. Use files in the cutting direction only, cutting away from your body. Don't rub back and forth.

File teeth should be kept clean. You can make a file cleaner with a 12- or 16-penny common nail. File a flat edge on the nail head; then draw this edge through the file teeth to groove it to the pattern of the file being cleaned. Make a handle for the nail shank by drilling a hole in a piece of hardwood.

If you're using a bench stone, be careful to grip it well above the lower surface of the stone so that you won't get cut by the axe or adze edge. The procedure is the same as sharpening a knife, only upside down; you move the abrasive instead of the tool. Find the correct bevel angle, then rub the stone back and forth until a wire edge is formed.

Dress the flat side of a single-bevel axe before shaping the bevel, and then leave it alone. Start with a belt sander, file, or a coarse diamond bench stone. Be sure to make contact with the area leading to the cutting edge. You could also take the axe head to a machine shop. When you get a burr, progress to a honing stone—a fine diamond—followed by a polishing stone. When polishing the flat side of a single-bevel axe, be sure to hold the stone flat against the bevel. Further work on the flat side is unnecessary and often destructive.

On a single-bevel axe, hone the beveled side only; once the flat side is truly flat, you never hone it. A little polishing is all that's necessary. On a double-bevel axe, hone both bevels. Stop honing when you feel a burr along the full length of the opposite side of the bevel.

Polish with a 4000 to 8000 water stone. Work at the bevel until you can feel a much finer burr than the one created by the honing stone. The bevels should shine.

Once your axe is sharp, make a blade guard to protect both the edge and yourself and others from injury. Sewn or riveted leather blade guards are best, but I often simply tie a slitted piece of hose over the edge.

Axe Techniques

Hewing is strenuous, precise, and potentially dangerous; body mechanics is important. You should work *with* gravity. Begin hewing with a wide stance. If you need to lean forward, extend your left leg (assuming a right-handed grip) so that your center of gravity remains within the base created by your feet. Work at developing a rhythmic action. Restrict body movements to one or two joints of each arm. To save energy, relax and immobilize body parts not involved in the work. Avoid wrist movement.

Bench axes are generally used with a chopping stump to support the work and act as a safety stop. The stump should be tall enough that you don't need to lean over it. A stump for hewing short work, such as cooperage staves, should be taller than one used for hewing larger materials. The stump must be stable. You can make a two-level stump by cutting a step in the work surface.

To prevent a piece from slipping sideways when you are hewing, hollow a groove or shallow cavity in the top of the stump. (You can do this with a chain saw. Be very careful to avoid kickback, using the lower tip end of the saw bar only.) The chopping surface should be kept clean, since grit will dull a sharp hewing axe. An inverted box makes a good protector when the chopping stump is not in use.

Hold the wood being hewed so that it's impossible to get cut. Place the end you are hewing on the stump, and hold on to the piece on the opposite side of the hewing. Never let your fingers grip the face being hewed. Also take a wide stance, with your right leg well back and away from the path of the axe if it should miss the wood being hewed.

Chop with a vertical swing whenever possible. Let gravity work for you. For angled cuts, tilt the wood to allow a vertical swing. The wood must be well supported by the stump, both so that it can't slip and to back up the force of the axe. Support is particularly important when hewing a thin and delicate piece that could break. It's sometimes convenient to support a piece at a horizontal angle, overhanging the edge of the stump.

Use the axe so that it slices, rather than trying to cut perpendicularly to the fibers. When hewing large chips, grasp the handle toward the end for a good swing. Swedish woodworker Jogge Sundqvist showed me how to "throw" the axe. You reach high above your head, take aim, and fling the axe into the work—*without releasing your grasp on the handle*. The technique is effective and not as difficult as you might imagine. Be sure to grasp the work a safe distance from the axe swing, and use a large, solid hewing stump. To hew away a large amount of wood, make a series of diagonal scoring cuts into the grain, then hew off the waste in line with the fibers.

For small, detailed work that requires control, hold the handle close to the axe head. Place your thumb around the inner side of the eye, and extend

Bowls and spoons carved by Drew Langsner, except the serving spoon on the left, which was carved by Wille Sundquist

your index finger across the outer side. Use a short, deliberate chopping action.

You can also use a bench axe as a giant chisel. Position the blade on the wood, then press down hard with your full body weight. This can be effective toward the end of a hewing job, when you don't want chop marks to show. Be sure to have the work safely and securely held.

Adze Techniques

Posture is particularly important when using an adze. Stand directly over the work or as close to it as possible, so that you don't have to reach out far from your body. Short hand adzes can be used with one or two hands. I generally use both hands, gripped close together on the handle. A variation is to grasp the adze with your right hand, then grip your right wrist with your left hand for added strength.

To control both depth of cut and the arc of the adze, press your elbows against your torso or thighs so that your lower arms swing in a constant radius.

As with all other hand tools, adzes cut with or across grain, but not against it.

Project: Hewing a Large Bowl

Tools. To hew a large bowl, you use a bench axe, hollowing adze, gouges, and possibly a plane, drawknife, and spokeshave.

The hollowing adze must have a curved edge when viewed in section and an exterior bevel (one on the outside of the curve). Some hollowing adzes that I've seen have an interior bevel and a poll. As sold, they're useless for hollowing. I bought one, ground off the original interior bevel, shaped an exterior bevel, and hacksawed off the poll since the adze felt too heavy. The tool works quite well, but I had to add to the cost of this adze a morning's labor and half a grindstone. It's worth finding (and paying for) a really good adze that will do the job as intended.

Materials. The type of wood you choose depends on the use your bowl will be put to. Usually, large bowls are hewed from soft woods, but many carved bowls have been made from walnut and other hardwoods, including burls. In Sweden, hewn troughs are generally paper birch. Actually, bowls can be hewed from almost anything free of knots. For help in choosing a wood, refer to the tables "Comparative Hardness and Softness" and "Comparative Freedom from Odor and Taste When Dry" in chapter 3.

Bowls that contact food must be made with a wood that doesn't impart an odor or taste. Linden, yellow poplar, and buckeye are traditional choices. Catalpa and butternut can also be used. I recently saw an advertisement for dough bowls made from water tupelo, guaranteed not to split. I haven't tried water tupelo, but it should be nice to work green. Water tupelo grows in river and coastal swamps from Virginia to Texas.

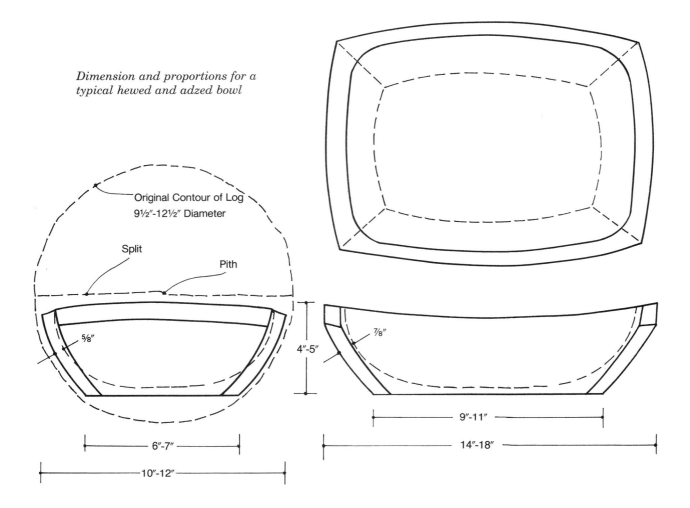

*Dimension and proportions for a
typical hewed and adzed bowl*

Original Contour of Log
9½"-12½" Diameter

Split

Pith

⅝"

4"-5"

⅞"

6"-7"

10"-12"

9"-11"

14"-18"

The design of a hewed bowl can take many shapes, but there are basic guidelines that enhance appearance while strengthening the bowl and lessening chances of checking. Most bowls are taken lengthwise from a log that has been split in half. Also, it is easier to make a shallow bowl with gradually sloped sides and a rounded interior bottom than one with steep sides and ends. Most traditional carved bowls are symmetrical, but asymmetric shapes can also be attractive.

Most often, bowl carvers begin by hewing the exterior, based on an idea that they have better control or can make more interesting forms than if they started by hollowing. I prefer to hollow the cavity first and will describe that method.

You need a log section without any end checks. The diameter should be slightly greater than the width of the bowl. The depth will be something less than the radius. A bowl that's about 15 inches long and 8 inches wide makes an excellent starting project.

Crosscut the log slightly longer than the finished bowl. Avoid knots and checks. To split the log in half, stand it on end, place a wide axe blade across the pith, and strike the axe poll with a wooden club. (Never strike the axe poll with an iron sledge or maul.) The first step is to hew a flat bottom. Support the split edge of the log half on your chopping stump. Tilt about 20° from vertical. Chop a series of scoring cuts. Then hew the bottom as flat as possible, eyeballing it from end to end at a low angle. At this stage, the bottom extends the full length of the log. After hewing, finish flattening the bottom with a plane. A jack plane with a slightly convex blade is ideal. Next, use the axe to rough out the rim. Hew the rim below the pith; if the pith were to stay, the bowl will crack as it dries. Use the same hewing procedure, starting with scoring cuts. The rim at this stage is usually parallel to the plane of the bottom. Don't be fussy, since the rim is easy to finish once the cavity is hollowed.

Using a felt marker or a soft pencil, outline the inner and outer edges of the rim. The sides should be thinner than the ends, which are much weaker end grain. Typical thicknesses are 5/8 inch for the sides and 1 inch for the ends. Extended handles will make the ends longer.

To adze the cavity, place the bowl on the floor or on a sturdy low bench. Secure it with end cleats or pegs, and a tightening wedge. If you can't put nails in the floor, nail the cleats to a piece of plywood that's wide enough to stand on.

When I use a short-handled adze for scooping or flattening, I like to stand directly over the work with my legs bent. To support my back, I prop both elbows against my thighs. I swing the adze with my lower arms. The radius of my swing is safe and easy to control, since both arms pivot from my fixed elbows.

Start adzing just past the center and chop toward the near end. At first, adze just a few central cuts. Then, turn yourself—or the bowl—around, and chop from the other direction toward the original cuts. Increase the size of the hollow by working from both ends toward the center. Don't adze close to the sides or ends until you have a good feeling of control and of how the chips come off. Check the depth with a ruler set against a stick placed across the rim. A conservative adzed bottom thickness is 3/4 inch. Adze the interior as nicely as possible, because subsequent gouge-work will be much easier to accomplish.

Hollowing a trough made from buckeye. The small, tightly curved adze is from Sweden. Note the grasp.

Finish the interior with the bowl secured to a workbench or a low bench. Use large clamps or a cleat-and-wedge holding system.

The bowl gouges that I use most often are a #8 sweep 35mm bent gouge and a #3 sweep 20mm straight gouge. I also like a #5 sweep 35mm bent gouge and a special dog leg gouge for cleaning the bottom, which is a bit tricky.

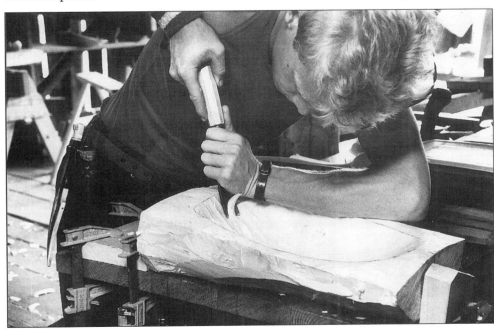

Jogge Sundqvist. Hollowing is finished with large gouges before the exterior is hewed.

Sharpening a Scraper

A scraper is a piece of saw steel with minute hook-shaped burrs on the edges that smooth wood. A common size is a 3-by-5-inch rectangle, but other sizes and shapes are available, including curved scrapers. (You can make a scraper of any shape from the blade of an old hand saw.) Properly sharpened, a scraper will remove tissue-thin shavings. A scraper has several advantages over sandpaper: It takes an even shaving, produces no sanding dust, doesn't cause grit to be embedded in the wood, and is inexpensive to use.

It's your job to put burrs on your scraper. The burr is located where an edge and a side come together. This intersection is called an *arris*. You can put one or two burrs on any edge.

First, square the edge with a mill file. Put the scraper in a vise so that an inch of it extends above the vise jaws. Place the file lengthwise along the top edge. Hold the flat of the file perpendicular to the sides of the scraper. Push the file along the edge, then lift it, and repeat the push stroke. You're done when the edge reflects light as a flat surface.

The rough arris burrs caused by filing must be removed. Use a flat, fine bench stone. Hold the scraper slightly askew on the stone, so that it won't wear a groove in the surface. Hold the scraper perpendicular to the stone, and rub it back and forth a few times. Then make a few light passes on the sides of the scraper.

The scraping burr is made with a burnisher, which can be any piece of round steel that's smooth and harder than the scraper blade. You can buy a burnisher, but a chisel blade or screwdriver shank works just as well.

Put the scraper back in the vise. A drop of oil helps the burnishing. Hold the burnisher with both hands. Lower the burnisher across the scraper edge. Tilt it about 7° from horizontal. Rub the burnisher along the edge of the scraper three or four times. You should now be able to feel the burr along the arris. You also can make a second burr by burnishing the other arris of the edge.

To use the scraper, tip it about 10° from vertical. Push or pull the scraper toward yourself. When scraping a flat surface, bow the blade slightly so that it cups into the wood. You can re-burnish several times before going back to squaring the edge with the file.

For gouge-work, I start using a mallet and then switch to using just body pressure. Hold gouges with both hands. Position your left thumb or fingers inside the flute, about 1/2 inch above the edge of the blade. Use the large muscles of your upper arms and the weight of your upper torso.

Because of grain direction, most gouge-work starts at the rim and progresses downward toward the bottom. Defined interior corners at the sides and bottom can be attractive, but a gently rounded interior is easier to make. The bottom of the bowl is the most difficult area to smooth because grain structure converges there from all directions. Quit when you feel that the cavity is about 95 percent complete. You'll do the final gouge-work and scraping or sanding after the exterior is shaped and the bowl has dried.

Hew the exterior at a chopping stump. Any sharp bench axe can be used, but a small broad hatchet is faster and easier to use than most double-bevel hatchets. Tilt the bowl as needed to take a vertical swing with the axe. Hew off the corners first, then shape the sides. Hewing the ends is the most difficult part. Hold your hatchet so that it takes an angled cut that slices across the end fibers. A design detail that makes this easier is a gradual slope with a vertical lip just below the rim.

It's important to stop often to view your hewing from all angles. Keep in mind the shape that you're after. Use your thumb and fingers to test for uniform thickness. Remember that the ends will be thicker than the sides.

Finish the exterior with a spokeshave, gouge or drawknife. For a rippled texture—which is harder to achieve than a smooth surface—use a gouge with a shallow sweep. Leaving attractive, even tool marks requires very sharp tools and considerable practice.

Shape the rim with a drawknife or a spokeshave. Observe the bowl from the profile and end views; the rim can be flat or dished at the sides.

When the rim is finished, you may want to do more gouge-work on the interior. If the wood is still wet, allow it to dry before doing the final surfacing.

Care is necessary to prevent cracking as the bowl dries out. Drying should be as slow as possible. An old Swedish method is to rub the interior and exterior end grain with a boiled potato. Another is to dry finished work in a pile or box of shavings. A contemporary equivalent is a sealed plastic bag. To slowly lower the moisture, air the bowl for an hour once or twice a day, turn the bag inside out, and put the bowl back inside.

Thin bowls are less likely to crack than thicker ones. One reason is that there is less moisture difference between internal and surface wood. Stresses tend to cause thin bowls to warp or change shape, rather than crack.

Once the wood is dry, final surfacing is done with sandpaper or a scraper. Sanding softwoods is effective in any direction to the grain. Scrapers must be used with the grain, or you'll get fiber tear-out. You can buy a curved scraper for the interior or make one from the blade of an old hand saw.

Dry bowls are usually given an oil finish. The most common traditional finish uses linseed oil—which can contain toxic additives. Recently, many bowl carvers have been using food grade walnut oil. Saturate the wood. If the oil is thinned by warming, it will penetrate better.

Using a Viking axe to hew the rim

CHAPTER SIX

Riving

Most greenwood crafts begin by dividing raw materials—logs, limbs, bark, or roots—into smaller, more workable dimensions. Wood is generally crosscut to length with a saw. Then, for division in width or thickness, green woodworkers put away their saws and get down to the serious business of *riving*

Riving—also known as *cleaving*—is a method of splitting wood that allows you to accurately control the process. The basic idea is simple. As with the bundle of straws, dividing wood fibers into bunches is easier than cutting across them.

Why rive wood with sweat and muscle, when power saws can rip materials to any precise dimension? The answer is that rived wood is always stronger than sawed wood because it follows the cellular structure of the material. This is especially beneficial if the wood is to be bent. Also, because rived wood follows cell boundaries, it resists weathering and has superior decay resistance.

Riving isn't a grueling job. For me, cleaving wood is a joy and always an adventure. In the best cases, riving is very precise, yielding exactly what's wanted and with very little waste. But you never know how a piece of wood will cleave until you're into it. Depending on material quality and your skill, riving waste can vary from almost nothing to considerably more than that of conventional sawing. Hidden knots, weak grain structure, unexpected decay, unusual fiber patterns, and twisted growth are a few of the surprises that may surface even if material is carefully selected. I've been riving wood for 22 years, but I'm challenged by every new piece of wood.

Since wood cleaves into natural divisions, flat planes and straight lines don't exist. If cleft wood for a potential chair rung takes a curve, it's either rejected or accepted, but not straightened out. By taking advantage of natural variations, you can make something stronger and more interesting than a piece of machine-shaped wood.

Materials

Although most hardwoods and softwoods can be split, many species are not suitable for controlled

riving. Quality material is important. Wood must be straight growing and free of knots and other defects. As a clue, bark furrows should be straight, not spiraled or bumpy. Whenever possible, wood for riving should be green—that is, saturated with water. For more details on selecting woods, refer to chapter 3.

Many ring-porous hardwoods cleave easily and predictably. These are deciduous trees which grow with distinct annual rings that clearly define early growth from late growth. They include most oaks, hickory, ash, locust, osage orange, and hackberry. White oak is the favored cleaving wood of many green woodworkers. One ring-porous hardwood that resists splitting is elm. Two diffuse-porous hardwoods that should be reserved for uses in which resistance to splitting is advantageous are black gum and hornbeam.

When you start riving, you'll quickly learn that some species cleave easily parallel to the rays. A few species, such as ash, rive tangent to the growth rings, but not radially. Straight-grained hickory will sometimes rive with perfect control irrespective of the growth rings or the rays.

The most incredible riving woods native to North America are the Pacific red and yellow cedars of the northwest coast. A prime specimen will cleave in any plane, regardless of growth-ring orientation. Before the introduction of European tools, Native American woodworkers were splitting 2-inch-thick cedar planks 2 to 3 feet wide and up to 30–40 feet long.

Tools

If green woodworkers were to adopt a tool to symbolize their craft, they would probably choose the froe. This wonderful tool is a combination of wedge and lever. It consists of a straight, double-bevel blade fastened at a right angle to a wooden handle to describe an "L." A froe can be factory-made, or crafted by a local blacksmith or welder.

Splitting clubs, *gluts,* and a *brake* are usually homemade. Iron wedges, a sledgehammer or splitting maul, and a polled axe are available at any good hardware store. Saplings, limbs, and roots are sometimes rived with a small hunting knife or a short-handled brush hook called a *billhook*.

The splitting maul or sledgehammer is used to drive iron wedges and gluts (wooden wedges). A splitting maul is a sledge whose head has a striking surface and a splitting surface. The splitting end can be used for rough splitting without wedges, but accuracy is important for most of our work, so we'll use wedges. The heads of mauls and sledges come in weights from 6 to 16 pounds. A 10-pounder is a heavy-duty tool; 8 pounds should be adequate for most craft purposes.

Green woodworkers use several types of wedges. Felling wedges are made for inserting behind a saw blade so that the kerf can't close during felling or bucking logs. Felling wedges are usually wide, thin, and fan shaped. Old-fashioned ones, for use with a two-man crosscut saw, were made of malleable iron. Their shape makes them useful for starting to rive a large log. Plastic felling wedges are made for use with a chain saw. They're fine for sawing timber, but not for splitting. Standard malleable iron splitting wedges are a necessity for this. You need two or three. You also need a few wooden gluts. Factory-made socket wedges, with a hollow steel point, a wooden body, and a ring to prevent splitting, will outlast many wooden gluts. But I make my gluts and discard them when they bust apart.

An axe is needed to sever cross fibers that occasionally connect the sections of a split. In chapter 4, we used a polled axe as a wedge to split blanks for spoon carving, and a wooden maul to strike the poll. *Never hit an axe poll with a sledge or go-devil. Also, never use an axe poll to strike an iron wedge.* Axe heads are not designed to be hit by steel or iron tools. They'll mushroom and may crack; more important, there is a danger of flying metallic chips.

You need two wooden clubs: a big one for splitting with a polled axe and a smaller version for hitting the froe. An excellent club can be made from the root cluster of a hardwood sapling. You can also use a hardwood limb or a sapling that contains a cluster of knots. Hickory, oak, beech, dogwood, and hornbeam are excellent. Since it resists splitting, persimmon is highly valued for making clubs, but since it is a medium weight wood, it can't be used for heavy work.

The big club can be about 30 inches long, with a dry weight of about 10 pounds. When fashioning the club from green wood, make it about twice as heavy

A Northwest Coast Indian box made from rived yellow cedar. The sides are a single plank which is kerfed at the corners, then steamed and folded. The fourth corner and the bottom board are secured with angled pegs.

as you need. The smaller froe club should be narrow, so that the froe blade can be pounded between the froe handle and the wood being rived after the blade has started a split. The head of a froe club is roughly 3-1/2 inches wide and 8 inches long. The overall length should be about 16 inches.

A *brake* is a holding jig that exerts counter pressure against opposite sides of a piece of wood during riving. It's typically nothing more than two roughly parallel members, between which the material is jammed. The two members can be splayed slightly to accommodate pieces of different dimensions.

A very good brake can be made from a narrow tree crotch. The lower stem end is rested on a log stump. The two branches are supported by two stout sticks that are inserted through the crotch from opposite sides. Each stick passes under the close branch and over the far branch. As one old timer interviewed by the Foxfire Project (see chapter 2) commented, the crossing sticks hold the fork up by "working contrary to each other."

Brakes are often improvised. I sometimes use my bench vise as a light duty brake. The jaws are set loosely. When riving wood in the barn, I've used the framework of a tractor implement. For splitting shingles, I have a small brake made from scrap lumber nailed to a big stump; it's nice to use because the stump provides a resting surface for the short pieces of wood.

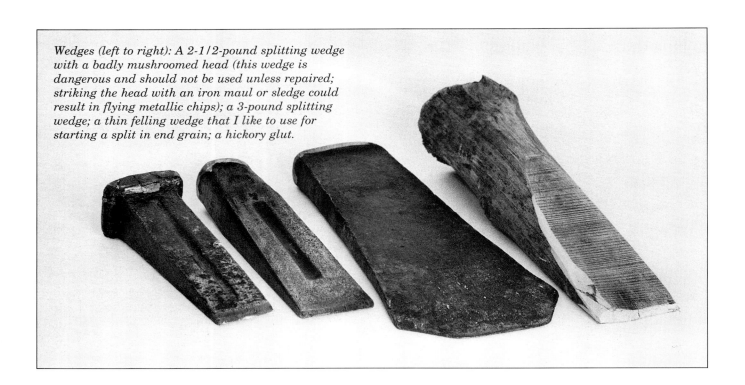

Wedges (left to right): A 2-1/2-pound splitting wedge with a badly mushroomed head (this wedge is dangerous and should not be used unless repaired; striking the head with an iron maul or sledge could result in flying metallic chips); a 3-pound splitting wedge; a thin felling wedge that I like to use for starting a split in end grain; a hickory glut.

The large club, hewed from the root node of a dogwood, is used to strike the poll of a single-bit axe. The small club, made from a knotty hickory sapling, is used with a froe.

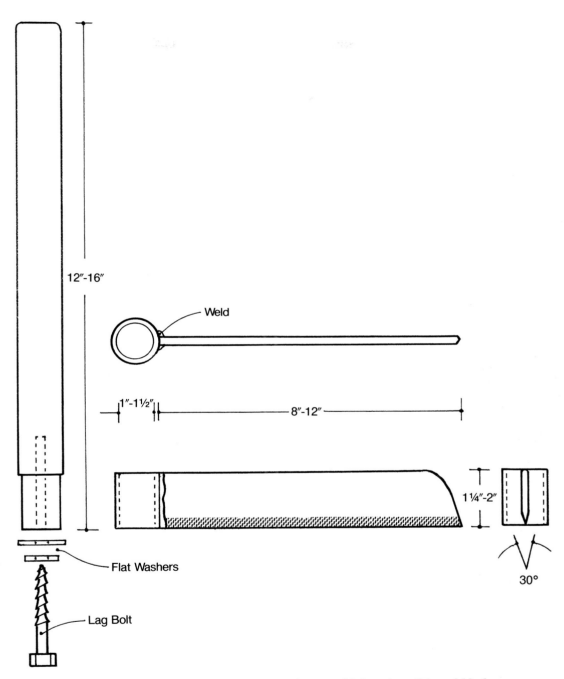

12″–16″

Weld

1″–1½″

8″–12″

1¼″–2″

Flat Washers

Lag Bolt

30°

Recommended froe dimensions. The eye is a piece of pipe welded to the mild steel blade. Traditional froes were made from a single piece of stock. The eye was shaped on one end and forge-welded to the blade.

Making a Froe

The traditional froe blade is a flat piece of steel bar stock, with an eye at one end fabricated by bending a loop and forge-welding it back against the blade. A contemporary method of making the eye is to weld a short piece of pipe to one end of a mild steel bar. You can buy a factory-made froe, but the ones I've seen require some modification to be usable. A welder or blacksmith can make one to your requirements. The dimensions that I give can also be used to modify a factory-made froe.

The blade can be common mild steel—high carbon tool steel isn't required. The blade should be 1-1/4 to 2 inches wide, 8 to 12 inches long, and 1/4 to 3/8 inch thick. The bevels are shaped with a grinder before the eye is welded. The enclosed bevel angle should be about 30°. Unlike true edge tools, the froe has its bevels eased into the sides of the blade; that is, don't "define" them. File or grinder sharpening is adequate.

To minimize wear on the froe club, round off the striking surface along the back edge of the blade. The inner diameter of the eye should be 1-1/4 to 1-1/2 inches. If the eye is welded, use "black" pipe, not galvanized.

A froe handle can be made from any straight-grained, tough hardwood. The length should be about 50 percent longer than the blade. If you shape the handle from green wood, be sure to dry it (so that it shrinks) before fitting one end to the blade socket. The grasping section can take any shape, but there must be a small shoulder at the business end to stop the blade from migrating upward. Some old froes were made with a tapered socket, like that on a mattock, and the handle was shaved to fit.

Securing the handle to a froe blade socket has caused grief for more than one would-be green woodworker. The froe blade is hit downward, but it reacts to resistance by moving upward. The shoulder on the handle stops this movement. But wedges will not prevent the blade from loosening and falling off the end. Instead of using a wedge, I secure the blade with a lag bolt and two or three stacked washers. The largest washer draws against the eye of the froe blade. Bore the lag bolt hole 1/16 inch smaller than the lag bolt diameter.

Riving Techniques

Several rules form the basis of all riving techniques. The process is essentially one of always splitting the mass in half. First, locating a split with even internal pressure on both sides is critical, especially when riving narrow widths with a froe. If one half of the split is narrower, it has less resistance, which tends to cause a split to "run" further toward the narrower side. Even side pressure isn't as important when splitting large sections of logs.

The second rule is that you must follow through with each split. If a piece of wood has an incipient crack, or if you strike the froe off center, finish riving it. Ignore this rule and you'll open two splits simultaneously. The results are loss of control and wasted material.

The third rule isn't as important, but it's a good one to follow. Always rive as close to the finished dimensions as possible. Close riving minimizes time spent shaving or hewing. Riving is the fastest way to bring materials to usable dimensions. In determining the width of rived materials, you need to strike a balance between riving close to finished dimensions and the possibility of unexpected run-out resulting in wasted materials. Experience helps in making the decision, but there is always an element of chance.

Before you start riving, you'll probably have to do some measuring and possibly crosscut material with a saw to appropriate lengths. With first-class material, you can crosscut very close to the final length. If there is any question about wood quality, allow some extra length in case you want to shift the final location of the piece. You can also rive a log into halves and quarters before crosscutting so you can see what it's like inside. (If the log is dirty, use an axe to remove the bark at the crosscuts before beginning to saw.)

Do some planning before starting a split. Usually, there are several possibilities. Riving typically begins with a progression of pie-shaped radial splits. Divisions tangent to the growth rings are commonly made later in the process. Wood that splits very true can sometimes be cleaved in a grid pattern. The advantage of a grid is that there's less waste; in comparison, the triangular and trapezoidal shapes of radial splits often require more shaving. Slabs from certain woods, such as cedar and cypress, can be cleaved in series from one side of a log that is first rived into a square cross section. Riving by division in half isn't necessary with cedar and cypress.

Hewing the handle of a small root club. The edge of the chopping stump is directly below the axe blade.

Making Clubs and Gluts

If you're using a root, dogwood is a good choice, because its root develops from a clump with many knotty radials. The knots make the head particularly durable. Most other trees grow deep taproots, which are tough but more likely to split. An alternative is a trunk or limb with a clear section for the handle and a cluster of two or three knots for the head end. A pair of clubs and several gluts can be made from the trunk of a single sapling.

To make a root club, fell the sapling about 3 feet above ground level. Dig out the root clump with a mattock. Wash and scrub it. Then shape and smooth the root with an axe or hatchet that you're not too fond of. Grit embedded in the root will ruin a good edge.

To form the handle, hew a wide V around the circumference just below what is to be the head. (You can also use a saw to cut a circular kerf.) Rive off or hew most of the waste to form the handle. Be careful not to hew or cleave deeper than the bottom of the hewed V ring. Use a drawknife to finish shaping the handle.

Allow the club to season in an airy shed before using it—if possible, for a full year or longer. Because the club is shaped around the pith, it builds up considerable internal stresses as it dries and shrinks. To minimize checking, dry the club slowly (like the wooden bowl in chapter 5). And don't store it in a dry, heated environment. Another tip is to make the handle about a foot longer than you'll need it. After seasoning, trim off the end, along with any checks that might have formed. You can also slow drying by coating the entire head with paint or end grain sealant.

Gluts are usually 2-1/2 to 3-1/2 inches in diameter and 10 to 12 inches long. The wedge shape is formed by hewing two converging sides to an enclosed angle of about 20°—roughly 8- or 9-inch sides for a 3-inch-diameter glut. The bottom 1/2 inch must be blunter, shaped to an enclosed angle of around 60°. To minimize damage from maul blows, bevel the edge around the striking end.

Although gluts are usually made from limbs or saplings, you can also rive rectangular glut blanks that don't include pith wood.

While making a glut, the round, tapered shape doesn't give you much to hold in a vise, a shaving horse, or by hand. Don't saw glut material to the length of individual gluts until they're finished. Instead, make them in a series from a sapling several feet long.

Gluts can be hewed with a bench axe, then dressed with a drawknife. I've also made gluts quickly with a band saw. The angled sides must be straight. In use, convex sides tend to pop loose; concave gluts drive in partway, but stop where the wider angle begins to enter the material. Like clubs, gluts should be air-dried before use.

Avoid using rived pieces that include the pith and innermost growth rings. You may be able to rive good materials close to the pith, but incorporating the actual pith usually leads to checking when the wood dries. It's often a poor idea to include sapwood and heartwood in a single piece, because the two could shrink differently during drying. If decay is a potential problem, split off all sapwood. (Compared to heartwood, sapwood deteriorates much faster and is more susceptible to wood-boring insects.)

You can draw on wet wood with a water-soluble pencil or a felt marker. Measure with a ruler, or just make appropriate marks on a piece of scrap wood. I often step off equal segments with dividers.

Begin cleaving by splitting any existing cracks. With radial divisions, follow the paths of visually exposed ray cells. For riving control and minimal waste, try to work out divisions that can be halved.

To rive a log, you'll need the bigger tools: a sledge hammer, iron wedges, gluts, and an axe or hatchet. If the log is a big one and you can't transport it, consider cleaving it where it lies. If you can avoid skidding the log, it stays clean. (Incidentally, paint a broad red or orange blaze on tools used in the woods. Leaves and dirt make a fine camouflage.)

Logs under 3 feet long can be set on end for riving. An advantage is that you can pound straight down, with gravity. Also, the ground resists the pounding force, and the log won't move. Longer logs are rived horizontally. It's often said that you should begin riving from the smaller, or upper, end of a log, but in my opinion there's no difference.

Let's imagine that we have a log that's 12 inches in diameter and 6 feet long. All of the initial splits will be radial.

Use body mechanics while splitting with a heavy maul. To minimize back stress, align your center of gravity over the base of your legs. For accuracy in swinging the maul, straddle the log and swing the maul between your legs.

Since you'll be hitting iron wedges with an iron maul, be sure to wear protective glasses.

Begin with a split into the end grain. Look for an existing crack, which will follow a ray plane. If the width of an existing crack is short, you can lengthen it by scoring along the ray. Use an iron wedge and the maul to form a row of end-to-end indentations. It's not necessary to score very deeply.

The impact from driving a wedge into a log lying on the ground will move the log away from you and absorb energy from the maul. The remedy is to place the opposite end against a post or other stationary object.

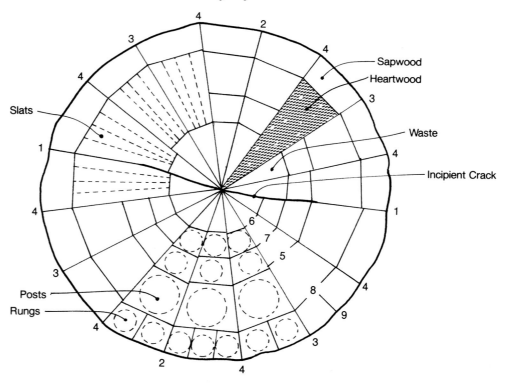

Schematic for riving a 12-inch log into chair parts, with numbered splitting sequence. The large broken circles indicate billets that will be made into posts; smaller broken circles indicate rung stock.

Drive an iron wedge into the scored line. I like to start with a wide, thin, felling wedge, but a standard splitting wedge will work. Stop pounding when the head of the wedge is within 1 inch of the log.

Drive an iron splitting wedge into the crack on the side of the log. As you do this, the first wedge should loosen so that it can be removed easily, but you may need to hit the sides of the wedge to get it loose. Again—and always—stop pounding when the head of the wedge is within 1 inch of the log. To lengthen the crack, leapfrog another splitting wedge in front of the preceding wedge, and continue to the end of the log. *Never put your hands inside the piece being split, in case it should snap shut.*

In many instances, the log halves will still be connected by a few interior connecting fibers. Use your gluts to widen the crack, placing them where the log is free of cross fibers. While the head end of a glut can take considerable pounding, the wedge end has no shear strength; intercepted cross fibers will split it.

After removing the iron wedges, you can safely use an axe or hatchet to sever connecting fibers in the crack. If a log still resists division into halves, rotate it 180° and drive in wedges from the other side.

Split the log into quarters and eighths with the same procedure. Whenever possible, locate splits to make segments that are equal in width.

Sometimes it might seem more economical to divide a log into thirds, but this would prevent you from driving wedges from one side of the log through the pith. In splitting a log, I would make eight rather than nine divisions. Dividing halved logs into thirds often works. Off-center riving into thirds is more likely to be successful during early phases of riving, when there's a large amount of mass (and resistance) on either side of the crack. Experience—and observation of how well a particular log splits— will guide your decision.

Use the froe, club, and brake to rive wood that's narrower than 4 or 5 inches. At the brake you can either rive a round sapling or you can continue cleaving splits that are radial or tangential to the growth rings. Position the wood in the brake so that it tilts toward your body. If you don't have a brake, place wood upright on a chopping stump or directly on the ground.

Here's where the key riving rules—equal division and going with any existing crack—become

When splitting a log, I usually begin by opening an existing crack often found at either end. I'm using a 10-pound splitting maul and a 3-pound malleable iron wedge. When striking iron against iron, always wear protective glasses or goggles.

crucial. Equal division means equal mass, not the halving of a lineal measurement.

Hold the froe with your left hand, with the blade horizontal and directed to the right. Locate the blade over the exact center of mass of the material being rived. With the club in your right hand, carefully strike the back of the froe blade directly above the material. As you raise and then lower the club, be sure not to move the froe. This is a common problem for beginners. Hold the froe blade securely in place, exactly where you want it.

The first blow with the club should drive the froe blade into the wood. If it doesn't, repeat with the blade in the exact same location. When the width of the blade is fully inserted, stop clubbing. Now pull down on the froe handle, so that the blade twists and exerts pressure on the two sides of the crack. As the crack opens, lower the blade deeper into the crack. If the blade is pinched too tightly to be lowered, lever the froe handle and insert a piece

To split short stock, such as chair posts, it's much easier to stand the log on end.

This brake is used to split stock from 3 to 6 feet long. It consists of a forked limb from a black locust and two short poles that are propped inside the fork.

of scrap wood (but not your hands) into the sprung crack. With the crack forced open by the scrap, lower the froe, and continue levering until the wood splits in half.

If the wood resists division, don't strain yourself in pulling the froe handle. The wood could suddenly pop open, and this could cause an injury. Instead, place the wood—with the stuck froe—on the ground with the froe end propped on a cross piece. Then drive an iron wedge into the side of the split, parallel to the froe blade.

If you're working with an eighth section, you may be at the right dimension for cleaving tangentially to the growth rings. This creates an inner triangle and an outer trapezoid. To equalize mass and side pressure, position the froe so that the triangular section is somewhat larger than the trapezoidal section.

At times you may want to influence the direction of a split as it develops. Even when riving begins at the center of mass, the split may run off center because of a hidden knot or slightly decayed sapwood (which is weaker than the heartwood) or because of uneven froe pressure. Twisted grain also can cause a split to wander. To alter the riving direction, lever the froe handle toward the thicker of the two sections. This usually requires rotating the wood 180°. The principle behind this technique

is that the split tends to travel toward the wood fibers curved downward under tension by pressure from the froe.

With experience, you can learn to notice and correct uneven side pressure by feel. One worker who rived a great amount of hazel told Herbert L. Edlin, author of *Woodland Crafts in Britain* (Devon, England: David & Charles, 1949, 1974), that once a cleft had been started he could keep it running with his eyes shut.

When you want to trim a piece of rived wood to a narrower width, you can sometimes use *off-center riving.* This is much faster than hewing or shaving with a drawknife. By positioning the froe off center, you can be fairly sure that the split will safely run out toward the narrow side. The method can be used to split a small usable part, such as a chair rung, from a much larger part, such as a piece of post wood that is oversized.

Back riving is the term I use for starting a second split from the opposite end when an attempted

Riving bucket staves with a froe and club

When riving narrow divisions, such as chair slats, place the froe with equal mass on each side of the blade. This brake was made of scrap lumber nailed to a large stump.

division runs out of control. Ideally, the two opposing splits will run together. If they don't, use a hatchet to separate the sections.

If you're making chair rungs or posts, you'll make both radial and tangential splits. Since radial splits are often more predictable, it's best to make them first. The illustrations of splitting sequences on pages 82 and 87 show typical examples. Be very careful in positioning the froe for each split. Plan a sequence of steps. Use corrective splitting when necessary. Don't be shy about taking some risks. By pushing your limits, you can hone your skills, and you may get extra pieces that would otherwise be wasted.

The procedure for riving large-diameter logs into shingles is basically the same. Crosscut a log section to length and stand it on end. Use a pair of dividers to step off 3-1/2-inch increments along the circumferential division between sapwood and heartwood. A 3-1/2-inch-wide split divides into eight shingles, each 7/16 inch thick at the outer edge. If the log diameter is greater than 24 inches, you may be able to rive an additional inner ring of shingles.

Start each split by scoring along a ray plane to the pith. Place the first iron wedge about 3 inches from the edge. Pound in a second wedge a few inches closer to the pith until the first wedge is loosened. Remove the first wedge, then drive a glut in its place. Later, when the glut is needed again, it can be worked back out by pounding the sides from opposite directions.

When you complete each split, leave the sections standing in their original position. Don't sever connective cross fibers until all the 3-1/2-inch wide billets are rived, so they support each other until the process is complete.

This is what I call off-center riving. The next split will be at the division between sapwood and heartwood.

Each billet is then rived by halving into eight shingles at a small brake like the one shown in the photo above. First, froe off the sapwood, which decays quickly and must be discarded. For shingles, all of these splits are radial. After splitting, shingles are edge-trimmed with a broad hatchet and smoothed with a drawknife.

Fine splits for baskets and chair seating are rived from saplings 6 to 10 inches in diameter. Wood quality must be close to perfect. Growth rings should be about 1/16 inch thick. Narrower growth rings tend to produce weak splits, and splits from thicker rings are usually too heavy to make good weavers or seating. Select a sapling that has grown straight, with minimal taper. Scattered pin knots, produced by leaflets that grow from the trunk surface, are often acceptable. White oak is the prime material for basket splits, but maple, hickory, and some conifers can also be used. The sidebar on page 89 explains how to make ash *splints* by pounding.

The method for riving fine splits is essentially the same as for cleaving wider pieces. Rive radially until splits are about 1 inch wide. Then rive off the pith and inner heartwood by cleaving tangent to the growth rings. Rive the trapezoid radially to create two narrow rectangular sections. Cleave these narrow sections in half tangentially. If you're riving white oak, this split should be at the division between sapwood and heartwood.

These squarish sections are dressed before proceeding to make the final splits. Use a drawknife at a shaving horse to carefully shave off the bark. Then square the sides by shaving on the ray plane until the width of each piece is uniform from end to end.

The final splits are made tangent to the growth rings. Use a small froe or a thick-bladed knife to start cleaving the squares. Be sure to divide the mass exactly in half. As soon as possible, grasp each half-section with your fingers and begin to pull the splits apart manually. If you're sitting, you can hold the wood between your knees. If you're standing, hold it under one arm. Correct for any tendency of run-out by pulling on and bending down the thicker section. Use a sharp knife to sever any cross fibers and to start the final splits. Continue halving splits until you reach the desired thickness. If the splits are wider than needed, you can trim them to size later with a knife, shears, or small tin snips.

West Virginia basketmaker Rachel Nash Law riving white oak splits

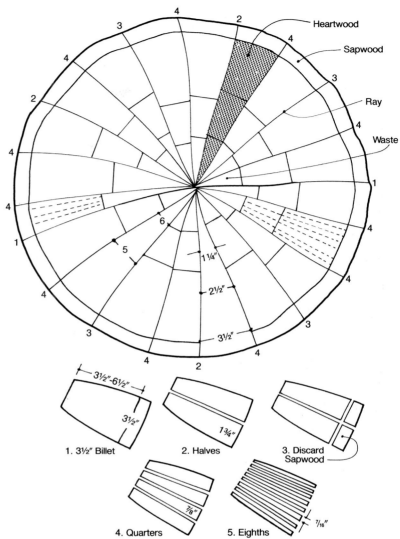

Sequence for riving oak shingles. The minimum log diameter is 20 inches. The sapwood, which decays much more quickly than heartwood, must be discarded. With a good specimen, it's often possible to rive billets for an inner ring of shingles (indicated by split number 6).

1. 3½" Billet

2. Halves

3. Discard Sapwood

4. Quarters

5. Eighths

A. Sequence for riving white oak basketry splits.
B. Sometimes a grid sequence can be used for splitting particularly straight-grained stock. The small center area of this hickory is heartwood.

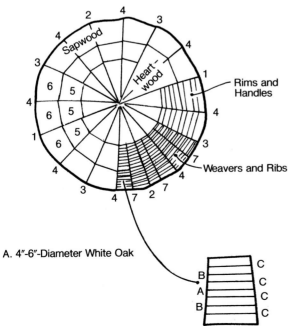

A. 4"–6"-Diameter White Oak

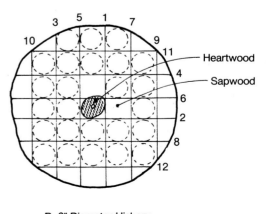

B. 6"-Diameter Hickory

Preparing to rive white oak basket splits. Use a drawknife to remove bark and to shave billets to a square cross section. The squares are then rived tangent to the growth rings.

The final white oak splits are started with a stout knife...

...then carefully divided by hand.

Ash Splints

Ash splits used for basketry or chair seating are called *splints*—with an "n." Freshly cut ash logs are pounded with a maul to crush large, early growth pores so that the wood delaminates along the growth rings. Ash baskets are usually made from black ash, also known as brown ash. According to Martha Wetherbee, the ash-splint basket maker who I'll introduce in Part Three, red ash and green ash work just as well. White ash is considered a second choice.

As with other riving materials, log quality is important. Logs should be clear and 5 to 10 inches in diameter. Splints from smaller saplings have too much cup. Fast-growing ash is best because the large earlywood pores crush easily. Ash for pounding can be felled any time of year. Work the log green, or store it under water until needed.

Remove the bark with a drawknife. Position the log so that it won't bounce around as you pound on it. An alternative, preferred by some ash-splint basket makers, is to split out quarter or eighth section radials. Then make a split with the growth rings to eliminate the inner heartwood. The ash splints are pounded from the resulting outer trapazoid section.

Use a sledgehammer or a polled axe. The edges of the striking tool should be rounded off so as not to damage the fragile wet wood. Pound in one area near an end of the log until you see the growth rings separate. Then pound toward the center. When an entire growth ring delaminates, remove it by cutting long, 1-inch-wide strips loose with a knife. Continue pounding and removing successive growth rings until the splints are too cupped or knotty to be used. Both sapwood and heartwood are usable; the difference is color.

Pounding ash by hand is hard work. Using a polled axe, Martha Wetherbee has pounded a log for as long as ten days to delaminate it. She now hires a man to operate an ancient trip hammer to make ash splints, and even using this machine, it may take a full day to pound a log into splints. But one log can make splints for many baskets.

Thick ash splints can be separated into two or even four layers. The technique is the same as dividing white oak splits. Use a knife to start, then peel splints apart by hand.

The natural divisions that follow the growth rings of ash splints are fuzzy and need to be smoothed with fine sandpaper when dry. The inner surfaces of splints made by dividing growth rings are very smooth and don't require cleaning up.

Coarse splits can be scraped smooth by pulling them under a stationary knife blade. Most basket makers do this from a sitting position. The knife blade is held against a thigh that is protected by a piece of scrap leather. If the pieces are too thick, they can be thinned with a drawknife at a shaving horse, as explained in chapter 7.

Project: Garden Hurdles

Garden hurdles are modular fence units that you can easily set up wherever needed. Anyone with a garden or livestock will find these hurdles useful. They're perfect for trellis crops, such as peas or cucumbers. These hurdles can also be an attractive, rustic addition to a flower garden. Hurdles are easily stored in a limited space when not needed.

Hurdles were originally used in England as temporary enclosures for sheep. Two types were traditionally made. Woven hurdles consist of a row of uprights called *standards,* which are woven together using thin, horizontal *withes,* usually willow or hazel. The result is a solid panel that makes a good windbreak. Rived hurdles resemble lightweight fence gates. Removable wooden pins are used to join a number of hurdles together. The gate hurdle is the type I will describe here.

Riving out hurdles is fun to do and a perfect project for learning the basics of riving.

Tools. You'll need a maul, wedges, gluts, a froe, a froe club, a broad hatchet, a brace with a 3/4-inch auger bit, an ordinary hammer, and a 1-inch chisel. You'll also need a crosscut saw to cut your logs to length. A drawknife and a shaving horse or bench-mounted vise are useful but not necessary.

Materials. Select a wood that rives easily and resists decay. Our hurdles were made with black locust for standards and white oak for crossbars and braces. Softwoods such as redwood or cedar can also be used.

Select good-quality logs, 8 to 12 inches in diameter. In the directions, dimensions for parts are for hardwoods. If you are using softwoods, which are weaker than hardwoods, increase widths and thicknesses about 50 percent.

Small pegs and dowels are rived from ring-porous hardwoods using a knife and hammer.

Rived hurdles can be used as a garden trellis or as temporary livestock enclosures.

Our hurdles are 6 feet long and 46 inches high, with seven crossbars and three braces. You can alter this overall size and number of crossbars, but these dimensions have worked well for us.

Rive the standards from your best wood, since they will take the most strain when put to use. The standards are 3/4 inch thick, 2-1/2 inches wide, and 46 inches long. Then rive the 72-inch-long crossbars, 1/2 inch thick by 2 inches wide. The braces can be made from rejected crossbars. Make them 1/2 inch thick by 1-1/2 inches wide. The vertical brace is 40 inches long; the diagonal braces are 50 inches long. Rived pieces can vary by 1/4 inch in thickness or 1/2 inch in width.

If the rived parts are too thick or too wide, shave them to size with a drawknife. Use a hatchet to point the lower end of each standard. Hew or shave both ends of the crossbars to fit rounded mortises in the standards. These measure 3/4 inch by 1-1/2 inches. A loose fit is acceptable.

The mortises are spaced as you choose. Start the mortises by boring two 3/4-inch holes on 3/4-inch centers. Chop out the waste with the chisel.

Bore 3/4-inch holes for the connecting pins midway between the two upper crossbars.

Fit all the crossbars into the standards. To square up the hurdle, put a nail or a dowel through the top and bottom crossbars of one standard. Use 6-penny galvanized nails or rived hardwood dowels (store-bought dowels are too weak and often fit too loosely). Then measure both diagonals of the hurdle. If the measurements differ, push the corners of the longer diagonal together. When the distances are close to equal—within 1/8 inch—you're square enough.

Nail or dowel the top and bottom crossbars of the other standard. Check for square again. Stabilize the hurdle by nailing—not doweling— the vertical and diagonal braces. Clinch the nails by pounding the pointed ends over on the back side. Then nail or dowel the remaining crossbars to the standards.

The removable pins should be rived from a tough, straight-grained hardwood. Cleave 7/8-inch squares, 8 inches long. Use a drawknife to round the shanks to an 11/16-inch diameter, but leave one rived end square so it can't pass through the 3/4-inch holes in the standards. Put a point on the other end.

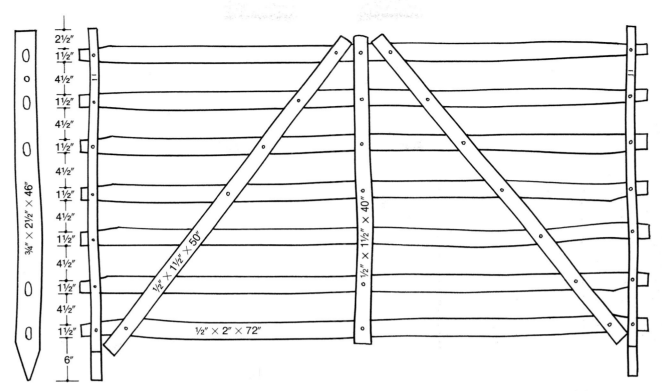

Dimensions for our rived sheep hurdles. The overall dimensions and number of cross bars can be modified to suit your requirements. The braces are clinch-nailed.

Labels within the figure:

3/4" × 2½" × 46"

2½"
1½"
4½"
1½"
4½"
1½"
4½"
1½"
4½"
1½"
4½"
1½"
6"

½" × 1½" × 50"

½" × 1½" × 40"

½" × 2" × 72"

Hurdles are joined end to end with removable wooden pegs.

CHAPTER SEVEN

Shaving

Shaving is a method of shaping wood using slicing tools such as drawknives and spokeshaves. Although related to knife-work, shaving is much faster. With practice, you can learn to do exacting work, taking deep or delicate shavings. When an expert shaves a piece of wood, each stroke counts, and there's a sense of authority that remains in the finished work. There's a definite sense of satisfaction in shaving a rived billet into a precisely shaped piece of wood, such as a chair post or a basket handle.

Straight-grained woods, both hard and soft, are particularly suited to shaping with shaving tools. Hardwoods are usually shaved green. Although dry hardwoods are difficult to shave, the finished surface can be particularly attractive. You can shave wet wood slightly oversize, allow it to dry (and shrink), and then carefully shave to final dimensions.

Wood for shaving is usually secured in a holding device, such as a shaving horse. You also can use a vise (a machinist's vise is especially useful) or *fids*, which are adjustable dogs with steel holding points. When a crooked knife is used, the work is held by a free hand.

Except for spokeshaves, tool control is by hand and eye, with no mechanical stops for depth or width of cut. Constant attention is necessary for producing good results.

Historically, many crafts depended on shaping wood by shaving. Coopers developed a variety of specialized drawknives. Ladder-back and Windsor chairs required shaving in their construction. For strength, the best ladder rungs and wagon spokes were once rived and shaved.

Drawknives and spokeshaves can be used to chamfer architectural beams, railings, and trim work. Tool handles can be shaved quickly and accurately. Wood to be turned on a lathe is often pre-shaped to a round configuration by shaving with a drawknife. Spokeshaves can be used to create a smooth surface on furniture where hand planes can't be used. After riving, shingles are dressed with a drawknife. Basket makers often shave their handles and rims. My first job with a drawknife was pointing half-round fence pickets for Reudi

Kohler, the Swiss cooper. Probably the most mundane application of shaving is removing bark.

The blade of a general-purpose drawknife is 8 to 10 inches long. Blades may be slightly convex when viewed either from above or from head on. For general use, I prefer a straight, flat blade, mainly because it's considerably easier to sharpen than a curved blade. Most drawknife blades have a single bevel, although some old ones are double-beveled. The advantage of a single bevel is that you can shave bevel up or bevel down, with different results. Old drawknife blades were often made from laminated steel.

Usually, both handles are set in the same plane as the blade and at a right angle to it. Drawknife handles should be securely attached, with the tangs riveted over washers or end caps. Some new drawknives have a button at the end of each handle to conceal a tang which is clinched over the wood. This inferior construction leads to loose handles.

Since drawknives were once very common, used ones are inexpensive. One good drawknife was the Greenlee, also sold under the brand names of Craftsman and Montgomery Ward. But there are many others worth owning. In selecting a used drawknife, examine the blade to insure that it's not warped, rusted, or badly pitted near the edge. If so, it will be difficult to restore and sharpen. The back edge of a drawknife that has been beaten down from abuse as a riving tool will require grinding. Loose handles can be fixed with epoxy; this works. An old narrow-bladed draw knife—narrow because it's been sharpened many times—can be excellent for shaving inside curves.

For flattening work, such as dressing chair slats or shingles, I prefer a drawknife with a slightly bowed shape and a single bevel on the concave side of the blade.

Some cooper's drawknives were made with one angled handle and one handle in line with the blade. These were used for chamfering the inner rim of a barrel, where the standard angled handle would get in the way.

The Swedish *bandkniv* (translated *push knife*) has both handles in line with the blade. It's used

My most used drawknife (top) has a straight, flat blade. It's easy to sharpen and works well as an all-purpose tool. The blade of the middle drawknife, from Germany, is slightly bowed when viewed from above. I use it to shape the edges of a Windsor chair seat. The bottom drawknife, a French Peugeot, has a blade that's bowed when viewed facing the edge. It's used to flatten chair slats and shingles.

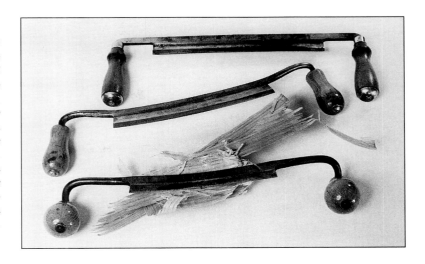

Vermont chairmaker Dave Sawyer shaving Windsor spindles from hickory

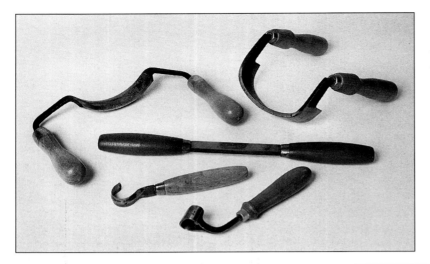

A few specialized shaving tools. A cooper's hollowing knife (upper left), an inshave (upper right), a Swedish push knife (center), a Swedish carver's hook (bottom left), and a scorp (bottom center).

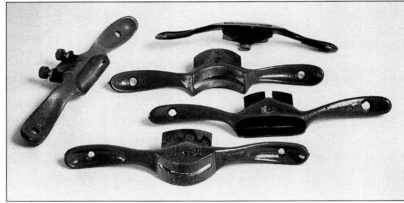

Spokeshaves. Extreme left: an all-purpose shave with a flat sole and two adjusting nuts. Top to bottom: a slightly convex shave, shop-made by modifying the sole and blade of a flat shave; a half-round shave; an adjustable-throat shave; a round-face shave.

where the handles of a conventional drawknife would get in the way. I find the push knife difficult to control. Instead, I use a spokeshave.

Hollowing knives are used primarily by coopers. For scooping, the bevel must be on the exterior side of the blade.

An *inshave* is a drawknife used to scoop chair seats and the cavities of large bowls and troughs. In contrast to a hollowing knife, the handles don't extend to the sides beyond the curved blade; instead, the handles angle back and upward just beyond the deeply bowed blade. For most uses, you need an exterior bevel.

Spokeshaves incorporate a sole and a blade depth control similar to that of a plane. Spokeshaves can be wood or cast iron. I use iron-body spokeshaves; the blades of some can be adjusted easily with knurled knobs, and I like the weight. But other green woodworkers prefer the lightness of a wooden spokeshave and the lower cutting angle of the blade—30° compared to 45° for an iron-body spokeshave.

Spokeshaves are often considered a finishing tool. However, they're also useful for general shaping work, especially for ornery grain. A sharp spokeshave with a fine blade setting works very nicely on end grain.

For your first spokeshave, I recommend one with an iron body, a flat sole, and knurled knobs for setting blade exposure rather than a central friction screw. It's worth paying a few dollars extra for a body of malleable iron; plain cast iron can easily crack. Two good models are the Stanley 151M ("M" for malleable) and the Record A151.

You might also be interested in a specialized spokeshave. A light, compact model can be used in confined locations, such as between hayfork prongs. With an adjustable-throat spokeshave, you can use a wide setting for hogging wood quickly and then narrow the throat for finish work or shaving difficult grain. Giant cooper's spokeshaves are useful for large-scale work, where a drawknife can't be used. An example is dressing the exterior of a barrel.

Half-round spokeshaves have a sole and blade that appear concave when viewed straight on. These are useful for quickly rounding drawknifed chair legs. The one model that I know of requires fine tuning before it can be used. (See the sidebar on page 100, "Modifying the Kunz Half-Round Spokeshave.")

Radius spokeshaves have a sole and blade that appear convex when held before you. They're used for shaving hollows, such as saddling Windsor chair seats.

A standard, flat-soled spokeshave can be converted into a shallow radius shave. Reshape the sole into a lengthwise curve with a flat mill file, then grind the blade to match. For work clearance, shorten the handle ends with a hacksaw, and then round the sharp edges with a grinder or a file.

The sole and blade of a *round face* spokeshave appear convex when viewed from the side (from the front, the blade edge is straight). These are used to shave concave shapes on something like the edge of a board.

Green woodworkers also use several one-hand shaving tools. American Indians and other northern nomadic craftspeople used *crooked knives* for both rough and detailed shaving work. The crooked knife is grasped palm up, with the crook of the blade directed up and inward, toward the user's body. The carver's thumb is braced against the end of the handle, which is angled something like a hockey stick. Birchbark canoe maker Henri Vaillancourt prefers using a crooked knife over a drawknife. Henri says he can position the wood with his free hand for better knife control and visibility than if the wood were worked with a drawknife and secured in a shaving horse or vise. *Carver's hooks* have short, curved blades. They're grasped palm up or down and, like crooked knives, are pulled toward the body. Carver's hooks are used to hollow the bowls of spoons, among other things. A *scorp* is a one-hand scooping tool with a blade shaped in a closed loop.

An obscure shaving tool that I plan to experiment with is the *block knife*, traditionally used for rough shaping of sabots (wooden shoes), bowls, and spoons. The straight blade, which resembles the drawknife, is attached at one end to an eye hook driven into a chopping stump. The other end has a long handle, bent at a slight angle to the blade. The work is placed on the stump, and the blade is pushed downward, as when using a paper cutter.

Shaving Horses

Any discussion of shaving wood would be incomplete without introducing my favorite holding device, the shaving horse. This ancient invention is a specialized variation of the low workbench that you sit on. The work is supported at a convenient height on an angled bridge and held in place by a pivoting arm operated with a foot treadle.

In my experience, a shaving horse is the superior holding device for most drawknife and spokeshave work. The wood can be gripped quickly and at a good position for most purposes. Ruedi Kohler told me that before workbenches with vises became common, shaving horses were also used to hold wood for sawing, chiseling, and boring.

Two types of shaving horses are known as the *dumb head horse* and the *bodger's horse*. The moving part of the dumb head is a single swinging arm that passes through mortises in the bench and the bridge. The bodger's horse utilizes a yoke that holds the work under a pivoting jaw mortised to two vertical members that pivot at the sides of the bench. Both horses are easily adjusted for holding wood of different thicknesses.

Of the two, I prefer the dumb head. Because the pivot is higher up, located at the bridge near the holding jaw, you get greater leverage from the foot-operated treadle. Also, the centrally located arm allows you to quickly reverse the wood without withdrawing and reinserting it, as must be done between the vertical side members that link jaw and treadle on the bodger's horse. On the other hand, the pivoting jaw of the bodger's horse holds with more friction and is less likely to cause indentations from pressure on the wood.

Shaving horses have either three or four legs. Three-legged horses are suited for outdoor work on uneven ground. See Appendix A for complete plans for building a dumb head shaving horse.

Sharpening Shaving Tools

Drawknives are sharpened slightly differently than other single-bevel edge tools. First, examine the blade. Use a protractor to check the blade angle. Look closely. If the bevel isn't flat, or if the back side is *dubbed* (slightly convex near the edge), the actual cutting angle will be wider than it may appear at first.

The enclosed bevel angle of a drawknife blade should be near 30°. The actual *cutting angle* is determined by how you hold the drawknife in rela-

A crooked knife, made by Henri Vaillancourt

tion to the wood. Thirty degrees is a good bevel angle because it combines sharpness with durability. A narrower angle is weaker. I've seen drawknives with bevels ranging from 20 to 50°; these extreme bevels should be reground.

The bevel of a drawknife can be slightly dubbed (convex). The bevel shape determines if a drawknife works well bevel up or bevel down. This is a major difference between drawknives and all other bevel edged tools.

If you use a drawknife bevel down, the bevel must be (very slightly) dubbed. If it is truly flat, you won't have control of the depth of the cut. The drawknife will dive in and won't come out. This is particularly true when shaving hardwoods.

Drawknives used bevel up will invariably have a slightly dubbed flat side.

Dubbing both the bevel and flat side isn't a good idea because you end up with an enclosed bevel angle that is too wide for shaving wood.

The edge of a spokeshave blade should be shaped just like a properly tuned chisel or plane blade. A spokeshave bevel can be either flat or hollow ground. A hollow grind makes honing and polishing at a consistent angle much easier. You can register the bevel on the bench stone using two distinct points: the cutting edge and the heel of the bevel. When a bevel is flat (and not hollow ground), it's very difficult to hold a perfectly steady sharpening angle.

As shown in the illustrations on page 98, the hollow grind shouldn't extend to the actual cutting edge or the heel. If it did, the bevel angle would be too nar-row, causing the sharp edge to break down quickly. Also, hollow grinding to the actual edge could cause overheating and loss of temper in the steel. Doing a good hollow grind requires practice, especially on a drawknife, because the blade is so long. At a standard bench grinder, the perpendicular drawknife handles will bump into the motor as grinding approaches the middle of the blade. For grinding a drawknife blade I use a slow-speed grinder with a stone that runs through a water trough.

Before grinding, position and tighten the grinder tool guide. Then rehearse a "motor off" pass from one end of the blade to the other. By inking the bevel with machinist's bluing or a felt-tip pen, you can see exactly where you're grinding.

At a grinder, always use eye protection. Wear safety glasses or use the transparent guard on the grinder.

With the grinder turned on, be sure to keep the drawknife blade moving constantly, with an even speed and pressure. This will give you an even cut.

Drawknives with straight, flat blades and a moderate hollow grind are easily honed using the tall bench stone holder described in chapter 4. The tall holder allows clearance for the perpendicular handles to pass above the workbench when you're honing and polishing the bevel.

Secure the stone holder between bench dogs, wedges, or the jaws of a vise. The holder must be positioned perpendicular to your body so that you face one end squarely. Start with a medium-grit diamond stone or an 800- to 1,200-grit water stone.

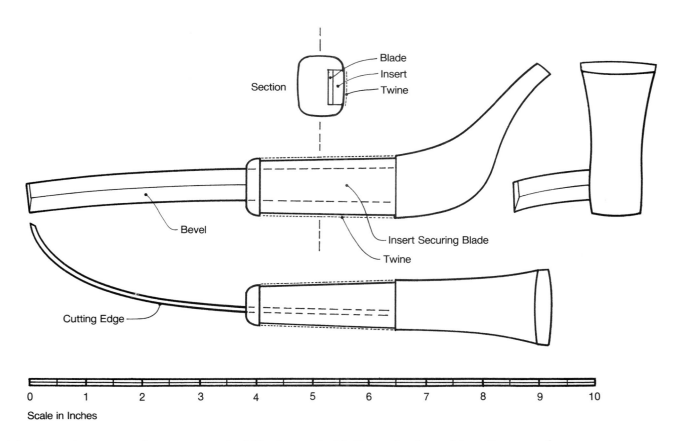

Section — Blade
— Insert
— Twine

Bevel

Insert Securing Blade

Twine

Cutting Edge

```
0    1    2    3    4    5    6    7    8    9    10
```
Scale in Inches

The dimensions, proportions, curve, and width of a crooked knife can be changed to suit your needs.

Making a Crooked Knife

I learned some basic metalsmithing and how to make a crooked knife when I visited birchbark canoe maker Henri Vaillancourt.

To make a crooked knife, only a few tools are required. The blade is crafted from a small, worn-out file. First, *anneal* (soften) the file by heating it to a dull red color. Then cool it very slowly. Henri's heat source in the bush is a tin camp stove. A good file is then used to shape the cross section of the blade. The old teeth are filed off, and it is made thinner and given a single-bevel edge.

Using a pair of pliers for tongs, reheat the blade. While it's red hot, bend the blade to an appropriate curve. The beveled edge is on the concave side of the curve.

To harden the blade, heat it red hot again, this time to the temperature at which it loses magnetism. The hot steel is quenched in water. At this stage, the blade is extremely brittle and could crack just by being dropped onto a wooden floor.

Tempering is the process of bringing the steel to an appropriate toughness for use The blade is cleaned and polished, then heated very carefully at a much lower temperature. When the steel turns blue, it's quenched again. The result is a blade that both keeps a fairly sharp edge and is flexible. Many woodworking tools are tempered considerably harder, at an even lower temperature to a "straw" color.

Attach the finished blade to a hardwood handle by fitting it into a shallow mortise carved into one side. The mortise is closed with a flush-fitting piece of carved wood. Then the lower end of the handle is wrapped with twine.

Five profiles for single-bevel edge tools. For most tools I prefer E, but C is correct for a drawknife that is used bevel down. A. Flat bevel. An excellent profile but difficult to shape and maintain accurately. B. Micro-bevel. Good for plane blades, since the cutting angle is constant. C. Rounded bevel. This common profile results from lack of control during honing. In a plane, fibers split in front of the edge. D. Full hollow grind. The narrow angle at the edge breaks down quickly. E. Partial hollow grind. Strong edge. This profile is easy to hone and works well with knives and shaving tools; the edge and the heel of the bevel create a flat registration plane.

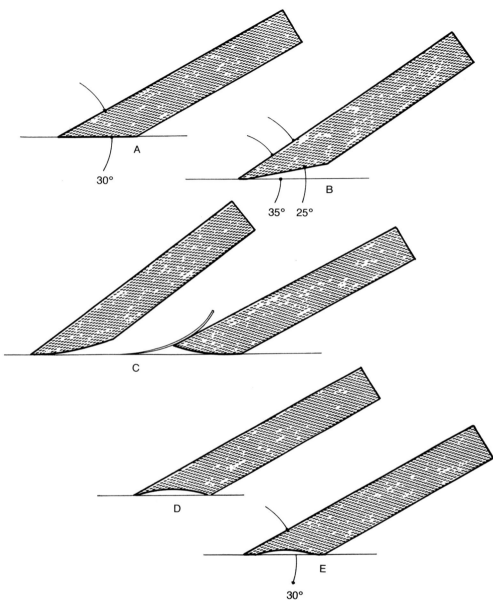

Before honing the bevel, dress the flat back side of the blade. You only need to do this once, not every time the edge requires sharpening.

Position the right end of the drawknife blade at the far end of the bench stone. Pull the drawknife across the bench stone, simultaneously moving it to the right so that when you reach the near end of the stone you're at the left end of the blade. Stated another way, you make a diagonal pass from the far to the near end of the stone. Using this method, the entire length of the blade is sharpened, and the stone wears evenly.

Press down hard, applying the weight of your upper torso. Hone until you can feel a wire burr begin to form along the full length of the bevel side of the blade. Then switch to a fine or superfine diamond stone or a 4,000- to 8,000-grit water stone. Stop when the previous abrasions are removed. The wire edge should now be so fine as to be almost imperceptible to the touch. The back side of the drawknife blade is now finished; only slight touch-ups will be required from time to time.

To sharpen the bevel, return to the medium-grit honing stone. Position the right end of the bevel at

Honing a straight, flat-bladed drawknife. Pull the knife diagonally across the bench stone. The tall bench stone holder provides clearance for the angled drawknife handles.

This spokeshave blade holder was made from a reject chair run. A kerf sawed at one end accepts the blade. For blade clearance, a wedge is removed from the bottom end of the holder. The blade is secured with a 3/16-inch stove bolt and a wing nut.

the far end of the bench stone. To find the bevel angle, first lower the heel to the stone, then drop to the bevel by lowering the handles.

Use the bench stone technique described above for honing the back of the blade. Stop when you feel a burr on the back of the blade. Then use a finer stone. Continue until the burr formed on the back of the blade almost disappears. Then flip the drawknife over—so that the bevel faces up—and lightly remove the burr from the back side of the blade. You're finished!

The next time your drawknife is dull, you only need to hone and polish the bevel side of the blade. Leave the back side alone, aside from removing the final, slight burr made by the polishing stone.

If a drawknife blade is bowed, with the bevel on the concave side of the curve, you won't be able to use a bench stone with the tall bench stone holder. Instead, hone and polish the bevel by steadying one handle against a fixed stop, like the shaving horse riser. Use a progression of cone-shaped water stone slips; they are available in coarse, medium, and fine grits. The convex side can be dressed with conventional flat bench stones.

Drawknives are relatively safe edge tools. Because of body geometry, it's nearly impossible to pull the blade into your chest. Most accidents involve cutting fingers or thighs on the sharp corners of the blade. To prevent cuts, round the corners of the blade with a bench stone or a file to a 1/8-inch radius.

Spokeshaves are sharpened at a bevel angle of 30°. Because spokeshave blades are so small, they're difficult to hold on to. The shop-made blade holder shown above is very useful. The blade holder also makes it easier to maintain the correct bevel angle.

As with the drawknife and all other single-bevel edge tools, prepare the back first. Make the back really flat. Next hone and polish the bevel.

Spokeshave blades are often wider than common 2-inch-wide bench stones. When you sharpen the bevel, position the blade at a diagonal so that it fits within the bench stone width. Skewing the blade also makes it easier to hold the blade at a constant angle as you rub back and forth.

Spokeshaves with curved blades require special sharpening stones. Cone-shaped slips are available in different grits. I secure the blade in a vise and work the stone over the stationary blade.

Inshaves are sharpened by securing the iron wings in a vise and moving abrasives over the

Pushing a drawknife into the shoulder of a tenon. A push stroke can also be used where edge grain rises away from the end of a piece of wood.

Modifying The Kunz Half-Round Spokeshave

The most common half-round spokeshave is made by Kunz in Germany. The ones I've seen require some handwork before they can be used. After completing these simple modifications, you'll have a fairly acceptable tool.

First, you may need to modify the blade curve to match the sole of the iron body. Then, redefine the bevel angle with a half-round mill file. The correct angle is 30°; as sold, the bevel is much steeper. Finish by honing with cone or gouge slips.

If the cap iron wobbles on the blade, a gap opens that tends to jam with shavings. Flatten the underside of the cap iron by filing the high points. The bevel of the cap iron must mate with the blade exterior. To make fine shavings you will need to narrow down the gap at the throat of the spokeshave. This is easily accomplished by inserting paper shims between the blade and the iron body. This modification can be made to any spokeshave or hand-plane.

blade. If shaping is required, I use a small drum sander with a sandpaper sleeve mounted to an electric drill. Use a bench stone on the exterior bevel. Clean up the interior burr with a cone-shaped slip.

Shaving Techniques

Riving and shaving are wonderfully complementary techniques. Both are based on using and working with straight grain. Drawknives are always used by cutting with the grain direction. When grain shifts, the wood is usually reversed end for end, and you shave from the other direction.

Drawknives are generally pulled toward your torso. It's also possible to push a drawknife, but control is much more difficult. The bevel can be positioned up or down, depending on the work at hand, the particular tool, and your preference. With the bevel down, the bevel acts as a fulcrum, resulting in depth control. Concave cuts must be done bevel down. Shave bevel up to make very straight cuts.

Shaving may be easier if you hold the knife in a skew position. Skewing reduces the effective cutting angle of the blade to the wood. This is because a skewed blade cuts at the angle formed by a *diagonal* section through the bevel angle. Skewing will help to prevent *pencil pointing* and *hourglassing*.

Sometimes large amounts of wood can be removed by combining shaving and splitting into a single stroke. Start by making a deep shaving. Once you're into the cut, rotate the drawknife handles upward to split off the waste.

Occasionally, wood may continually slip out of the shaving horse jaw, especially if it's very hard or wet, or when you are hogging large shavings. If a billet slips loose, it punches you in the belly. To eliminate this painful annoyance, you can increase holding friction by tacking leather or inner tube pads to the jaw or the bridge of the shaving horse. Pads also keep the jaws from denting the work.

Exercise: Shaving Cylinders

Shaving a cylinder from a rived, squarish billet will give you hands-on practice with several shaving techniques. A typical rived billet—for something like a ladder-back chair rung—would be about 1 inch square and 15 inches long. We want to finish with a 3/4-inch-diameter cylinder. Any type of straight-grained wood will do for practice. If you use a hardwood, it should be green.

In most cases, work with any natural curvature in the wood. Straightening out a curve necessitates

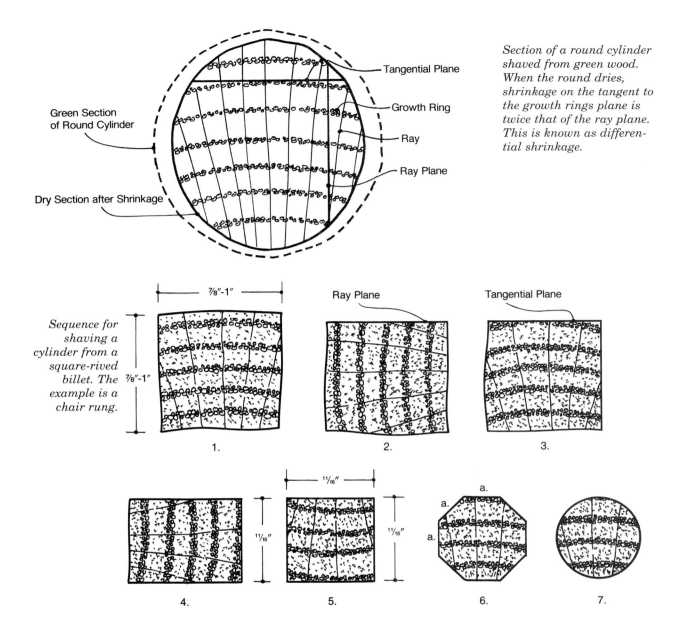

Section of a round cylinder shaved from green wood. When the round dries, shrinkage on the tangent to the growth rings plane is twice that of the ray plane. This is known as differential shrinkage.

Tangential Plane

Growth Ring

Ray

Ray Plane

Green Section of Round Cylinder

Dry Section after Shrinkage

Sequence for shaving a cylinder from a square-rived billet. The example is a chair rung.

⁷⁄₈″-1″

Ray Plane

Tangential Plane

1.

2.

3.

4.

5.

6.

7.

¹¹⁄₁₆″

a.

cutting across fibers, weakening the wood. Instead, try to use natural curves as an interesting feature. Often, crooks are hardly noticeable in a finished piece. Sometimes crooks can be hidden. A crooked rung can go under the seating or be used as a point of interest. When you can't work with a natural curve, discard the wood.

Begin by cleaning up one side of the billet. Usually, I shave the best side first. With hardwoods, start by shaving on the *ray plane* (that is, across the growth rings). The ray plane is generally easier to cleave and shave than the growth ring plane. Just remove enough wood to create a flat surface. Work from both ends of the billet, reversing the wood end for end as necessary.

Rotate the billet 90° to dress an adjacent growth ring side. You're now on the tangential plane, which forms a tangent to the growth rings. Again, do the minimal amount of work.

When the second side is flat, rotate the wood another 90° so that the other ray plane faces up. Start reducing the billet to thickness by chamfering the corners to the desired dimension. Then shave down the flat.

Swiss cooper Reudi Kohler hollowing a very short bucket stave. Wood is secured between a breast bib and a ledge at the end of the shaving horse bridge.

Rotate the billet again and shave the other growth ring plane to thickness. Be sure to shave chamfers at the corners before shaving the flat.

Next, convert the square billet into an octagonal section by chamfering all four edges. Rotate the billet 45° onto one edge, and shave a chamfer on the upper edge. Make the chamfers about one-fourth of the width of the billet. (To hold square billets on edge, you may want to saw or chisel a small V-cut under one side of the shaving horse jaw.) Reverse the billet end for end and shave the opposite chamfer. Then chamfer the other two edges, working from both ends.

Continue shaving by rotating the piece until the original flats and the new chamfers are equal width. You should now have a very nice octagonal section billet.

Use a spokeshave to round the octagon. Begin by shaving off the edges. Spokeshaves work equally well as push or pull tools. Practice working in both directions. Skewing is helpful. If your spokeshave jams with shavings or chatters, the blade either is set too deep, inserted upside-down, or needs sharpening.

There's no need for cylinders, like posts and rungs, to be perfectly round. I often leave narrow flats. There's an old German saying that "God loves a little unevenness, but not too much."

Exercise: Shaving Wide Flats

Another good exercise is shaving a flat board from a wide, rived billet, as you would if shaving a chair-back slat or shingles. The rived billet should be 2 to 3 inches wide, approximately 15 inches long, and 1/2 inch thick.

Here's where I like to use a bowed drawknife. The bowed blade flattens wide stock much more quickly and easily than a straight blade. The blade is slightly convex, with the bevel on the inner side of the curve. (With the French Peugeot drawknife, the peculiar ball-shaped handles allow holding at a range of wrist angles.)

First, examine the rived stock for warp. A slight warp can often be removed. Hold the blank just below eye level so that you can sight from one end to the other end, and look for a twist along its length. Shave the best side first. Correct any warp by shaving off a triangular corner slab from the high corner of each end. Check your work often. Small mistakes are preferable to large ones. When the warp is removed, carefully dress the entire surface.

Shave the piece to the desired thickness from the opposite side. Start by shaving off any high areas. If you're making chair slats or anything else that will be bent, be sure to work for uniform thickness. Overly thick areas will resist bending, and thin spots will buckle. It's surprising how accurately you can test for even thickness by running the material between your thumb and fingers.

As the shaved board gets thinner, it will tend to bend under pressure from the drawknife. If this becomes a problem, support it with a board set on the bridge. The support board can be something like a scrap 1 by 3, roughly 2 feet long.

The edge of a board can be shaved in several ways. If the board isn't too wide or long, you can secure it vertically with the shaving horse jaw. Another method is to hold the wood between a notch in the bridge and a *breast bib*—a wooden plank suspended by a string around your neck. For dressing the edges of chair slats, I hold the wood in a bench vise. I rough-trim with a drawknife, then finish with a spokeshave or a plane. (To dress shingle edges, I use a broad hatchet at a chopping stump.)

Project: A Grass and Leaf Rake

During our years of homesteading, we've found that there's no substitute for a wooden-tined rake for gathering leaves and grass clippings. I've made rakes following several traditional patterns. This one comes from Finland. The rake is an excellent learning project, in addition to yielding a useful garden tool. The design is simple. However, making a nice one is a challenge.

Edge shaving a post and rung chair back slat. Sometimes a bench vise is the best holding device.

Tools. Drawknife; spokeshave; ripsaw; crosscut saw; 3/8-inch chisel; 1-inch chisel; brace (or electric drill) with three bits (5/16 inch, 3/8 inch, and 7/16 inch); shaving horse; C-clamp; tape measure; and 12-inch ruler.

Materials. Ideally, the handle, head, and disk will be ash, because this wood combines strength with light weight. White or red oak, hickory, black locust, walnut, pecan, and hackberry can also be used. The tines should be as tough as possible and might be made of black locust, hickory, oak, or osage orange. Traditionally, the Finns used lilac.

The handle should be rived to about 1-1/2 inches square. You can also use a straight, thin sapling. The handle's length ranges from 70 to 80 inches.

First shave the handle to a square section, 1-1/8 inches on each side. Leave 5 inches at one end square, and round-shave the remainder. Then shave the last 6 inches of the rounded end to a blunt point so that the rake can be stuck into the grass when not in use.

Bore two 3/8-inch dowel holes in the squared neck, centered 1-1/4 and 3-1/4 inches from the end.

Next, saw the slot in the neck to accept the disk. Use a ripsaw to make two parallel kerfs. The slot is 3/8 inch wide and 4 inches deep. Use a chisel to remove the waste wood between the kerfs.

Rive the wood for the rake head. In Finland, a slightly bowed rake head is common. Although the bow is attractive, it's not necessary, and making it requires a naturally bowed billet. The rived blank should be about 1-1/4 inches wide by 1-3/4 inches deep. The length can range from 24 to 32 inches, depending on how you plan to use the rake.

Shave the head 1 inch wide. The central 4-inch section, which holds the disk, is shaved 1-3/8 inches in height. From there, make a graceful curve down each shoulder to a height of 1 inch. The bottom of the rake head should be perpendicular to the two sides. Don't round the ends or chamfer the upper edges until later, after boring and mortising are completed.

With a pencil, draw the 3/8- by 4-inch mortise

The wooden tines of this rake are ideal for gathering clipped grass, hay, and leaves. The traditional design is from Finland.

on the outer side of the head. Use a square to transfer the outlines of the mortise to the bottom and up onto the inner side. Draw a centerline down the length of the mortise outline.

Clamp the rake head, inner side down, over a piece of scrap lumber to a sturdy bench. (The seat of your shaving horse can be used.) Bore a row of closely spaced 5/16-inch holes down the center of the mortise, passing straight through the head into the scrap wood. A piece of masking tape wrapped around the bit can serve as a depth gauge.

It's important to make the holes parallel to the side of the rake head so that the drill will emerge within the mortise boundary. To align the drill, place a square on the bench top, blade up and perpendicular to the rake head. Align the bit so that it's parallel to the blade of the square.

Use a 1-inch chisel to clean the mortise sides and a 3/8-inch chisel to clean the ends. With sharp chisels, you can pare using hand pressure and body weight. Or, you can strike the chisel with a wooden mallet or a steel hammer. (I prefer using a hammer when the chisel handles are hooped or made of impact-resistant plastic. A wooden mallet absorbs impact that should be driving the chisel.) Chisel to a depth of about 1/2 inch, then turn the rake head over and finish chiseling from the other side. The mortise is completed when the interior walls are

flat or slightly undercut (concave) when gauged from one side to the other.

Use a pencil to mark out the centers of the rake tines. The two inner tines are centered 1/2 inch out from the outer disk mortise. The end tines should be centered 1-1/2 inches from the ends of the head. Spaces between the tines can range from 2-1/2 to 3-1/2 inches.

Clamp the head to the bench top, with the scrap board in the middle. Bore the holes carefully, using a square for alignment.

Finish the head after the disk mortise and tine holes are made. The ends of the head are rounded and slightly tapered, as viewed from above. Once the proportions look right, spokeshave a 1/4-inch-wide chamfer along both upper edges. The chamfer tapers out at the ends.

For the disk, rive a blank 5/8 inch thick, 4-plus inches wide, and about 12 inches long (the finished 7-1/2-inch length is a difficult size to shave). Drawknife the disk blank to an even 3/8-inch thickness, then saw it off to 7-1/2 inches. The oval shape could be sawed out, but you'll have more fun shaping it with a drawknife and a spokeshave. Draw the disk outline, then place the blank in a vise. Shave with the grain, working from the mid-sides to the ends. A sharp spokeshave works nicely on the end grain.

Shaved dowels are used to secure the disk and for the rake tines. Rive and shave them from green

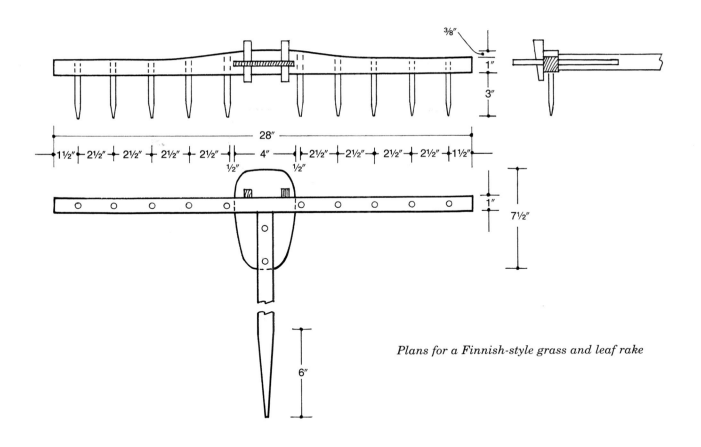

Plans for a Finnish-style grass and leaf rake

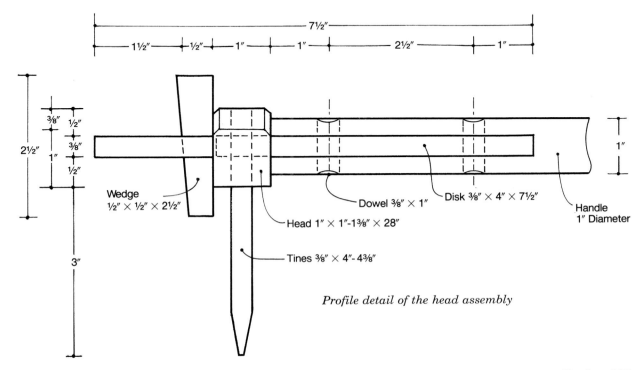

Wedge
½" × ½" × 2½"

Head 1" × 1"-1⅜" × 28"

Tines ⅜" × 4"- 4⅜"

Dowel ⅜" × 1"

Disk ⅜" × 4" × 7½"

Handle
1" Diameter

Profile detail of the head assembly

or dry wood. If you're using green wood, shave the dowels about 1/16 inch oversize. After the dowels have dried, shave them again to an exact 3/8 inch. The tines must be thoroughly dried before they're installed, or they'll shrink and fall out. Commercially manufactured maple dowels are weak and not straight grained. Don't use them.

Rive dowel stock about 1/2 inch square and 12 to 15 inches long. The rake tines will be 4 to 5 inches long, and you'll need 10 to 16 of them, depending on your spacing. While you're at it, rive and shave a few extra dowels for replacement tines if the originals break. You'll also need two dowels, each 2 inches long, to secure the disk to the handle.

Make a dowel-hole gauge in a dry hardwood board. For green wood, bore several 7/16-inch holes; for dry wood, use 3/8-inch holes.

It's important to use the same 3/8-inch bit for boring the gauge, the handle, and the tine holes in the head, because there's often a considerable variation among same-sized boring bits. Also, standard auger bits are actually 1/64 inch larger than nominal dimensions. Auger *dowel bits* are sized exactly, but they are no longer manufactured.

Shave the dowels into squares, followed by octagons, and finally rounds. If you're using green wood, shave to a diameter of 7/16 inch. Use a narrow support stick under the dowel stock. When you're finished, put the dowels in a warm place, such as above a wood stove or a water heater, to dry and shrink for a few days.

When the dowels are bone dry, shave them to 3/8 inch. The fit in the test gauge must be squeaky tight. Use several holes, as they tend to enlarge with each test fit. Keep dry dowels in a closed plastic bag until they're fitted to the rake head.

To locate the disk dowel holes and the tapered wedge mortises, insert the disk into the handle, then fit the rake head over the disk. Be sure that the disk and rake head are correctly positioned. With a pencil, mark the centers of the dowel holes, and scribe a line across the outside of the head. Then take everything apart.

The holes in the disk are *draw bored* (offset) from the holes in the handle to insure that the dowels won't loosen. Pencil a cross mark for the center of each dowel hole about 1/16 inch closer to the head end of the rake disk than the test-fit pencil marks.

Next, pencil on the disk the outlines of the mortises that will house wedges to secure the rake head. Pencil the mortise on the upper side of the disk, forming a 1/2-inch square. The inner edge of

the mortise should be 1/16 inch beyond the line you drew across the rake head; this offset insures that the head will fit tightly against the handle when wedged. Pencil the lower side of the disk mortise, 1/2 inch wide by 7/16 inch deep, and offset it too, 1/16 inch on the inside edge. The 7/16-inch dimension creates a 1/16-inch slope for the wedges.

Clamp the disk over a scrap board on your workbench. Bore 3/8-inch holes at the offset dowel marks and in the centers of the wedge mortise outlines. Use a 3/8-inch chisel to chop out the mortises. By eye, pare the outer wedge mortises to angle slightly inward. The wedges slope about 8°; at this angle an 8-inch chisel will tilt about 1 inch from vertical. The exact angle isn't critical. However, a shallow angle holds a wedge much better than a steeper angle.

The two wedges can be shaved from a 10-inch blank rived about 3/4 inch square. First shave two opposite sides to a width of 1/2 inch. Shave the third side lightly, in line with the wood grain. Shave the fourth side to a taper beginning 2-1/2 inches from each end. At 8°, the small end of the wedge will be 1/4 inch wide. Saw the wedges off the ends of the blank.

Saw the dry dowel stock to the length of the tines. With a knife, chamfer one end to make the tines easier to insert. (The actual pointing is done after the tines are in place.)

Support the rake head on two blocks so you can hammer the tines straight through the 3/8-inch holes. They should fit tightly. Glue can be used, but broken tines are easier to replace if they can be hammered out with a drift (a punch with a blunt end). If tines are loose, tighten them with tiny wedges. Use a 3/8-inch chisel to split the top of the loose tine. Split out wedges 3/8 inch wide by 3/4 inch long from a 3/4-inch block of straight-grained hardwood. Put a touch of glue on the wedges only. Then hammer the wedges into the splits in the tines.

Insert the disk into the slot in the handle. Chamfer one end of the 2-inch dowels, then hammer them home. Saw off the extending ends flush with the handle. Slip the head over the disk, and tap in the two wedges.

Now point the tines. Place the assembled rake, tines down, on a piece of scrap board set on a workbench. Pare the points with the 1-inch chisel; work with the bevel facing outward.

Finish the rake with tung oil thinned with about 20 percent turpentine. A second oiling, applied after the first coat has hardened, will give the surface a handsome, durable finish.

CHAPTER EIGHT

Boring

Drilling a hole in wood has long been an essential technique for most woodworkers. Greenwood joinery commonly utilizes round mortises fitted with cylindrical tenons. Drilling also speeds up the clearing of waste from rectilinear mortises.

Boring tools remove material directly from the bottom of a cavity. Hole diameter is constant as depth increases. *Reaming* enlarges the diameter of a hole by removing material from the sides. Because reamers are tapered, the sides of a reamed hole are angled. Reaming is advantageous where tenons tighten under pressure. The mortises for the legs of a Windsor chair are reamed.

Hand-powered boring tools, such as a brace and bit, are simple machines. Hole profiles are determined by the configuration of the bit, not the skill of the operator. Mechanical depth stops and various guides and jigs can make the job easier still.

One of the early wood drills was the *spoon bit*, which is shaped like a gouge but with an upturned, spoonlike cutting edge. Spoon bits date back to the Roman Empire.

Spoon bits cut by boring and reaming. With each rotation, the bit cuts through alternate quadrants of end grain and long grain, resulting in a slightly oval hole.

Because spoon bits lack a pointed lead, you can drill almost all the way through a post or board without coming through on the other side. But the rounded nose makes it somewhat difficult to start a hole at a precise location, especially on a curved surface such as a chair post.

On a *duckbill* spoon bit, the sides are tapered slightly narrower than the cutter width. This reduces friction as boring depth increases. The duckbill shape allows the bit to slop around at the bottom of the hole, resulting in a hole that is wider at the bottom than it is at the opening. If mating tenons are made slightly bulbous—something easily done with a lathe—the undersized mouth of the mortise traps the tenon. The tenon can't come out, although it can loosen and rattle.

Spoon bits are still used by woodworkers who prefer authentic period methods. But spoon bits were historically replaced by more complex boring

The bore and waste made by an antique duckbill spoon bit, used here with a Spofford brace. The sample was sawed open after the hole was bored.

tools, such as twist bits and augers.

An *auger bit* combines several features, each with a specialized function. The working end includes a pointed *lead screw*, one or two *spurs*, and one or two *cutters*. The lead precisely locates the hole. The screw pulls the cutter into the wood, controlling the bite taken with each rotation. The spurs, which extend ahead of the cutters, score the circumference of the hole. The cutters slice off the waste. Cutter shavings are removed from the hole by the spiral auger. The end of the shaft is usually a tapered square shank for use with a brace. Other augers are made to be chucked into electric drills.

Auger bits are manufactured in various patterns. The shank of a Jennings pattern auger bit consists of two continuous spirals that wind around each other. The less expensive Irwin auger bit has a coarser lead screw and a single spiral that winds around a substantial shank. The cutter heads of both are similar. The Jennings pattern can be advantageous when boring very hard wood. For boring most woods, the Irwin is faster, and the heavy shank is less likely to bend. A *ship auger*, which is also called an electrician's auger, has one cutter, a single spur, and a deep-walled spiral that forces it to bore straighter than a conventional auger, which can be deflected by grain angle. The shank end is generally six-sided for use with an electric drill. Ship augers are made in diameters from 3/8 inch to 2 inches. A common length is 18 inches, with a 12-inch auger.

Jennings and Irwin auger bits are manufactured in 1/16-inch increments, from 1/4 inch to 1 inch in diameter; and in 1/8-inch increments, from 1-1/8 inches to 1-1/2 inches. The sizes are numbered in sixteenths: #4 is 1/4 inch, #10 is 5/8 inch, #20 is 1-1/4 inches, and so on. The diameters of many auger bits are actually 1/64 inch larger than their nominal dimension. For true sizes, I use Irwin dowel bits (but these are no longer manufactured).

Twist bits are designed for drilling metal but are often used in wood. Quality twist bits are made from high speed steel, an alloy that holds a good edge and resists overheating. Polished flutes reject shavings considerably better than the unfinished flutes of cheap twist bits. Standard diameters run from 1/16 inch to 1/2 inch in increments of sixty-fourths and hundredths. Twist bits in larger sizes are also available.

Twist bits are usually sharpened on the side of a 100-grit grindstone. Inexpensive sharpening jigs are available, but twist bits can also be sharpened freehand, by eye. Carefully duplicate the original configuration.

The *brad point* is a special woodworker's version of the familiar twist bit, for use in wood only. The design of the cutter includes a short lead point and two spurs that prescore the diameter of the hole. The best brad-point bits have knife-edged vertical spurs and polished flutes. The spurs on less-expensive brad points are made by flaring the cutters at a reverse angle—the profile resembles a butterfly. Compared to standard twist bits, brad points are easier to center, and they cut cleaner holes. Because of the complex shape, sharpening is difficult, especially with the smaller sizes. Common sizes are from 1/8 inch to 1/2 inch in sixteenths, and from 5/8 inch to 1 inch in eighths.

The *Forstner* wood bit and its younger nephew, the Stanley *Power Bore*, are made for use with an electric drill, but they can also be used in bit braces that have universal jaws. Instead of spurs, Forstner bits ride on two quarter-circle scoring rims. Neither style has a spiral to carry out shavings. The shank is considerably smaller than the cutting head diameter. Shavings exit as a hole deepens. If they don't, you need to withdraw the bit periodically, or the shavings will jam the bit in the hole.

The lead point on a Forstner bit is short, and the curved rims are very low, allowing you to bore very close to the bottom of your material without coming through the back side. The holes are exceptionally clean. Using a drill press, Forstners can cut at any grain angle, including end grain, without deflection. They can also be used to cut overlapping holes.

The standard Forstner shank is cylindrical, but some combine a tapered square section—usable in any bit brace—at the end of the round shank. Forstner bits are manufactured from 1/4 to 1-1/16 inch in 1/16-inch increments, and from 1-1/4 to 2-1/2 inches in 1/4-inch increments.

Due to the limited clearance within the cutting head and the rounded rim, Forstner bits are not easy to sharpen.

The Power-Bore bit is made with a 1/2-inch lead, one 1/4-inch spur, and a single cutter. Sizes are from 3/8 inch to 1 inch, in eighths. I've noted considerable variation in diameter within each nominal size. The shank is ground with three flats for a Jacobs-type chuck. The steel is soft; after about a dozen sharpenings, I toss them.

What's good about the Power-Bore? First, it makes a clean hole, as quickly as a Forstner does. Because of the soft steel, the lead and spur are easily shortened. (Use a small, triangular file.) If necessary, you can file or grind down the sides of the cutter to special diameters. Most important, Stanley and Irwin manufacture extensions which are very useful for freehand boring.

When they were introduced, Power-Bore bits cost considerably less than Forstners; more recently, the cost of Forstners has fallen, whereas Power-Bore prices are rising.

Bit braces were originally developed for use with spoon bits and reamers. Early versions held bits in various odd ways; some bits were permanently attached. The Spofford split socket brace, which uses tapered, square-shank bits, was invented in 1859. I like to use a Spofford brace because there's no chuck mechanism, which invariably wobbles.

The modern shell chuck, with adjustable jaws and a ratchet advance, was patented in the 1860s. Shell chucks are made with two types of jaws. An *alligator* chuck has two jaws which pivot from the

Wood-boring bits (left to right): Jennings, Irwin, Forstner, Power-Bore (new), Power-Bore (with shortened lead and spur).

bottom of the chuck jaws. This limits use to tapered, square-shank bits. The jaws of a *universal* chuck can open and close either parallel or at an angle to each other. Universal chucks hold tapered square shanks and parallel shanks with flats. Chucks with three and four jaws have also been manufactured.

Sweep refers to the diameter of a circle described by the crank of a brace. Common braces have a 10- or 12-inch sweep. Eight-inch sweep braces are nice for boring small-diameter holes and for working in close quarters. Sweeps of 12 or 14 inches are recommended for boring holes larger than 1 inch in diameter and for working in very hard wood.

Hand-powered eggbeater drills and breast drills are made for use with twist bits and brad-point bits from 1/16 inch to 3/8 inch. Drill gearing develops speed, but there's very little power behind the bit.

Sharpening Auger Bits

Auger bits are commonly neglected, but sharpening them is not difficult. A sharp bit will pull itself into the wood, requiring little downward pressure on the brace. Boring wide holes in hard wood requires muscle power, but the work should be in turning the brace, not in getting enough advance.

Bits are sharpened with a special auger bit file, which has two elongated, flat tapers at opposite ends of a central shank. The file teeth of one end are on the flat sides; the narrow edges are smooth. At the other end, the teeth are on the edges, and the flats are smooth. With this arrangement, there's no danger of accidentally filing two adjacent planes at once, which would be easy in the crowded interior architecture of an auger bit. Auger bits larger than about 5/8 inch can also be sharpened with a small, three-cornered file, like the ones made for sharpening hand saws.

First file the spurs. If the spur is wedge shaped, it should be thinned to a knifelike section. File the leading edge on the inside of each spur until you raise a burr on the exterior. Remove the burr with one or two very light file strokes on the exterior.

To sharpen the cutters, rest the lead point on a piece of scrap wood, tilting the auger shank away from your line of vision. File the interior bevel of the cutters to about 30°. It's easy to file the cutters at a steeper angle, but resist the temptation. When you raise a burr on the lead side, lightly file it off. Be sure to keep the file flat, so that the lead of the cutter doesn't become dubbed over.

Two common brace bit chucks. The less expensive alligator chuck (left) works well with conventional tapered square-shank auger bits. The universal chuck (right) also holds round- and parallel-sided, hexagonal shank bits.

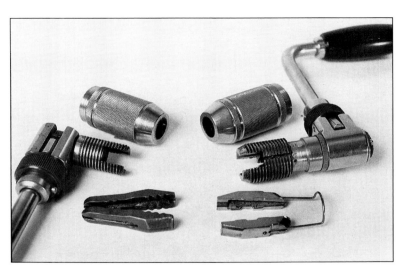

In recent years many green woodworkers have taken to using hand held, variable speed electric drills for many boring tasks. The new, better quality cordless electric drills are especially useful; they have impressive torque and can be operated at very slow, safe speeds. Some of my colleagues also use a drill press. But personally, I prefer free-hand boring for most green woodworking, including making chairs.

Boring Techniques

Boring wood by hand is commonly looked upon as a monotonous activity, to be avoided whenever possible. (The adjective "boring" is derivative.) Personally, I enjoy drilling holes, if the wood isn't extremely hard or ornery. And boring compound angles can present some good challenges. Often, holes must be bored at different angles, and sometimes in mirrored pairs. You have to stay alert at all times; mistakes can be disastrous to the work.

While helping students learn how to make greenwood chairs, I've probably encountered more mistakes during boring than in all other phases of construction combined. The fastest learners sometimes make the worst errors. Boring angles can be complicated and confusing, but there are several methods for getting your bearings.

Most drilling tasks can be jigged. To bore the compound angles for the legs of a Swiss two-board chair, Ruedi Kohler uses a boxlike jig with alignment holes that's placed directly over the seat blank. Drill press tables can be tilted. On a radial drill press, the head itself can be set at an angle.

I prefer to bore freehand, although I do use visual alignment aids and depth stops. Without a mechanical jig, you must keep alert at all times and also develop skills in eyeballing.

Boring angles can be referred to as simple (perpendicular) or compound. When perpendicular, the drill appears square to its base when viewed from any direction. A compound angle tilts from the surface, in one or two directions, depending on how it's viewed.

Any boring angle can be located by determining the intersection of two planes, or one angle and the lean direction. Angles are often specified in relationship to a horizontal (level) or vertical (plumb) reference. Level and plumb references are particularly useful for boring into irregular shapes, such as logs or chair posts. A line level can be taped to boring tools and angle gauges, such as squares and sliding bevel gauges.

Using a horizontal plane as a reference, it's always possible to rotate your sighting position until a compound angle looks vertical from your vantage point. (This is easy to understand if you imagine yourself walking in a circle around a leaning tree. Regardless of the lean, from two opposite positions the tree appears vertical.) This viewpoint is the *lean direction*. The *lean angle* is the angle formed when the lean direction is seen as vertical.

Compound angles can be measured and notated from a model—either a mock-up or an object being reproduced—and from drawings. To take angles from drawings, use two perpendicular views, usually one head-on and the other from a side. You will have two lean angles. For the lean direction, you need a plan view, as seen from above. The angles are copied with a flat plastic drafting protractor. A second kind of protractor, consisting of a rectangular steel plate that is etched with a 180° arc and that has a pivoting leg, is used for measuring angles of things such as a model. Either protractor can be used to set bevel gauges.

Most boring at perpendicular and compound angles is done from a vertical boring position. The piece is secured to a horizontal surface—usually a workbench—with clamps or a three-peg-and-wedge holding system (see sidebar on page 113). The boring tool is positioned by referencing against two gauges placed perpendicular to each other. Eyeball your boring position by tilting the boring tool so that it appears parallel to each guide when viewed from respective viewpoints.

One way to bore a compound angle is by tipping the drill in the lean direction at a specific lean angle. To insure that the drill is correct, adjust a sliding bevel at the lean angle, and place it parallel to the lean direction. Then set a square perpendicular to the lean direction. From perpendicular vantage points, the gauges and the bit will be parallel.

In a second method, you use two lean angles and sight against two sliding bevels, set perpendicular to each other. Lean direction isn't considered.

It's possible to bore compound angles by eye. For a set of compound angles, such as the legs of a bench, you can bore the first hole by eyeballing the drill shank from two perpendicular directions. (A bit extension helps to increase accuracy by magnifying any errors.) After the first hole is bored, insert a first leg into it. Refer to the first leg as a mirror image of an adjacent hole. Bore the second hole, insert another leg, and continue the set.

For horizontal boring, the drill is always held level. One advantage is that you can bore a series of holes using a level as a constant reference. I use

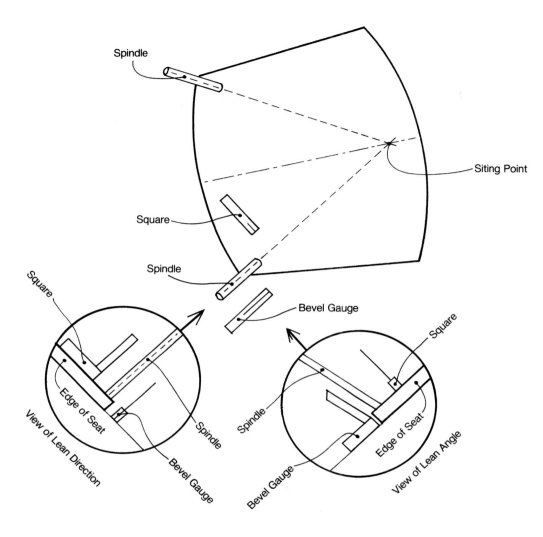

Siting the compound angles of a chair spindle by combining lean direction and lean angle. The chair seat is shown on a flat surface.

horizontal boring for the rung mortises in the posts of a ladder-back chair. The holding device can be a bench vise or a three-peg-and-wedge system on a wall. To insure that the drill is horizontal, tape a line level to the bit shank. The addition of a bit extension exaggerates angular fluctuations and makes sighting easier.

Stand with your feet about 18 inches apart. Steady the brace by holding the knob just inside your left or right hip joint.

On a ladder-back chair, the rungs intersect to form a trapezoid. The boring angle for rungs coming into a post is often perpendicular. To bore the intersecting rungs, you must rotate the post to the correct angle. Usually, the first set of rungs is already attached to the post. (If not, insert a dummy rung in one of the holes.) To set up the rotational position, tape a line level to a sliding bevel set at an angle taken from a model or drawing. Hold the sliding bevel with the bubble centered in the level. Rotate the post until the attached rungs are parallel to the angled leg of the sliding bevel.

You can also make special angle gauges for specific projects. My "Potty Seat" (not patented) combines the various angles of a ladder-back chair in a single gauge. The outer angles represent the rung-post angles and their relationship to the back slat mortises. The gauge has a hollow center, so that a line level can be taped parallel to one side.

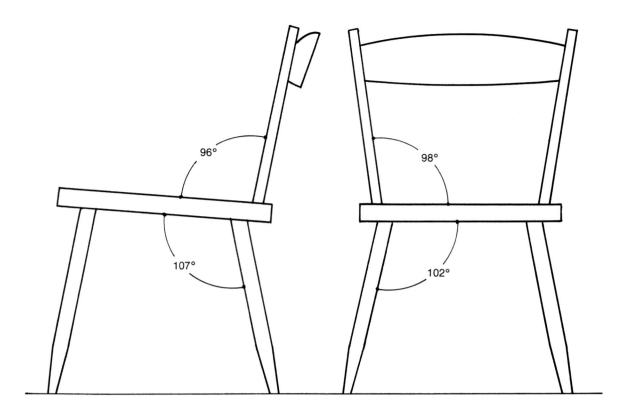

Measuring compound angles using drawings of front and side views. Note that the side views are measured from the tilted seat, not a horizontal plane.

96°

98°

107°

102°

Boring Tips

Freehand boring is dependent on accurate eyeballing. My best tip is to check alignment from two vantage points at right angles to each other. With auger bits, you can stop boring at a very shallow depth—the lead screw will hold the brace in position—and then step back to check the angle from both views. Or you can rely on a helper to align the setup. Mirrors and lines on the floor or a wall can also be used. (Plastic mirrors survive abuse in the shop.)

Depth gauges keep you from drilling too far. You can wrap a piece of tape around the drill shank, but I prefer a mechanical gauge that physically limits the bore. For twist bits, you can buy small collars that are held in place by a set screw. Or, drill a hole through a small block of wood that's just the right length to stop boring when it reaches the material being bored; the block must be positioned against the chuck. For auger bits, I use a Stanley No. 47 depth gauge. This neat device is a spring with a ball-shaped end that makes a warning noise when it contacts the wood, without preventing you from boring deeper. Unfortunately, these are no longer available.

The exit end of a hole bored through a piece of wood is often marred by torn fibers. If you clamp the material on top of a piece of scrap wood, you can bore straight through the work and into the scrap without tear-out. There must be close contact between the two pieces. Another method is to bore a hole partway from opposite directions. This works particularly well with bits that have a long lead screw; stop boring when you see the tip of the lead coming through. Turn the wood over and finish boring, using the lead prick to center the bit. If you're boring at an angle, reversing direction can be confusing; the second pass must mirror the original angle.

By drilling from both ends, you also can make deep holes that might otherwise wander out of alignment. An example would be boring for deep mortises, such as for the wedges of a trestle table. Again, careful alignment from two vantage points is the key to success.

When a bit doesn't cut cleanly, it requires sharpening and possibly reshaping of the cutters or spurs. Auger bits may have been filed at too steep a cutting angle.

The Three-Peg-and-Wedge Holding System

Three pegs protrude from holes bored in a bench top or any other horizontal, vertical, or tilted surface. The pegs should be hardwood and at least 3/4 inch in diameter. Two pegs are placed in line, as a base for the material to be bored. The third peg is placed above the base to secure the work plus about half the width of a wedge. Wedges of different widths can be used in combination with material of varied dimensions. The enclosed angle of the wedge should be no more than 10°, or it will loosen too easily.

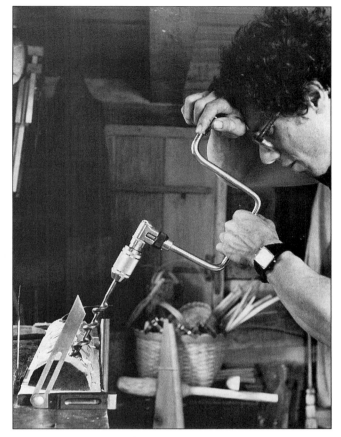

Horizontal boring using a three-peg-and-wedge holding system. The drill rig consists of a Power-Bore bit, a bit extension, a line level, and a bit brace with universal jaws. The bore depth gauge is a piece of tape wrapped around the Power-Bore shank.

Boring a compound angle using two lean angles. The siting guides are two sliding bevels, positioned perpendicular to each other.

A pair of lightweight, rived and shaved trestles. The legs and cross pieces are white ash.

This "Potty Seat" is used to set up front and back post boring angles for my ladder-back chairs.

For tips on boring into the side of a cylinder (such as rung mortises in a ladder-back post), see the project description in chapter 10.

Project: A Pair of Lightweight Trestles

I first saw these trestles while visiting my friend Daniel O'Hagan. Daniel had been doing some carpentry for a neighbor when he discovered that the neighbor didn't have any sawhorses. Daniel quickly made a pair, using a split sapling for the trestles. He liked them so well that he made another set for himself. When I returned home, I made these.

These trestles are lightweight and strong. They stack nicely, since there are no braces between the legs. Making them will give you practice doing vertical boring of compound angles. We'll do some horizontal boring while making the stool in chapter 10, which you should preview before building the trestles.

Tools. The standard riving tools; bit brace; 1-inch auger bit; two sliding bevels; drawknife; spokeshave; a fine-toothed crosscut saw; chisel; carving knife; two large clamps; shaving horse; and a 2- to 3-pound hammer or mallet. A workbench with a vise is useful but not necessary.

Materials. For the two trestles, you need a sapling, 4-1/2 to 5-1/2 inches in diameter and 24 to 30 inches long; for the legs, enough wood to split and shave eight 28-inch legs. My sawbucks are ash, which is strong and light, but any strong,

straight-grained, ring-porous hardwood is appropriate. Yellow pine can also be used. You also need material to make eight small wedges, and white or yellow glue.

Rive the leg blanks, about 2 inches on each side. Shave them into squares, 1-1/2 inches on each side, then into octagons, and finally into rounds. Wet rounds should be air-dried a few days, then "superdried" in a warm place, such as behind a furnace or wood stove, so that they won't shrink and fall out of the trestles. The tenons will be shaved just before assembly, after the wood has thoroughly dried.

Work on the trestles while the legs are drying. Both trestles are made by splitting or sawing the sapling in half. (I ripped mine with a chain saw, since I wasn't sure if my ash sapling would split straight, and I had only one piece to use.) Flatten the inner surface with a plane. Remove the bark with a hewing hatchet or drawknife.

The mortises are bored from the bottom of the trestle. Use two clamps to secure the trestle, flat side down, over a piece of scrap wood. The end to be bored should overhang the scrap so you can see the auger lead when it starts to exit.

Locate each pair of mortises at centerlines, 2-1/2 inches and 5 inches from either end of the trestle. Because the trestle is exceptionally narrow, the mortises are staggered, rather than located opposite one another.

The leg angle as viewed from the end of the trestle, called *splay*, is 20° from vertical. From the side, the leg *cant angle* is 13° from vertical. Set two sliding bevels to these angles. (You could also use cardboard triangles cut out to these angles.) Place the 20° gauge on the bench top parallel to the end of the trestle; set the 13° gauge parallel to the side of the trestle.

The first hole can be at the 2-1/2-inch or 5-inch location. To determine the placement of the bit, hold the drill parallel to the end sliding bevel, then locate it perpendicular to the tangent of the half-round side. At the correct position, the lead screw should point near the center of the trestle top. When viewed from the end of the trestle, the auger will appear parallel to the 20° sliding bevel. Shove the lead into the wood so that it won't slip.

While holding the brace at the 20° angle, shift your viewpoint to one side. Now tilt the brace to the 13° side angle. (This is where beginners will appreciate a helper!) Start boring. Stop as soon as the lead screw can hold the brace at the angled position in the wood.

Step back a few paces and view the bit from the end and side views. Judge the angle of the bit in comparison to both sliding bevels. They should appear parallel to the bit. Adjust the brace as necessary; use your sense of judgment, shifting the brace up or down, left or right. Take about two turns of the brace to set the new angle. Then check your alignment once more. Continue boring until the lead just begins to poke through the trestle surface. Then stop, and back out of the hole.

Bore the other three holes. Be careful to make the correct bevel setups for each leg.

Rotate the trestle, so that the top side faces up. Clamp it in position on the scrap board. To prevent the trestle from rolling, slip two or three wedges under the curved bottom.

Set up the sliding bevels, with angles mirroring the positions when the bottom was bored. (The splay and cant angles are now directed inward.) Finish the holes by boring through the lead-pricked centers.

Once the leg blanks have dried, you can work on the tenons. The length of the 1-inch-diameter tenons is determined by the depth of the trestle

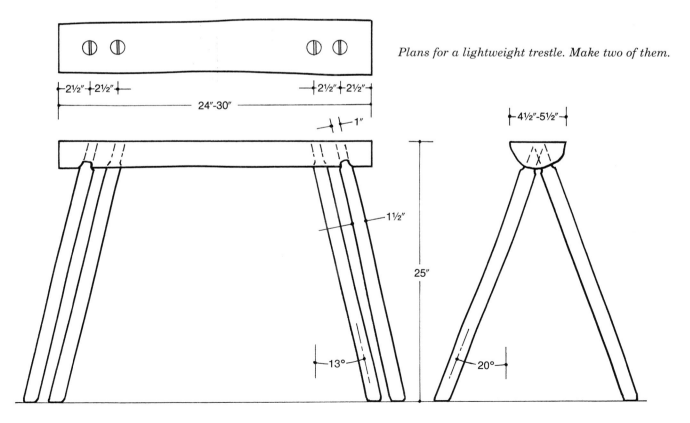

Plans for a lightweight trestle. Make two of them.

The tenon wedges must be perpendicular to the long fibers of the trestle.

mortises. Find the deepest mortise, and make all the tenons the same length. (Mine were 2-1/2 inches.) Any excess length will be trimmed after the tenons are in place.

To accurately size the tenons, make a gauge by boring three or four 1-inch holes through a piece of dry hardwood about 1/2 inch thick. Make several holes, since they'll become larger with use.

To make these big tenons, I start by sawing a shallow kerf, about 3/16 inch deep, around the circumference of the leg. This can be done at a shaving horse or with a bench vise. Begin shaving the tenon with the drawknife bevel facing down. To shave up against the shoulder, reverse the drawknife and push it into the saw kerf. Use the hole gauge often. The tenon should fit through, but quite tightly. (If one of these long tenons gets shaved too small, don't worry. The tenon will probably tighten up when it's wedged into the trestle.)

When the tenon diameter is right, carve a small chamfer on the end. Since loads tend to concentrate at the square shoulders, you can also drawknife a chamfer at the tenon shoulders for added strength. Make a 2-inch-deep saw cut through the center of each tenon for a wedge. Saw the kerf tangent to the growth rings.

To make the wedges, rive two or three 12-inch-long blanks about 1 inch wide and 1/4 inch thick.

Shave a 2-inch-long wedge from one end of a blank, then saw it off and make another wedge. When the first blank becomes too short to shave, switch to another piece.

Place the trestle upside down on two pieces of scrap wood. Leave clearance for the tenons to exit. Brush glue in one mortise and on one tenon. Orient the tenon so that the wedge kerf is perpendicular to the long fibers of the trestle. Use a hammer or mallet to drive the tenon into the mortise. (I use a 3-pound mallet with rawhide inserts that fit into an iron head.) Stop when the tenon shoulders engage the cross piece.

When all four legs are in place, turn the sawbuck over. It will probably wobble. We'll level it after the other sawbuck is put together to make a matched pair.

Right now, you need to drive in the wedges before the glue around the tenons dries out. Put a little glue on each wedge, and hammer it in until it fits tightly. Use a 12- to 16-ounce steel-headed hammer. Remove glue slop around the tenons with a dampened cloth. Trim the protruding tenon ends with a saw or chisel.

Assemble the second sawbuck. Then level both sawbucks with adjustment wedges, and saw the legs to final lengths. Details for this procedure are given near the end of the stool project in chapter 10.

CHAPTER NINE

Bending

There's a magic in bending wood that reminds me of a blacksmith shaping hot metal at a forge. You work the material quickly, with deliberate actions. Jigs must be just right. All necessary tools are within arm's reach. As with blacksmithing, you must finish a hot bend before the wood loses its heat. Also, there's an element of risk and suspense. With tight bends, you can expect some failures even with experience.

Wood bending is particularly suited to the needs of green woodworkers. North American Indians have bent wood to make snowshoes, sleds, toboggans, and canoe frames. On the Pacific Northwest coast, Indians crafted rectangular storage boxes from rived cedar planks. Corners were made by carving kerfs across the grain, heating, and folding. The fourth corner and a bottom plank were fastened with pegs or lashing. Even logs were bent. After a cedar dugout canoe was adzed from a log to a uniform thickness of two finger widths, the hull was filled with boiling water. As the wood softened, the beam was widened by wedging sticks across the hull.

The slats of a ladder-back chair are always bent. If the chair is to be comfortable, the back posts must be curved. (On Shaker side chairs, which aren't particularly comfortable, the back posts were usually straight.) Windsor chairs of all styles have a bent back rail. On a continuous-arm Windsor, a single 5-foot rod is bent into a triple curve to form both arm rests and the back support. Thin-rived Windsor back spindles sometimes require *straightening*—wood bending in reverse. Other uses of bending by green woodworkers include basket frames and handles, wooden bucket hooping, tool handles, canes and shepherd's crooks, and the rims of large wool-spinning wheels.

Bending has several unique advantages over other shaping methods. Bent wood is much stronger than wood shaped by cutting across the long fibers. This advantage is particularly true when the wood is rived instead of sawed. (In industry, sawed lumber with a grain run-out of 1:15—which means that in a 15-inch board, the grain moves to the side 1 inch—is considered prime material. Rived stock has

A jig used to bend back slats for ladder-back chairs

little, if any, run-out.) Since it's stronger, bent wood can be used in smaller dimensions and, therefore, be considerably lighter than wood shaped by sawing. There is also a savings in materials.

There are a few disadvantages to wood bending. Because bent wood springs back slightly after forming, it can be difficult to match paired components. Due to fluctuations in wood moisture content, unrestrained bent wood, such as a bent hayfork, can change shape long after bends are set. Wood bending requires flawless materials, and even then failures are possible. Bending wide stock is much easier than bending deep-sectioned stock.

When wood is bent, the fibers on the outside of the curve are stressed in tension. At the same time, the inner curve is forced into compression. As in a loaded beam, somewhere in the middle there is a neutral axis which is neither tensed nor compressed.

Wood can be *plasticized*—made more bendable—by the use of heat and moisture to temporarily soften the cellular structure. *Limbering* is a technique of gradually creating a curve by flexing wood several times before bending it to the required radius. On a deep bend, the outer curve may stretch 2 percent while the inner curve compresses as much as 30 percent.

Bending the back rail of a continuous-arm Windsor

Stretching on the outer curve is insignificant relative to the extensive compression of the inner curve, where cell walls deform into microscopic folds and wrinkles. There may also be a small amount of cellular slipping.

Because green woodworkers use wet rived stock, radical bends can be made with low-tech methods. Bending sawed, dried lumber requires tension straps and other specialized equipment. Green wood plasticizes better and more quickly than dry wood. Because of high moisture content, green wood conducts and holds heat much better than dried wood.

In extreme bends, hydrostatic pressure within the cell walls of saturated wood can cause failures; lowering the moisture content to 30 percent may help.

Bending stock must be high quality and free of defects such as knots, insect holes, incipient decay, and checking. You can expect both successes and failures, even using wood species rated highly for bending. Tests by the U.S. Department of Agriculture Forest Products Laboratory haven't determined any correlation between weight or growth rates and bending qualities. A table rating bending qualities of wood species is included in chapter 3.

Because of variation within species, you should experiment with woods in your area. Windsor chairmaker Dave Sawyer observed that North Carolina hickory growing on our farm woodlot didn't bend as well as the hickory he uses in New England. Henri Vaillancourt, founder of the Trust for Native American Cultures and Crafts, says that the Indians of Quebec, Canada, prefer to bend snowshoes from yellow birch, not white birch. Henri has found that New England white birch is too weak, so he uses white ash. Black ash bends easily, but it wears quickly. For snowshoes, maple wears well, but the uneven grain is difficult to work and to bend without failures.

Bending Equipment

Thin green stock, such as that used for snowshoes and lap-strake boat planking, is sometimes bent cold by nailing or riveting into its bent form. Heavier

Bending forms for basket rims and handles used by Martha Wetherbee

stock requires plasticizing with steam or hot water and the use of bending jigs. The use of heat may make an unrestrained bend more permanent.

A commonly used jig for flat curves consists of a form board shaped to the interior curve of the bend, screwed to a base of plywood or lumber. The bent piece is held in place between the form board and pegs with wedges. A separate jig is required for each shape. In a more flexible—but less exact—arrangement, a tabletop or a wide, thick board is drilled with a grid of holes. Pegs are inserted to describe the interior of the desired curve. Other pegs, used with wedges, are placed in holes to secure the bent wood on the exterior of the curve as it sets.

When I was making hayforks, I used simple frame jigs that form bends in both width and depth simultaneously. The hayfork handle is made with an S curve, as viewed from the side, while the tines are bent in compound curves, as viewed in plan view. The jig consists of a shallow frame of 1 × 4s, with holes in the sides that are fitted with removable dowels. I've used these jigs to bend hundreds of hayforks and also the back posts of ladder-back chairs. To change the curve, I just bore different dowel holes in the sides of the frame.

The chair post jigs that I currently use are made from a 1-inch-thick board with a notched keeper board screwed to the base to hold the posts in place. One form holds two posts, positioned back to back. I like these jigs which are easy to make and don't take up much space in storage or when used.

In designing any jig, the curvature should be slightly exaggerated to compensate for the effect of springback. A change from one material to another could require jig modifications.

The steamer I use was put together in about half an hour. The steam chamber is a box of rough pine lumber nailed together. It's better than most pipe steamers, since the wood box doesn't cause much condensation. Inside the box there are six cross dowels, located about 1 inch above its floor, to keep the pieces being steamed out of the condensation on the bottom and to allow steam to circulate freely. The ends of the steamer are plugged with removable pieces of foam rubber.

The steamer rests directly on a 2-1/2-gallon pot, which is heated on a stove or a hot plate. Steam enters the chamber through a pot-sized opening cut in the bottom. Because the steamer is narrower than the pot, I cover the extra width of the pot top with two wooden lids, one on each side of the box.

This frame jig bends hayforks in two planes. Adjustments in the profile bend can be made by relocating the large, middle dowel.

To monitor the temperature in the box, I insert a deep-fry dial thermometer into an end. These are available at supermarkets and hardware stores for a few dollars. The maximum temperature that I achieve is 195°F, which seems to be adequate.

The chamber should not be larger than necessary. Mine was made for steaming the back rail of a continuous-arm Windsor and is 62 inches long, 4-1/2 inches wide, and 5-1/2 inches high.

Wood Bending Techniques

Careful shaping—especially thicknessing—is important. Bending forces tend to concentrate and cause failures at abrupt changes in dimension. Thick areas resist bending; thin areas tend to collapse. The thickness of a chair back slat should be uniform.

A purposefully made taper in thickness can be used to modify the radius of a bend. Examples include the irregular curves of a snowshoe frame, some basket handles, and the bent back posts of ladder-back chairs.

Smooth surfacing will minimize failures such as cross grain slivering. A slight chamfer at the edges of square section members also helps to prevent tear-outs.

Wooden bucket hooping provides an interesting illustration of the importance in careful thicknessing and detailing. Bending the hoop seldom presents a problem. But when the hoop is put in place and driven tightly against the staves, the entire hoop is forced into tension. A slight imperfection in

the wood or the dimensions of the hoop usually results in a failure. To a point, hoop strength increases as the thickness is reduced.

Generally, bending billets should be rived and shaped so that bends are parallel with the growth rings. This isn't always possible, but chances of success are greater. In the case of multi-dimensional bends, such as the back rail of a continuous-arm Windsor, growth rings can be oriented in either dimension.

The cross section of the wood being bent should be wide, not deep. Deep-sectioned bends tend to buckle at the sides. Do any mortising or boring after bending.

It's usually worthwhile to shave and bend extra pieces, especially if you need matched parts such as chair posts, because some are likely to fail during bending or to set with unexpected curvatures.

Limbering may help with both cold and hot bends. The wood should be flexed only in the direction of the bend. The contact surface of a limbering fixture should be curved, to spread out the compression forces and to prevent dents in the wood. I sometimes bend the wood against my leg. After limbering a hot bend, I often reheat the wood for the final jigged bend.

Boiling works as well as steaming. The disadvantage is that large boilers are cumbersome. Boiling can be used to advantage on a long piece if only one end requires bending. Boiling water can be ladled over thin stock, such as chair slats, bucket hoops, and basket handles.

A simple, but effective, steamer, made from pine boards nailed together. Both ends are plugged with pieces of foam rubber. The block of wood on top is a balance. (The heating element of this particular hot plate is small and tippy.)

Limbering a ladder-back post. If the wood seems stiff, I'll put it back in the steamer for a few minutes before bending it in the jig.

Allow an hour of steam—or boiling—time per inch of thickness for air-dried wood and half an hour per inch for green wood. Longer steaming times may help, but the wood can also be weakened if it begins to "cook."

It's important to work quickly once the wood is removed from the heat. Wear neoprene gloves. Be sure to have everything close at hand, including a supply of twine and a selection of C-clamps in different sizes. These can save the day, as we'll see below. A helper will be appreciated, especially by beginners.

About an hour after executing a bend, it's often possible to remove the wood from its jig and tie the bend in place with twine. This is useful if you have

Bending a ladder-back post. A second post will be bent on the other side. The posts are held in place with pre-knotted loops of twine.

Project: A Firewood Carrier

For years, I stubbornly hauled firewood to our kitchen by the armful. I've tripped on the way, I've balanced a full load in one arm so that I could open the door, and so on. Now, with a firewood carrier, I can haul twice the load with half the effort. When it's raining, I have a free hand to carry an umbrella. The carrier can also be used to store firewood once it's in the house.

The design for this carrier was developed by Vermont Windsor chairmaker Dave Sawyer. The carrier may look small, but it easily holds about 50 pounds of firewood. With two carriers, you can carry two moderate loads and stay balanced.

Here's a second use for the carrier. If twine or hickory bark is woven around the frame like a chair seat, it's transformed into a very nice indoor swing for a small child.

Before starting this project, preview chapter 10.

Tools. Riving kit; drawknife; spokeshave; brace; 7/16-inch auger bit; 5/8-inch Stanley Power-Bore or Forstner bit; ripsaw; tape measure; shaving horse; steamer; simple jig (described below). Also needed are white or yellow glue; twine; and four 3/4-inch cut nails or brass brads. The leg spreader requires a nominal 1 × 8, 14 inches long, and eight 1-1/2-inch box nails.

Materials. This firewood carrier can be made from any ring-porous hardwood (except elm). The one in the photo on page 123 is red oak. White oak, ash, hickory, and hackberry are also good choices. You could use beech, maple, birch, or walnut, but with these semi-diffuse porous woods it's necessary to saw out the parts, rather than rive them, and shaving will be a fussier job because the grain is not particularly straight.

The bow is made from a small-diameter log at least 60 inches long. Rive out a blank roughly 1-1/4 inches wide and 3/4 inch thick. The width should be tangent to the growth rings so that the piece will be easier to bend. Trim the piece to 58 inches.

Shave the blank to 1 inch wide and 1/2 inch thick. Begin with a drawknife, then use a spokeshave for final surfacing.

Pencil a conspicuous mark around the center of the bow. Measuring out from the center, make marks at 1, 3, 7, and 9 inches on both sides. These marks indicate where the bow is thinned to 5/16 inch so that the bent handle will be straight across the top. *All of these thinned areas are located on the inner side of the bow.* Make two more marks, 16 inches from the ends, to indicate how long to saw out the legs.

to bend several pieces from a single form.

Setting time for bends depends on several factors, such as wood species, moisture content, wood thickness, and bend radius. Setting time is much quicker in a dry, warm environment. A simple kiln heated by a radiant heat lamp to 120° to 140°F works very nicely, but any warm, dry place will work just as well. (Instructions for making a low-tech kiln are included in chapter 10.) You know a bend is set when the wood rattles in the jig or springs back just slightly when untied.

On each half of the bow blank, shave the two 5/16-inch-thick areas for the corner bends. The transition from a thickness of 1/2 to 5/16 inch occurs between the marks at 1 and 3 inches, and between 7 and 9 inches. Shave the 2-inch-long area in the middle of the bow to a thickness of 7/16 inch.

Carefully ripsaw the legs to the 16-inch marks. (If you have a band saw, use it.) It's important to saw opposing pairs of legs to equal widths or the legs will take dissimilar bends. Use a spokeshave to round all corners (except inside the legs) to a radius of about 1/8-inch. About 1-1/2 inches in from the end of each saw kerf, wrap the legs tightly together with twine to prevent the bow from splitting when the legs are bent.

Make the leg spreader from a 3/4- to 1-inch board, 7-1/2 inches wide and 14 inches long. Use a drawknife and a spokeshave to bevel the long sides to about 24° from the original edge angle. On the long sides, set pairs of nails, spaced 5/8 inch apart and 1-5/8 inches from each end. Let the nail heads protrude 3/4 inch.

This firewood carrier can be used to haul 50 pounds or more. For a balanced load, make two.

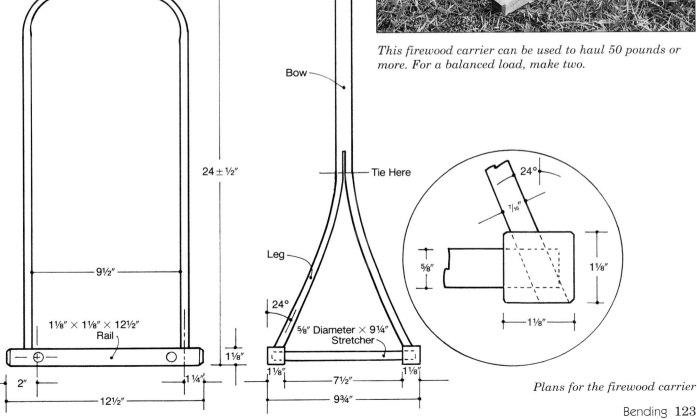

Plans for the firewood carrier

Steam the bow for about half an hour. If you don't have a steamer, you *might* succeed with green wood by ladling boiling water over the handle area and the leg bends just before bending them. With your gloves on, remove the bow from the steamer. The first bends form the handle. Limber the bow at the handle "corners" by bending it across your knee. Be sure that the thinned, 5/16-inch-thick surfaces are on the inside of the bend. Don't limber the center handle area. Bend the bow until the ends are 9-1/2 inches apart, and then restrain the sides by tying with twine.

Next, limber the curves for the legs. (If you're not steaming, ladle more boiling water over the legs before limbering the bends.) Make gradual curves by limbering along the length of each leg.

Insert the legs between the nails on the spreader. Observe the bow from different angles to see if it's smooth and symmetrical. Make adjustments while the wood is still warm and supple. Tie the bow into the position in which you want it to set.

Dry the bow in a warm place. The ends must be thoroughly dry at the time of assembly.

Rive the 9-inch-long stretchers about 7/8 inch square. Shave the green wood to 3/4 inch in diameter. Air-dry the stretchers for a few days, then super-dry them. For a "kiln," use any dry place that's between 100° and 140°F. When the stretchers are bone dry, spokeshave them to 5/8 inch in diameter. For a test gauge, bore a 5/8-inch hole in a piece of scrap hardwood. The fit should be squeaky tight. Do this shortly before assembly.

Rive the 12-1/2-inch-long rails roughly 1-1/2 inches square. Shave them to 1-1/8-inch squares. Use a spokeshave to chamfer the edges at the ends.

Bore 5/8-inch-diameter mortises, centered 2 inches from each end. Bore into the growth ring plane (perpendicular to the rays). Make the holes 7/8 inch deep. Because the wood beyond the hole is only 1/4 inch thick, use a Forstner bit or a Stanley Power-Bore bit with a shortened lead point. These bits are discussed in chapter 8.

The 7/16-inch-diameter holes for the legs are centered 1-1/4 inches from the ends of the rails and 5/16 inch from the inner side. The boring angle is 24° from vertical; set a sliding bevel to that angle for a guide. Use a conventional auger bit with a screw-type lead point. Stop boring just as the lead point begins to emerge through the rail. Then finish boring from the other side.

To take advantage of differential shrinkage (as explained in chapter 10), orient the stretchers so that their rays are in line with the rails.

Put the frame together with white or yellow glue. Yellow glue dries faster and has somewhat

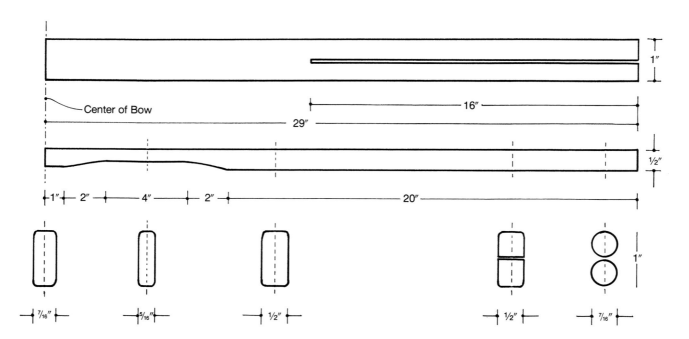

Dimensions for shaping one-half of the bow. In the plan and profile drawings, the thicknesses and widths are shown at twice the scale of the length.

better moisture resistance. I use both, depending on circumstances. (I use white glue for complex glue projects and for teaching. Yellow glue is preferred for production, especially when clamps are in limited supply.) Before the glue sets, make sure that the frame is flat. If it isn't, put one rail in a vise and twist the other rail until the frame lies in a flat plane.

Once the bow curves have set, you can adjust the lengths of the legs. First, re-tie the twine at the crotches to compensate for wood shrinkage during drying. Stand the bow on a flat surface, and wedge up the legs until the bow stands straight. Then scribe a line around the legs with a compass set at the height of the shortest leg, as measured from the flat surface. Saw the leg tips off at the scribed lines.

Next, make the round tenons at the leg ends with a spokeshave. The tenons are 7/16 inch in diameter and 1-3/4 inches long. Size the tenons in a 7/16-inch test hole bored in a piece of dry hardwood. Dye transfer (described in chapter 10) is a useful method for accurate sizing. Before assembly, use a scraper or sandpaper to smooth the inner sides of the legs.

Fit the leg tenons into the holes. Use glue. Observe the wood carrier from different angles. Final adjustments can be made by driving the legs further into the stretcher mortises; do this by striking the bottom of the stretchers with a hammer. When you get the bow just right, saw off the ends of the tenons where they protrude through the bottom. If the tenons are loose, chisel slots across the ends and glue wedges into the slots. The procedure is similar to wedging loose rake tines, discussed in chapter 7.

Bore a 1/16-inch-diameter hole through each tenon from the inner side of the rails. Tap a nail, sized slightly larger than the holes, into each. Leather supply stores carry 3/4-inch cut nails that are perfect; you can also use small brass linoleum tacks.

When the firewood carrier is assembled, scrape or sand any rough surfaces. For a finish, use two coats of tung oil.

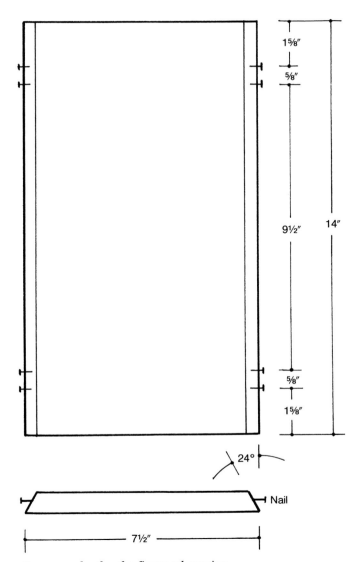

Leg spreader for the firewood carrier

CHAPTER TEN

Joinery

The strength of a greenwood joint depends to a great extent on the maker's understanding and use of the drying characteristics of wood. Factors include the orientation of growth rings and the relative moisture content of mortises and tenons. Although greenwood joinery generally uses bored mortises and cylindrical tenons, the principles can also be applied to conventional rectilinear mortise-and-tenon joints.

A ladder-back chair frame is a perfect example of greenwood *wet/dry* joinery. The vertical posts have bored mortises, into which are driven horizontal round tenons. The construction of a Windsor chair is also based on wet/dry construction. Other examples of greenwood joinery include the rake, sawbucks, low bench, and firewood carrier covered in chapters 7 through 9.

It is often said that a wet mortise, such as a rung hole bored in a green chair post, will later shrink and tighten around a dry tenon. But joints often fail sometime after construction. Chairmaker John Alexander and wood scientist R. Bruce Hoadley decided to find out why. They learned that loosening follows periods of high humidity, which causes the fibers of swelling tenons to crumple from extreme compression. With a change to low humidity, the moisture content drops and the tenons shrink. Cyclic changes in wood moisture content are also a contributing cause of failure with socketed wooden tool handles, such as axes and hammers. The key to wet/dry joinery is a joint that works when wood *shrinks and swells* with changing environmental conditions.

In the case of ladder-back chair construction, another factor is *racking*, the lateral forces applied to the frame during use. Leaning a ladder-back on the rear posts puts tremendous stress on the joints—particularly those in the side panels. The structural weakness of a ladder-back chair is that it lacks triangulation.

I made my first post-and-rung chair in the summer of 1979, during John Alexander's first class at Country Workshops. That winter, I made about a dozen more chairs. In the March/April 1980 issue of *Fine Woodworking* magazine, R. Bruce Hoadley

wrote on the weakness of the conventional ladder-back joint, and I began to fear that my chairs would soon fall apart. But 15 years later, my original chairs are still as tight as they were when I put them together. These chairs have been in constant use, with no particular care other than the fact that they're not left outdoors. Our environment is less than ideal for preserving furniture. The summer weather is humid, and our log cabin, which is heated by a wood stove, is quite dry during winter.

What holds these chairs together? Dealing with wood moisture content is crucial, but other factors are also important. The result is a "belt and suspenders" approach to greenwood joinery.

Control of wood moisture content at time of assembly is most important. Parts are shaped sloppy-wet and green but dried within specific ranges of moisture content before assembly. Final sizing of tenons must be done after all shrinkage has taken place and the wood is thoroughly dried. Theoretically, tenon moisture content (m.c.) should be close to 5 percent, but sound joints can be made with tenons that are somewhat wetter, probably up to 8 or 10 percent m.c.

During assembly, mortise wood, such as posts, should have a 15 to 20 percent m.c. Some of the shrinkage, from loss of bound water, will already have taken place. If moisture content is higher, there's a chance that mortise wood will split as it dries around the tenon. In the humid eastern United States, wood dried in a shed stabilizes at an equilibrium moisture content close to 20 percent.

When the relatively wet mortise is joined with the dry tenon, the mortise shrinks slightly and the tenon swells and tightens as it absorbs moisture from the mortise wood. Tight, long-lasting joints are dependent on an optimal balance of swelling and shrinkage.

The environment that a joint is subjected to should also be considered. In the arid West, moisture content for both mortises and tenons should be relatively lower.

Orientation of the tenon in the mortise is very important. Wet wood shrinks about twice as much tangent to the growth rings as it does on the perpendicular ray plane. A round, green cylinder will dry and shrink into an oval cross-section. Tangent to the growth rings, many green woods shrink 10 to 15 percent. On the ray plane, potential shrinkage is 5 to 7 percent. The heavy hardwoods commonly used for greenwood joinery are among the species that shrink the most.

Since the lengthwise shrinkage of wood is only about 1/10 of 1 percent, a mortise or tenon made from green wood will have almost no lengthwise shrinkage.

Selection of wood species and quality is important. For a green wood joint, use strong, straight-grained, easily rived, ring-porous hardwoods such as hickory, ash, white and red oak. Black locust and black walnut are harder to work but are appropriate also. Diffuse-porous hardwoods such as birch, beech, and cherry can be used, but components are difficult to rive and shave using these woods.

Wood for wet/dry joinery should be free of defects such as rot, bug holes, and knots. For strength, the growth rings of ring-porous hardwoods should be at least 1/16 inch wide, and preferably 1/8 inch or more.

In designing a joint, you want to orient the zones of minimum shrinkage in the plane of maximum stress. On a ladder-back chair, both direct load and lateral racking stress the top and bottom of the post-and-rung joints; there is very little pressure on the sides of the joints. The tenons of a ladder-back chair rung should be assembled so that the rays are vertical (parallel with the length of the post).

The joint must also have adequate depth. The diameter/length ratio should be at least 1:1-1/2. Shorter tenons pull loose too easily and have too little surface area for racking loads to bear upon. A common ladder-back post-and-rung joint is 5/8 inch in diameter and 1 inch deep.

It's unwise to lengthen a tenon so that it extends through the post, because the exposed tenon end will cycle more moisture than if it were in a conventional stopped mortise.

Both the mortise and the tenon should have smooth surfaces. The ragged fibers of a rough surface are structurally weak, make a poor glue surface, and are subject to moisture cycling.

Although many greenwood chairs have been made without glue, I use it. Glue slows down moisture exchange within the joint. Even though the stressed surfaces in the joint mate end grain against long grain, modern glues do provide some

This post section, which was assembled without glue, was put in a vise, and the rung was twisted using a pair of Vise Grips; it won't come out.

bonding strength. Glue also works as a lubricant during assembly.

For greenwood joinery I use white glue. Yellow glue has greater moisture resistance, but it grabs immediately in a tight joint. There is no possibility of making an adjustment. Don't allow white (or yellow) glue to freeze.

Real hide glue is possibly the best glue to use. This is because the joints can be dissolved in alcohol if a repair should ever be necessary.

On a ladder-back chair, rung tenons can also be secured within the post by interlocking with the tenon of an adjacent rung. The second rung slightly overlaps—and cuts through—the tenon of the first rung. When I assemble a chair, I bore and assemble the joints of the side panel before proceeding with the overlapping perpendicular joints of the front and back panels.

The bearing surfaces of a tenon should be carefully dimensioned and can be oversized by about 1 percent. The nonbearing surfaces—the sides of a rung joint—can be a slightly undersized.

During my early years as a chairmaker I actually pared away a thin slab from the sides of the tenons. This was supposed to reduce the possibility of the post splitting when the mortise shrinks in width.

Another detail that I've abandoned is cutting a shallow ratchet shaped notch or groove on the bearing surfaces of the tenon. When the mortise end-grain swells, fibers supposedly lock into the groove.

In recent years I've come to believe that neither of the above techniques (slabbing and grooving) are actually helpful.

A moisture-resistant finish helps to minimize moisture cycling. For ladder-backs, I use tung oil thinned with a little turpentine. Tung oil dries hard and has a subtle luster. A mixture of tung oil and urethane varnish will provide better protection from moisture than a straight oil finish. I paint my Windsor chairs with 3:1 mixture of satin enamel and satin urethane varnish.

Checking Moisture Content

With experience, you can judge the approximate moisture content by knowing the history of a piece of wood after it was cut and by sensory tests of feel and sound. When two pieces of dry wood are knocked together, the wood "pinks." In contrast, wet wood "thuds." If you hold a piece of dry wood to your cheek, it feels warm; wet wood feels cool. Try these tests using samples that you know to be wet, air dried, and bone dry.

It's instructive to have some ballpark figures to go by. Outdoors, in the eastern United States, wood air-dries to 15 to 20 percent m.c. In the West, wood will air-dry to 10 to 15 percent m.c. Indoors, above a stove or gas water heater, with a temperature of 90°F or so, wood eventually drops to 5 to 10 percent m.c.

After shaping parts, weigh them periodically as they dry. Small parts, such as chair rungs, can be weighed as a set. Pencil the weight and date on the parts. When weight loss levels out, they're as dry as your current conditions will get them.

This system can be improved by first drying a test sample in a low oven until you're sure it's bone dry. If you're drying rungs, saw off a 2-inch-long piece as a sample. Weigh it, then dry it in the oven until it stops losing weight. Dry the rungs along with remains of the test rung, from which you periodically cut off a 2-inch sample to weigh and compare to the bone-dry sample.

To determine the percentage of moisture content, use this formula:

$$\text{moisture content} = \frac{\text{green weight} - \text{dry weight} \times 100}{\text{dry weight}}$$

A moisture meter is useful, but they cost between $75 and $200, and I don't know of any production green woodworkers who use one.

Techniques

Traditionally, round tenons were usually turned on a lathe. Cylindrical tenons can also be shaped with a *hollow auger*, which is a circumferential cutter turned with a bit brace. Turned and hollow-augered tenons are always shouldered; the tenon's diameter is less than the section it's made from.

I made the tenons for my first dozen chairs with an antique A. A. Woods adjustable hollow auger. With a little practice, it works quickly. A problem with the hollow auger is that the knife cuts by scoring across the fibers. Even with a very fine adjustment, the fibers at the surface of the tenon are partially severed. For a good joint, the surface must be smooth. With a coarse wood like oak, the effect can be quite rough.

During my second year of chair making, I switched to turning tenons on a spring pole lathe. Turning takes more time, but the results seem to be worth the extra effort. Hickory and even ash can be turned to a smoother surface than oak.

The shoulder of a tenon is a point of weakness. Loads concentrate at the angular change in dimension. A 7/8-inch-diameter rung with a 5/8-inch tenon may look strong, but the rung is weakened at the shoulder, where it enters the mortise.

While I was turning tenons, John Alexander was experimenting with shaved, shoulderless tenons. The shaved rung is nearly uniform in diameter from end to end. (In practice, only the tenons are closely sized, while the middle section is shaved by eye.) When you first see them, thin rungs with shaved tenons may look weak, but they may be stronger than heavier rungs with shouldered tenons. Shaved rungs are also lighter in weight and they use less wood. Shaving is a little slower than turning, but the result is a strong, resilient tenon that follows the natural fibers. The only tools needed are a spokeshave, a carving knife, and a shop-made tenon gauge. I now shave tenons whenever possible.

The shaved tenon method can be refined by finishing sizing with a fine rasp or a strip of sandpaper pulled back and forth over the tenon like you do with a rag when polishing shoes.

Another way to make tenons is by carving them with a knife. This is the slowest method of all, and unless you're quite skilled, it's not very accurate. Carving could be appropriate if you need to make shouldered tenons and a lathe isn't available.

With any tenoning method, aim for a squeaky-tight fit, particularly on the areas tangent to the

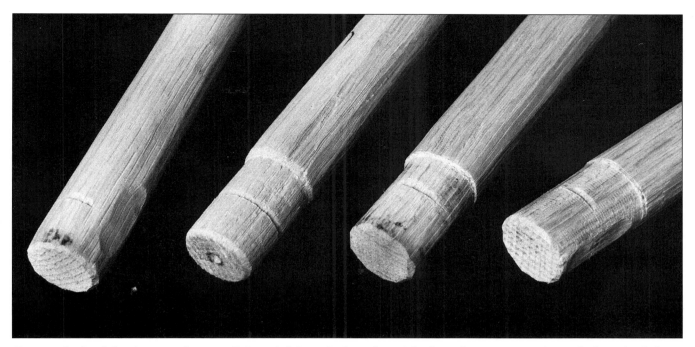

Four methods of shaping round tenons (left to right): spokeshaved straight from the rung, turned on a lathe, whittled, hollow-augered.

growth rings. Turned tenons can be sized on the lathe with outside calipers or a shop-made "go/no-go" gauge. (This is a C-shaped cut-out in a thin board or piece of plastic; you size the tenon by fitting it in the mouth of the C, which is cut to the appropriate size.) Shaved and carved tenons are sized with a simple hole gauge. This is a piece of dry hardwood with several sample holes bored in it.

I use a dye transfer technique to determine where a tenon needs further shaving: I coat the inside of the gauge holes with soft pencil lead. When a tenon is inserted, areas of tight contact pick up the dye. A slight chamfer at the ends of the tenons makes them easier to insert in a hole gauge or in the actual mortise.

The most difficult part of shaving tenons is avoiding "pencil-pointing," caused by shaving over areas that already fit. It helps to skew the spoke-shave and to adjust the blade finely. You can also try pushing the spokeshave, so that you can begin each stroke just ahead of the high area that you're after. When pushing, be careful not to make rungs shaped like an hourglass—caused by shaving the center part of a rung from both ends.

Regardless of how they're shaped, tenons should be prepared with two points in mind.

1. The wood must be bone dry—5 to 8 percent m.c.—when it's brought to final dimensions.

2. You should orient the tenon in the mortise so that the ray plane runs lengthwise, parallel to the long fibers of the mortise, and against the racking direction.

Mortises can be bored vertically or horizontally. I use both methods, depending on circumstances. For mortising ladder-backs, I prefer horizontal boring. The main reason is that I can use a level taped to the bit extension as a consistent plane of reference. I bore vertically for most simple tasks and for the many different compound angles of a Windsor chair seat.

Mortising bits are discussed in chapter 8. I generally use standard Irwin auger bits for mortises that go straight in or at moderate angles. For ladder-back mortising, I use a 5/8-inch Stanley Power-Bore bit with a shortened lead. Forstner bits are also good, but they are difficult to sharpen, and most Forstner bits cannot be chucked into a bit brace.

Drying Methods

Green wood should be air-dried a few days before you put it in an oven to dry, to avoid end checks, warping, and interior honeycombing.

An ideal temperature for oven drying is 120° to 140°F. Any dry place over 90° will work, but the process is slower. Over 160°, wood can char or even-

The tenons of turned Windsor legs and stretchers are quickly super-dried in hot sand. The middle areas, which will contain bored mortises, remain at a higher, air-dried moisture content. Keep the temperature below 150°. Periodically stir the sand, or there will be a large temperature variation getting hotter closer to the bottom.

tually ignite. Rushed drying can also cause interior honeycombing.

You can probably find a place in your home or shop that works well enough for oven drying. A rack above a wood stove or a gas water heater is all that's needed for drying small amounts of wood, especially if you're not rushed.

The posts and stretchers of Windsor chairs require a more specialized drying method. The tenon ends must be bone dry, while the middle areas should be air dry, since they contain mortises. The trick is to dry the ends in sand heated to 110° to 140°F. Use clean, dry sand and a thermometer to monitor the temperature. The heat source can be a stove or hot plate. Tenons are "cooked" when they become oval. Stretchers with two tenons have to be dried at both ends. If the heat source is a radiant

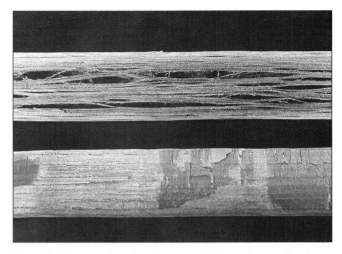

Top: Split rung showing honeycombing—the result of drying green wood too quickly. Bottom: The beginning of scorching—caused by a temperature above 160°F.

stove, wrap the middle area of the wood with aluminum foil to keep it from drying.

Project: A Post-and-Rung Stool

This project was selected as an example of wet/dry joinery and for practice with horizontal boring. The design derives from similar stools made by the Shakers; the main difference is that this one is shaved, not turned. For details on how to make a post-and-rung chair with slats and a bent back, refer to John Alexander's book, *Make a Chair from a Tree* (Astragal Press, 1994), or attend a workshop.

Tools. Riving kit; shaving horse; drawknife; spokeshave; knife; tape measure; small combination square with level; 2- to 3-pound hammer or mallet; crosscut saw; pencil; brace; 5/8-inch bit; chair stick (see the illustration on page 133); shop-made post/rung shaving gauge; tenon-sizing gauge; white glue. Optional: workbench with vise; bit extension; line level; 24-inch bar or pipe clamp.

Materials. For shaved chairs and stools, use straight-grained ring-porous hardwoods that split and shave easily—white and red oak, hickory, and ash are excellent. My preference is for white oak posts and hickory rungs. White oak posts are resilient and beautiful. Hickory rungs are tough, and the cream color of seasoned hickory is a nice contrast to the white oak.

Reject any wood that contains defects, such as knots, rot, or bug holes. I generally avoid riving billets that contain sapwood and heartwood in one piece. Oak sapwood decays quickly; rungs can be

The original Country Workshops electric wood kiln, made from a 55-gallon steel drum. The heat source is a 500-watt radiant lamp mounted in a chick brooder socket fitted with an aluminum reflector. The curved metal shield deflects direct radiation, causing heat to circulate evenly throughout the kiln. A heavy blanket doubles as insulation and a door.

made with oak sapwood if the wood is used shortly after felling. You can test for incipient decay by attempting to break a dry rived rung billet. Put the billet in a vise and bend it. If the workbench isn't bolted down, it should tip over before the billet breaks. Hickory and ash sapwood are fine for rungs or posts.

Rive the posts 1-3/4 inches square and 20 inches long. Rive five or six, so that you have extras in case of mistakes or warpage during drying, or so that you can make test joints.

Rive six rungs 7/8 inch square and 13 inches long. Rive nine or ten rungs 7/8 inch square and 17-3/4 inches long (extras can be cut down for short rungs).

Before shaving parts, make the chair stick and the sizing gauge that is used to measure the diameter of posts and rungs. For the sizing gauge, use scrap wood, Masonite, thin metal, or plastic. The gauge is 2 by 3 inches, with two notches that correspond to the diameters of the posts and rungs. One notch is 3/4 inch wide, the other is 1-3/8 inches wide.

Markings on the chair stick indicate the location of mortises, the lengths of posts, and so on. Rung lengths can be marked on the back of the stick. Once you try a chair stick, you'll not want to use a tape measure or yardstick. Make the chair

A Low-Tech Wood Kiln

For Country Workshops, I rigged up a simple kiln that oven-dries rungs for ten chairs, taking them from a 20 percent m.c. to 7 percent m.c. in about 36 hours. The housing is a clean 55-gallon steel drum with one end cut out. The other end has three vents for moisture to exit. (The back end could be cut out entirely, allowing access from either direction.) The drum is placed on its side across a pair of sawbucks. Wedges prevent the drum from rolling.

The heat source is a 500-watt clear (not red) radiant heat lamp, used with a chick brooder lamp holder and a wide aluminum reflector. The lamp is centered on the bottom of the drum, facing up.

The drying rack is a rough wooden frame made of 1 × 2s, held above the floor of the drum by four 8-inch legs. Half-inch hardware cloth is tacked to the bottom to prevent rungs from rolling off the rack.

A piece of sheet metal, about 2 by 3 feet, is placed between the lamp and the rack to keep the wood from being charred from direct radiation.

The door, and insulation, is provided by a heavy blanket draped over the kiln. I use a thermometer to monitor the interior temperature; it stays about 135°F with one lamp.

stick from a piece of wood that's about 1/4 inch thick, 1-1/4 inches wide, and a few inches longer than the posts. Beveling one edge will make accurate measurements easier.

The first step at the shaving horse is shaving all the posts to 1-3/8-inch squares. Follow the grain, even if this results in crooked posts. After squaring, work each post individually. Use the chair stick, always measuring from the bottom up, to make a pencil mark at the beginning of the taper for the bottom end of the posts. Shave the lower taper while the posts are square. The bottom of the post is 1 inch across. If the tapered end curves or bows, you can make an adjustment by shaving more taper off one side or another. When you examine the post, look down its length; this view provides the most telling story. Then shave the post into an octagon, followed by a cylinder. Set shaved posts aside and let them air-dry to 15 to 20 percent m.c. This might take two weeks indoors or a month in an airy shed.

All the rungs should be shaved to 3/4-inch squares as a set before shaving them into octagons and cylinders. Be sure to follow the grain. Reject banana-shaped pieces. Rungs with a double or triple curve—and ends that are more or less in line with each other—can be kept. Air-dry the rungs for a few days. Then kiln-dry them with whatever setup is available.

Tenons are spokeshaved when the rungs are bone dry. First, check the lengths. They should be uniform within 1/16 inch. While working on one rung, you can keep the others in a dry environment—in a plastic bag, over a stove, or under a lamp. In humid conditions, rungs will swell within 30 minutes.

Make a tenon-sizing gauge from a piece of dry hardwood about 1/2 inch thick. Bore three holes with the same 5/8-inch bit that will be used for the actual mortises, and number them. You will start out using hole #1 and, when it enlarges, continue to use it for the initial test fit, but use #2 for the final fit. Move on to #3 when hole #2 seems a little loose.

Use a fine rasp or coarse file to carve a slight chamfer around both ends of each rung. Initial sizing is done with a spokeshave. Set a small blade exposure. I usually shave from the middle of the rungs toward the near end. When I start to get close, I mark the inside of my test holes with ink or soft lead pencil to reveal high areas to shave down. Final sizing is done with the rasp or strip of sandpaper (cloth backed sandpaper works best).

Size the tenons for a very tight fit tangent to the growth rings. The final fit in the test gauge should be squeaky tight and hard to pull out. Renew a slight chamfer around the ends so the tenons cannot jam on the mortise wall during assembly.

For mortising, you need to orient boring in relation to the grain direction of the posts. The posts will shrink in width twice as much across the growth rings as they will across the rays. Since posts will have mortises at right angles to each other, I compromise so that mortises in both planes shrink about the same amount. Do this by looking down at the posts and rotating them so that the rays are angled diagonally across the stool. Just for looks, you can also orient the posts so that the growth rings curve with the pith side facing inward, as they did on the tree. Pair the posts into left and right sides. (For this stool, the short dimensions are called the sides.) With a pencil, draw a vertical orientation line down each post where the side rungs come in.

To locate the mortises, use the chair stick, measuring up from the bottom of the posts and the stick. The tops of the posts run randomly over-length—they're trimmed after assembly. Hold the chair stick next to each post and transfer rung tangent lines on the chair stick across the vertical orientation line on the post. Mortises for the side panels are bored just above the tangent lines shown on the chair stick. The mortises for the front and back will be bored after the side panels are assembled. Draw a circle above each tangent line. With the circles, you won't make a mistake by boring on the wrong side of the tangent lines or by using a tangent line as a boring center.

Set aside the posts for one side panel so that you won't accidentally work on them until after the first side panel is assembled.

I prefer horizontal boring for these mortises. Use a waist-high vise or a three-peg-and-wedge holding system. Position the post so that the lengthwise orientation line faces you. The post is horizontal, but it doesn't have to be perfectly level. With a vise, I secure the post to bore the middle and top mortises first. (The vise jaws grip the lower half of the post.)

I use a brace with universal jaws. For a bit, I like a 5/8-inch Stanley Power-Bore. (With this bit, the lead point must be filed down to about 3/16 inch, as noted in chapter 8.) You can also use an auger bit with a shortened lead, or a Forstner bit.

My boring system also includes some other accessories. The long shaft of a bit extension minimizes boring slop and makes aiming more accurate. I tape a carpenter's line level to the extension. I also use a depth gauge (Stanley #47), set to 1 inch. If you don't have a depth gauge, wrap tape around the bit 1 inch above the cutters.

The most difficult part of boring into a round post is aiming the auger bit directly at the post center of mass. If you miss the center, the auger side spur could emerge through the back side of the post before you've bored a full inch.

Bore the middle mortise first. To locate the bit, kneel so that you can sight straight down the length of the bit shank. Check the line level to make sure that the bit is horizontal. Because you are looking at a cylinder, the center of your eye's iris must be level with the center of the bit shaft. (The bit extension helps here, too.) If your eye is too high or too low, the horizon lines that define the edges of the round post will shift from the horizontal center of mass. Use eyeball judgment to move the bit up or down so that it's centered on the post. Then locate the circumference of the bit against the tangent line. Finally, press in the lead so that the bit won't slip.

A shaved stool. Posts and rungs are oak. The seating is hickory bast.

Plans for a post-and-rung stool. The chair stick is used to transfer dimensions to the individual parts. Rung dimensions are on the other side of the stick.

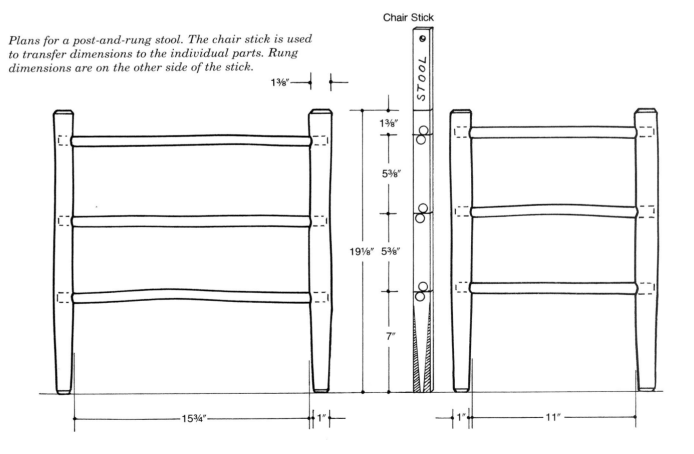

A plastic sizing gauge, with notches to measure the diameter of posts and rungs. Shave all the parts to a square section before shaping into octagons, and finally cylinders.

Diagram on the floor shows the boring orientation in relation to the growth rings and rays of the posts. The arrow on top of the post indicates the rays. The vertical pencil line is the boring axis for the short side rungs.

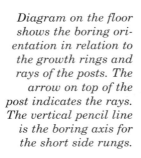

Stand up, legs apart, to bore the mortise. Place the brace knob inside your right hip socket. Make sure the bit is level. Use a square to insure that you're aimed perpendicular to the post.

As you bore the mortise, keep an eye on the shavings. If they stop ejecting, immediately withdraw the bit. Power-Bore and Forstner bits easily jam. Stop boring when the gauge bumps the post.

Next, bore the top mortise. Even if the post is crooked, aim for the center of mass.

If the post is held in a vise, it's necessary to shift it before boring the third (bottom) mortise. It's important that the post is not rotated when you move it. To prevent rotation, use an alignment dowel—a 6-inch length of rung—with another line level taped to it. The bubble on the dowel must read level before and after moving the post. Now bore the bottom mortise. Again, aim for the center of mass. Don't try to make a straight line from one mortise to the other.

Repeat the mortising procedures for the second post. The only difference is that the second post is a mirror image of the first.

Using a chair stick to locate boring tangents on the back posts of my daughter's youth chair. Make a separate stick for each design that you build.

Boring rung mortises. Proper vertical positioning of the bit relative to the cylindrical post is critical. Before boring, site the bit by aligning your eye with the leveled bit extension. Then equalize the spacing on the post above and below the bit.

An alignment peg (with a taped-on level) is used to reposition the post so that the bottom mortise can be bored.

You're now ready to assemble a side panel. But before putting the panel together, clean up the posts. Spokeshave and scrape off all the pencil scribblings and smudges. This is the best time to smooth the surfaces.

Check the rungs for even length and for proper fit in test holes. Decide which rungs will go where. Unattractive but strong rungs are used at the top, since they're hidden by the seating. Crooked rungs can be attractive if you plan where to put them. If a rung has a slightly loose tenon, use it in a middle mortise, where there's less stress. To start, you need three short side rungs. Keep the other rungs dry.

To spread glue, I use an old toothbrush. Keep a clean damp rag ready for cleanup. Put glue on the tenons at one end of the three short rungs. Brush glue in the mortises of one post.

Place the post on the bench top above a workbench leg or on a log stump. A helper will be appreciated. Be sure that the mortise is securely backed by the work surface to guard against the possibility that a tenon will break right through. As you insert the rungs, make sure that the rays are oriented lengthwise, parallel with the long fibers of the post. Curved rungs are oriented crown up.

Knock the tenons in with a mallet. (I use a 3-pound iron mallet with rawhide inserts, but wood and Computhane mallets can also be used.) When you hit a rung, you will hear "bong, bong" and then "thud" as it bottoms in the mortise. Don't be afraid to hit the rungs hard. If the wood is sound, the rungs can take it.

After three rungs are seated, measure their lengths and sight across the ends of the tenons. If the center tenon protrudes, try to pound it further in or saw off the extra length. Re-chamfer the ends if necessary. Don't worry if the rungs do not line up in a straight row. They will pull together when the opposing leg is fitted.

Brush glue on the exposed tenons and in the mortises of the second post. Be sure that the posts match (top mortises with top mortises, and so on). Position the initial assembly with the first post on the work surface, rungs pointing upward. You may have to pull or push the rungs around to line them up with the mortises of the second post. Tap on the second post to start it onto the tenons. Once all the rungs are started, hammer on either post until the second tenons are about halfway in.

Stop to check alignment. View the panel by looking across the rungs. If the panel is warped, put one post in a vise, or on the bench top, and twist the other post in the appropriate direction. When the panel is flat, proceed by pounding the posts until all the tenons seat.

If a tenon won't seat, or if pounding makes you nervous, you can pull the tenons in with a bar clamp or pipe clamp.

A try square and level are used to orient the side panels before boring the front and back rung mortises.

When all the tenons are seated, check the spacing. The side posts should be 11 inches apart. Also, check alignment again, and correct it if necessary. Use the damp rag to clean up glue slop before proceeding with the second side panel. Then stop and admire your accomplishment.

The assembly of the second side panel is identical to that of the first, except that this panel mirrors the first one.

To bore mortises for the front and back panels, put either panel into a vise or three-peg-and-wedge holding system. Use a combination square or a try square with a taped-on level to orient the rungs vertically. Make sure that you're about to bore in the right direction—toward the other side panel.

When you bore the front and back panels, overlap the side mortises by about 1/16 inch so that the rungs will interlock with one another. Make the overlap equal for all the mortises; uniformity is more important than the actual amount of overlap. *Be sure to mortise below the side rungs.* Bore all 12 mortises—6 in each side panel.

Brush glue in the six mortises of one side panel and on one end of all the long rungs. Start pounding the rungs in. When all six rungs have bottomed, check lengths and alignment of tenon ends. Brush glue on the opposing tenons and in the mortises of the other side panel. Bend the rungs as needed, and start hammering on the posts.

Once all the tenons are started, stop to check alignment. View the stool by looking across the front and side panels to opposite rungs, and down the panels at a close angle. If the stool is lopsided, determine which direction could be shortened to straighten things up. Put the appropriate post on the floor and bear down on the frame. Dave Sawyer calls this "chair wrassling." Then pound the tenons home.

Measure between the front and back posts; they should be 15-3/4 inches apart. Check alignment and "wrassle" the stool into shape if necessary. If it's stubborn, run a bar clamp from the top of one post to the bottom of an opposite post. Leave the clamp in place overnight.

Chances are that your assembled stool wobbles a bit on the floor. The easiest way to level it is to find out which posts act as a fulcrum and then saw or rasp them down a little. But this isn't a good method, since the seat will not necessarily be level. Instead, first level the seat by placing wedges under the posts. Place the stool on a flat surface, such as a table saw. Check for level by taking measurements from the floor to the top of the front and back rungs. Play with the wedges until you get the seat just right.

Next, scribe a cutting line around the bottoms of the posts. (Use a compass or a pencil held at a constant height with an appropriate shim.) The scribing height is the distance from the tabletop to the bottom of the shortest post. Scribe around the other three posts at this height. When you saw off the post bottoms, align your saw blade with the scribing lines on the other posts. A fine-tooth dovetail saw works nicely.

Saw off the random tops of the posts, leaving at least 3/4 inch above the top of the side rungs. Marking the posts by measuring from the table at 3 or 4 places will help in getting a square saw cut.

Chamfer the top and bottom ends of the posts with a sharp chisel, used bevel up. I also pare the

Chair Doctoring

A mistake can usually be corrected. Mortises may be bored in the wrong location or at the wrong angle. Short and long rungs can get switched. Posts have been assembled upside down. I've seen all these problems, and worse.

If an incorrectly bored mortise is discovered before assembly, you can plug it and bore again. Make the plug from an extra rung. See that it fits tightly, and use glue. If the correct mortise will overlap the plug, a Forstner bit will work very nicely, but other bits can also be used. If a rung is in the post when the mistake is discovered, saw it off and you have a built-in plug. A rung joint may pull loose, but properly sized tenons won't come apart.

When a post boring mistake is discovered after assembly, you can save the rungs by splitting off the post with a chisel. Figure out what went wrong, then bore mortises in a spare post and reassemble the stool.

If you discover that tenons are undersized before boring, you can switch to a smaller bit. A 9/16-inch mortise will do, although it looks undersized. It's possible to grind or file a Power-Bore bit about 1/32 inch undersize. You can also increase the tenon's diameter by gluing a nylon stocking over the end or by driving a tiny back wedge into a kerf at the end of the tenon as it's pounded into the post mortise. For successful back wedging, careful planning is necessary. Don't make the wedge too big. If you do, you may split the post, or you may not be able to drive the tenon in.

In the case of a terrible disaster, remember that a loser project can be a good learning experience. Saw some joints in half to study how the chair works and what went wrong. Try to pull some joints apart. Try stressing some rungs. Subject joints to several cycles of changes in humidity. Long rungs can be sawed off and recycled as short rungs.

Before glue sets, "chair wrassling" can often be used to even up alignment of front and rear panels caused by minor boring irregularities. Bar and pipe clamps can also be used.

tops of the posts just slightly convex—like the floor of the Parthenon, a very slight dome-shape looks much better than a flat saw cut.

Before putting on a finish, do a final scraping job and possibly a little sanding. For a polished surface, a brisk rub with dry spokeshave shavings will work better than sandpaper. I don't try to remove *flats*, the subtle planes left from shaving, but I remove irregularities that would draw attention.

For a finish, I use tung oil cut with about 15 percent turpentine, or a proprietary penetrating oil. I never use stain or coloring agent. Apply the oil with a clean rag. Rubbing heats the oil a little and this improves penetration. In a few hours, you can apply a second coat.

Since air hardens tung oil, it should be stored in an airless container. You can put marbles into the can to displace air as the tung oil is used up. Or, you can transfer the oil to a plastic bottle and then squeeze out the air before putting on the cap.

Instructions for weaving the seat with hickory bast are given in Appendix B.

Wille Sundquist, carving a spoon at our North Carolina home in 1977.

Swiss Kufermeister Ruedi Kohler planing the interior of a coopered bowl. Photo taken in 1980 when Ruedi was 79.

PART THREE
Profiles

Vermont Windsor chairmaker Dave Sawyer

CHAPTER ELEVEN

Meet Some Green Woodworkers

While shaving bucket staves or assembling a chair, I sometimes pause to daydream. I usually work alone, but when I think about woodworking, friendships with other craftspeople often come to mind. My experience as a woodworker has not been one of isolation. Through teaching and travel, I've discovered that green woodworking is a common interest for an uncommon group of people. Much of what I've written has been learned from other woodworkers and my students. When I began to write this book, I started out by visiting several colleagues.

* * *

I met Rachel Nash Law when we were looking for someone to teach white oak basketry at Country Workshops. At the time, the Laws lived in a large frame house on the main street of the small town of Beverly, West Virginia. When I drove around the alley to the rear of the house, I saw Rachel working in an enclosed back porch. A large German shepherd greeted me with enthusiasm. So did Rachel.

Rachel was busy weaving a large, double-handled white oak basket. She smoothed several oak splits by pulling them under a knife blade pressed against a leather pad on her thigh. She worked

White oak basket artisan Rachel Nash Law

An almost-finished melon basket with two swing handles

A square to round white oak basket by Rachel Nash Law

Rachel's die used to form oak rods

quickly and expertly, and we began talking about baskets and basket makers. I soon realized that Rachel was a person who was dedicated to her work, but who also valued her friendships and enjoyed sharing her extensive knowledge of basketry.

I asked how she became involved with basketry. Rachel replied that her father, who is an inventor, made baskets as a hobby. Rachel made her first baskets in 1964 when she was nine. As a teenager, she came under the tutelage of a local basketry researcher and teacher named Catherine Candace Laird. After high school, Rachel studied at the International School of Interior Design in Washington, D.C., and at the Virginia Polytechnic Institute and State University at Blacksburg, where she received a B.S. in interior design.

In 1978, Rachel completed a one-year course in willow basketry at the *Staatliche Fachschüle für Korblechterei und Mobelbau* (National School of Basket Making) in Lichtenfels, West Germany. She also did field research and museum studies in Holland, France, England, and Scotland.

When she returned to the United States, Rachel made baskets for her livelihood. Examples of her work have appeared in numerous exhibits, including one at the Renwick Gallery at the Smithsonian Institution. More recently, Rachel had been researching basketry history, writing, and teaching.

Rachel is influenced mainly by the traditional forms, techniques, and materials of the Appalachian region. Her baskets are made in a wide range of styles. One of her specialties is the melon-shaped basket, which is started by making a frame consisting of two hoops lashed together at right angles to form the rim and handle of a basket. She often makes baskets with one or two swing handles, instead of the more common rigid handle lashed to the horizontal rim. For these baskets, the ribs are cylindrical rods, and the weavers are thin, narrow splits.

With the exception of a neatly crafted willow basket, the work that I saw was white oak. Rachel's baskets aren't fussy or precious, but everything is made very carefully with precision and a relaxed sense of expertise. I particularly liked her interpretations of Appalachian basketry, which are innovative but remain rooted to traditional forms. She also enjoys experimenting with different techniques.

From 1982 through 1986, she was writing a book on white oak basketry with a friend, Cynthia W. Taylor. They have done extensive fieldwork in central Appalachia, interviewing traditional basket makers and photographing historical collections. Published by the University of Tennessee Press in 1991, their book is titled *Appalachian White Oak Basketry*.

During their research, Rachel and Cynthia learned about certain European basket makers who came to this country and adapted oak rod in order to make willow-style baskets like those they knew from the old country. Rods are cylindrical, not flat, and are shaped with a die—a steel plate drilled with holes ranging from 1/2 to 1/8 inch in 1/64-inch increments. The plate is bolted to a sturdy bench.

To demonstrate making oak rods, Rachel first rived some white oak splits and quickly cleaned them up with a drawknife. An end of each split was rounded and chamfered to get it started through one of the larger holes in the die. For this operation, Rachel wore leather gloves and used Vise Grips to pull the oak splits through the die. The split was quickly rounded and then made smaller in diameter by pulling the oak through successively smaller holes in the die. When rods are used in a framed melon basket, the ends must be tapered with a knife.

* * *

Martha Wetherbee lashing rims and handles to miniature ash splint baskets

Martha Wetherbee is possibly the best-known basket maker working in the United States. Her reputation has been carefully earned. In the mid-1970s, Martha became interested in making reproductions of ash splint baskets originally produced by the Shakers. She investigated Shaker collections and original documents, and taught herself basketry while working at the Canterbury, New Hampshire, Shaker community. Since then, she's exhibited extensively and written about Shaker basketry for woodworking and home furnishing publications.

When I knocked on the door of her picturesque rural New Hampshire cottage, I didn't recognize the woman who welcomed me. It was Martha—but with a short, curled haircut. I had seen only photos of her with long straight hair that hid part of her face.

I followed Martha into the living room, a scene of basketry in action. Martha introduced me to her husband, Nathan Taylor, who was busy weaving one of the smallest baskets I had ever seen. This work

requires concentration, but Nathan was more than amenable to taking a break to tell me about ash splint basketry and the Martha Wetherbee story. A table in the middle of the room was piled with stacks of miniature ash splints, many less than 1/8 inch wide and only 8 to 10 inches long. As Nathan talked, Martha resumed her work, which was binding rims and handles to a group of even smaller baskets, ranging in diameter from 1 to 2-1/2 inches.

I learned that Martha doesn't personally do all the work on the baskets which carry her name. Nathan's son, Eric, works full time at basketry, and Martha and Nathan employ a number of part-time basket weavers and a man who operates their ash splint pounding machine. They also hire a bookkeeper and, because there is so much correspondence involved in the business, a part-time secretary.

The Martha Wetherbee Basket Shop is located in a two-story building that looks like a small New England carriage house. Downstairs is the produc-

An ash splint Shaker reproduction by Martha Wetherbee

Pounding brown ash splints at Martha Wetherbee's

A Shaker pattern "kitten head" basket, and the mold that it's woven over. Height to rim, 2-1/2 inches; diameter, 3-1/2 inches.

tion room, crammed with stationary power tools, molds, piles of splints, and dozens of baskets in various stages of construction. The second floor combines a salesroom with the shipping department.

While we talked, my eyes and hands wandered about the living room. As could be expected, we were surrounded by baskets. Martha and Nathan have an outstanding collection of antique Shaker baskets, as well as Shaker oval boxes. Shaker baskets are notable for meticulous craftsmanship, uniformity, and a careful sense of proportion: Martha referred to the designs as "streamlined." The Shaker baskets range from very small, fancy baskets, with splints exactly 3/32 inch wide, to full-sized work baskets. Some of the utility baskets are lined with cotton ticking. Others have wooden skids riveted to the bottoms. Martha's baskets were also on display. The only difference that I saw between the originals and Martha's reproductions was age. The old Shaker baskets take on a tawny color and show signs of wear. In contrast, new ash splint doesn't have much character.

The first thing that I learned about Shaker baskets—and Martha Wetherbee reproductions—is that they were made to exacting standards. Designs were perfected and then put into production; parts for individual baskets were completely interchangeable. To do this, the Shakers used molds, and they developed specialized tools and machinery. But unlike many other crafts that became mechanized, Shaker basketry stayed at a high level of quality. Of course, the weaving has always been handwork.

Martha Wetherbee baskets are woven with brown ash splints. Quality ash is hard to find, but she recently found a dependable source in Maine.

The first step in making an ash splint is removing the bark with a drawknife. To release the annual growth rings, the surface of the log is repeatedly pounded until the porous rings of annual earlywood fibers crush and delaminate. For years, Martha—or sometimes an assistant—pounded logs by hand with the poll of an axe or with a sledgehammer. As did the Shakers, Nathan eventually set up a mechanized trip hammer to take over this laborious job.

The pounding machine is located in a shed, which also houses a table saw and a shaper. The machine, which makes a loud, repetitious thumping noise, is an ancient-looking Bradley's Cushion Hammer, a behemoth originally made for repairing automobile bumpers. The device is a conglomeration of heavy belts, cams, and levers powered by an electric motor. The logs can be 5 to 10 inches in diameter and 6 to 10 feet long. They are suspended from a chain attached to an overhead trolley that rides on an I-beam track.

The man who works at the trip hammer, a retired truck driver named Alvin, told me that the machine was three to four times faster than pounding by hand. I'm sure this is true, *if* you could keep up the pounding continuously. Alvin said that with the machine, it could take a full day to pound and peel a good-sized ash log.

Each time a growth ring delaminates, Alvin uses a knife to cut strips, about an inch wide, which are easily lifted off the core of the log. The process continues until the splint quality degenerates; inner splints are spoiled by knots formed during early years of growth, or when the diameter gets so small that they are too curved to be usable.

Before the splints are woven into baskets, they must be dressed and cut to narrower widths. Most splints are peeled into two layers, and the best can be subdivided again to yield four full-width pieces.

Next, the splints are slit into the widths required for weaving baskets. For this process, Nathan built a slitter that uses interchangeable spacers and knives that attach to a stationary base. To use it, you simply pull the original-width splints through the slitting blades.

For uniformity, the baskets are woven over wooden molds. The actual weaving is handwork, and the weaver must pay attention at all times. The result is a basket that is perfectly symmetrical. Martha, Nathan, Eric, and several part-time employees—who work mostly at home—do the weaving.

One advantage of uniform weaving is that standard rims and handles can be produced. These heavier parts are made from white birch, a wood chosen for its light color and good bending qualities. In a nearby pavilion, Nathan has set up a small band-saw mill. Clear birch logs are sawed into flitches—slabs, with the bark edges intact—to a thickness of 1 inch. To make the larger rims, the flitches are resawed into 1/2-inch strips, then run through a half-round molder. A sander is used for final thicknessing and to taper the ends. The blanks are boiled in an open trough, then bent on jigs. After bends set, the handles and rims are given a final touch-up at a drum sander.

That evening, the living room table was cleared of basket materials and we ate take-out food from the Chinese restaurant in Sanbornton. When we finished, Martha got back to the work of lashing miniature rims and handles to her tiny baskets.

Martha and Nathan shared their ideas about what they're doing. Nathan pointed out that a division of labor is not inconsistent with practices of the Shakers. Martha said that she didn't see any reason why crafts should be priced so low as to keep the makers perpetually impoverished. Their prices in 1986 ranged from $59 to $349. She said that while their prices may appear high, they are a fraction of what's paid for comparable antiques. Martha Wetherbee's baskets are a business, much as production basketry was for the Shakers.

I mentioned that Shaker baskets were made to be used and not for collectors. Personally, the miniature baskets didn't interest me. I prefer working baskets that the Shakers produced for hauling apples and wood chips, and finer baskets for herbs, stitchery, or baked goods. Martha responded that it's hard to earn a living making the larger baskets, even with the prices that they currently ask.

Martha and Nathan also talked about new areas of interest that they're expanding into. Martha was working on two books, *The Shaker Basket Story* and *Legend of the Bushwhacker Basket*, which is about Taghkanic baskets, named for a region of eastern New York State where two large, isolated families produced baskets for sale for generations. After more than ten years of making Shaker reproductions, Martha and Nathan were developing new designs. According to Nathan, the new baskets follow Shaker traditions, as if Shaker designs had continued to evolve to the present. They also were beginning to offer workshops in ash splint basketry and were looking into selling ash basketry kits, tools, and molds.

* * *

*Henri Vaillancourt
shaving cedar with
a crooked knife*

Henri Vaillancourt has been making birchbark canoes since he was 15 years old. When I visited, in November 1985, Henri had built almost 100. His canoes are made to order and are sold by length. In 1986, the price was $300 per running foot. A typical Vaillancourt canoe is about 16 feet long. During the last few years, he has built 3 or 4 canoes a year, working five 80-hour weeks on each.

Henri lives in Greenville, New Hampshire. Finding his place was easy. He prefers to work in front of his shop, and there were two or three newly finished canoes on the lawn, plus several older canoes in a nearby lean-to.

My immediate impression was a sense of Henri's profound respect for the Indians that originally made birchbark canoes. The design is fully

A new Vaillancourt birchbark canoe made in 1985.

functional—obviously highly evolved. Visually, the shape is exciting. Henri's canoes are put together with care, skill, and attention to detail.

Henri has dedicated his adult life to the crafts of North American natives. Therefore, I was somewhat surprised to see the European influence in the design of the combined shop and residence he built. The motif of his living quarters is derivative of timber frame with masonry in-fill, and includes a bay window and a rather decorative balcony. The overall effect is pleasing and comfortable.

When I arrived, Henri was busy making railing styles for the balcony. While we talked, Henri sat on the floor, working with a crooked knife, a rasp, and sandpaper. He said that he had tried cutting the curved styles with a bow saw but was uncomfortable using it; he didn't have a vise to hold the boards. For me, it was a treat to see a crooked knife used expertly and in an unconventional application.

Henri showed me other crooked knives of various shapes, used for specific kinds of work. He has made most of his while in the bush of northern Quebec with his Cree Indian friends.

Learning to make birchbark canoes was a slow process, demanding museum research and trial and error. By the time Henri happened to see someone else building a birchbark canoe, in 1980, he had already been making them for more than 15 years.

The canoes Henri makes are identical to those produced by several Algonquian tribes who dwelled on the Penobscot River in Maine. They're not copies of any particular canoe, but combine many of the features used by this tribal group. Henri said that if his were thrown into a group of canoes from that

A detail of the Vaillancourt canoe

period, he doubts that anyone would pick them out as being unusual.

His woodworking techniques are also authentic. Henri's canoes are built like those of the early l9th century, if not pre-Columbian. The use of steel tools among the Algonquian Indians goes back about 300 years; nails have been used for more than 150 years.

The canoe ribs and planking are split and shaved cedar. The gunnels are spruce, and the braces are birch. Bark for the skin is white (paper) birch, which can be peeled in late spring or early summer. Good-quality bark doesn't delaminate; it should be about 1/8 inch thick. The lashing is spruce roots. The caulking, used at bark seams, is a mixture of rosin and lard.

Henri maintains that he's not interested in being an innovator. His goal is to make the best canoe possible. He feels that generations of canoe

makers have developed the craft to a point that is close to perfection. He believes that his recent canoes represent a high standard of quality in details and finish.

Henri is also interested in other Native American crafts and in the Indians who continue to live close to the old traditions. In addition to building canoes, Henri makes traditional Indian snowshoes and crooked knives.

In the mid-80s, Henri devoted a considerable portion of his energy to documenting remaining traditional Indian crafts and ways of living. The Trust for Native American Cultures and Crafts, which he founded, sponsored field research, including the production of videotapes of Native Americans doing traditional crafts. The Trust published Henri's first book, *Making the Attikamek Snowshoe*, which details the construction of one of the most sophisticated and beautiful Native American snowshoe

Attikamek pattern snowshoe made by Henri Vaillancourt

styles. The Trust has also produced several documentary videos, including "Building an Algonquin Birchbark Canoe" and "Beaver Tail Snowshoes." The book and video are available from The Trust for Native American Cultures and Crafts, Greenville, New Hampshire.

* * *

*Bowl carver,
furniture sculptor,
and house builder
Dirk Rosse*

When I spoke to Dirk Rosse on the phone, he said he was very busy building a speculation house. Since he hadn't been carving lately, he couldn't do a demonstration. I was welcome to visit, but he would probably be working on the "spec" house.

The Rosses live several miles out of Millbrook, New York. Their driveway passes through a short strip of eastern hardwood regrowth. The first building I noticed was a long, open-sided shed overflowing with logs, slab wood, lumber, and old machinery.

Then I saw the Rosses' house. Instinctively, I knew it was owner-built by an artist/craftsperson. The two-story structure combines white plaster work, weathered wood, and a long window wall facing a garden. The beams are uneven, and the finish on the plaster isn't slick; I found the building attractive.

Dirk and Johanna Rosse met me at the door. Johanna, who speaks with an accent—she's Dutch—offered to show me around. The entry room contains a display of craftwork for sale, mostly Dirk's wooden bowls and cutting boards, and also Johanna's hand-dyed yarns and knitted wares. I had a feeling that the display was situated near the door so that the Rosses could show visitors their crafts for sale while preserving their privacy.

Johanna Rosse knitting in the Rosse living room

As we entered the living room, Johanna explained that when Dirk originally built the house, it was supposed to become his workshop. But Dirk found that he preferred working outdoors. Johanna said that the flagstone floor and uneven trowelled plaster are not easy to clean; she keeps the house spotless.

The wall to the right of the entry is dominated by a large masonry fireplace that reminded me of American Indian adobe work from the Southwest. Except for a few antiques, which appear European, the furnishings are Dirk's work—a large, free-form swivel chair made of weathered roots or limbs, and a built-in desk, couch, and cabinets.

Johanna asked if I had eaten lunch. I had. But it would be an opportunity to talk with Dirk—maybe my one chance. Johanna served a hearty soup, freshly baked dark brown bread, cheese, and coffee.

Dirk Rosse was born in 1925, in New City, New York, but raised in Holland. The Rosses moved to Millbrook in 1952, when the area was in economic decline. They were looking for a way to live economically and self-sufficiently, in harmony with nature.

For Dirk, woodworking has never been a business, but rather a way of living quietly in the country. He enjoys working alone and said that if he had helpers, there would be too much to sell and that he wouldn't find time to work.

Dirk Rosse isn't your typical idea of a green woodworker. He doesn't do traditional woodworking. But he does work directly from logs, and his work shows great respect for raw materials. His woodworking combines a variety of influences. "I was first inspired as a child by Dutch wagon makers," he said, "some with sidelines of milking stools and wooden shovels, and by the wooden shoemakers who turned willow and poplar trees into shoes." His designs are mostly contemporary, often experimental, and usually personal. He remains interested in traditional European folk forms and American Indian artwork. Organic shapes and natural processes of growth and decay also influence his work.

Dirk gets materials from a variety of sources. Bowls are often made from lappings—rejected timber—left by commercial loggers. Tabletops might be

Walnut bowl by Dirk Rosse

crotch wood, unusable by the local sawmill. A curved cherry limb can become part of a piece of furniture. Sometimes he cuts trees from his own property or purchases a log from a neighbor. For more conventional furniture—generally made as a special order—he uses custom-sawed lumber, which is air-seasoned in the woodshed.

Some of Dirk's bowls are variations of traditional carved bowls. A few are symmetrical and conventional, but most are imaginative, biomorphic forms. Some reminded me of seedpods, and others worked with natural deformities in the wood. Black walnut, butternut, and cherry are among his favorite materials. He sometimes leaves gouge marks for a textural effect, but all his work is carefully finished.

Dirk Rosse is an energetic worker. In a good day he can make 12 small bowls. He starts by roughing the exterior of a bowl with an electric chain saw. To hollow the interior, he makes a series of cross-fiber cuts with the chain saw or a circular saw. Removing the center, and the remaining work, is done with gouges, spokeshaves, and other hand tools. When the bowls dry, he sands them by hand if the gouge marks will remain. Most of his bowls are disk-sanded—some are smooth, others are given a rippled texture. His usual finish is boiled linseed oil thinned with turpentine.

Rosse markets through craft galleries, from home, and at an occasional crafts fair. Dirk said that specialty food stores can be an excellent outlet for small items like bowls and cutting boards. His proximity to New York City and other urban centers is a definite advantage. Surprisingly, local people provide only a few sales.

Earning a living doing crafts isn't easy, even for the Rosses with their talent, energy, and experience. As the Millbrook area developed and their children grew older, their cost of living increased. Dirk said taxes have skyrocketed. Johanna pointed out that woodworking is not their sole means of income. Johanna teaches kindergarten. She also does professional knitting, besides keeping house, gardening, and doing their bookkeeping. They own a small rental cottage, which Dirk built. The speculation house was taken on for two reasons: to make money, but also because Dirk enjoys building. Dirk said he would be back to carving and making furniture once the house was finished.

* * *

John Alexander teaching ladder-back chairmaking at Country Workshops, Marshall, North Carolina

John Alexander has considered making chairs for sale, but rejected the idea because his main interest in woodworking is historic research and technical exploration. Instead of getting into production, he's decided to stay with his "cash crop"—being a lawyer, which allows the time and energy to pursue his various interests.

In 1985 I spent a three-day weekend at the Alexanders' newly renovated inner-city row house in Baltimore. John has a shop in the house but, in the year that they had lived there, he had not had time to set it up. Part of my mission was to help get the shop in order. I also wanted to photograph chairs and baskets in the Alexanders' collection and hoped to do some hands-on woodworking with John.

John started making stools and children's chairs in 1968, in a neighbor's basement workshop. His materials came from a lumberyard, and he soon acquired a lathe, band saw, and drill press. Somewhere, John read that green wood is easier to turn than dry wood. He tried it and was impressed. When a local craft group asked John to give a lec-

One of John Alexander's ladder-backs

ture on chair making, he intended to do a lathe demonstration. For safety reasons, he wasn't allowed to. At that time, he was roughing out green turning stock with a drawknife. John's wife, Joyce, suggested that he shave the chair parts to their finished dimensions. This was the beginning of John's exploration into shaving chairs from green wood.

This adventure in woodworking has been inward, as much as it has involved studying history, wood technology, and shop techniques. John says that when he visited the Sabbath Day Lake Shaker community in Maine, he "went to see the furniture, but stayed to meet the Shakers." Learning to share has been an integrated part of John's woodworking.

John is an *amateur* woodworker in the full sense of the term. While a production craftsperson needs to get work accomplished, an amateur can take extra time to think about what he's doing, to experiment, to put effort into developing and refining designs. I've had a feeling that some of John's best craft ideas come to him on his way to work and during trials.

When he discovered green woodworking, John tapped into an ancient tradition. At the time, a few isolated craftspeople were making chairs the old way, from rived wood. John studied both their methods and old chairs to find out why some chairs hold together while others loosen at the joints. John went on to conduct tests with wood scientist R. Bruce Hoadley to find out what actually happens when a chair joint is subjected to cycles of moisture and frequent mechanical stress.

Table by John Alexander; white oak basket by Louise Langsner

The shaved ladder-back chairs John makes combine traditional and contemporary elements. His objective is to make a lightweight chair without compromising strength. The craftsmanship is straightforward. In my opinion, his chairs set a new standard of comfort for this type of furniture. Over the years, John has also made a few tables with frames made from green wood, using wet/dry joinery.

John's skills as an attorney have been applied to woodworking, in that he has kept thorough notes of his investigations over the years. In 1978, John was satisfied that he knew how to make a chair and why it worked, and he turned his notes into a book, *Make a Chair From a Tree* (originally published in 1978 by The Taunton Press, reprinted in 1994 by The Astragal Press). The next summer, John began teaching chair making at Country Workshops.

John has also investigated paneled chests that were made of green wood during the 17th century. The construction is similar to a timber-framed building. The components—posts, rails, and panels—are rived from wet red oak. The principles of green woodworking, such as grain orientation and differential shrinkage, play an important role in design and layout, but the technology is applied differently. The mortise-and-tenon joints are rectilinear, and the parts are flat, with right angles. After the stock is rived, most of the work is done with chisels and hand planes.

It took us most of Saturday to organize John's workshop. On Sunday morning, we were joined by Carl Swensson, a highly skilled craftsperson whose main interest is Japanese woodworking. John and Carl sharpened tools while I built a cardboard mock-up of a simplified 17th-century chest.

John's green wood had been air-drying since the move to the new house, so it wasn't particularly wet when we got to it. Working the oak was tedious, but we did manage to split out and plane a set of posts and eight rails. We used grooving planes to make housings for the side panels.

I had hoped to see an assembled chest before leaving. But on Monday I was busy taking photographs, and John decided to work on a series of test joints. John explained that experimenting with tools and joint theory was just as important to him as getting the chest together.

*   *   *

*Dave Sawyer
riving hickory
for Windsor
spindles*

Dave Sawyer lives with his wife, Susan, and their three young children in a rambling frame house on the outskirts of East Calais, Vermont. When I arrived, I was greeted as a member of the family. We exchanged warm hugs and news about our families.

During my visit, Dave offered his full services. One request that I had was to photograph the bending of a back rail for a continuous-arm Windsor chair. Dave agreed to split out the wood and shave the rail so that I could observe the full process.

Dave's shop used to be the living room. It's just the right size for one person, plus an occasional helper. Two people working full time would be a crowd. You don't see an overwhelming tool collection in Dave's shop. Along one wall is a massive German workbench. A few tools—a drawknife, two or three spokeshaves, and an antique Spofford brace—hang on hooks above one window. Other tools are conveniently tucked away. Dave's lathe—a sturdy cast iron machine, perhaps 50 years old—is in front of the window of the adjacent wall. To the

Dave Sawyer made this high chair for his son, Jonathan.

right is a tin wood stove. In addition to heating the shop, the stove is used to boil water for the wood steamer and to dry wood on a rack suspended from the ceiling. Dave also has a band saw. The most prominent piece of equipment is a long-legged shaving horse that matches Dave's physique. The boys' Lionel trains often occupy a third of the floor space. To the left of the doorway is a small desk, which serves as an office.

Out on the back porch, Dave had a hickory sapling, saved for Windsor back rails. Within a few minutes he split out several billets and chose one for the continuous-arm Windsor. I noted that David's movements are very economical. He tends to do exactly what's necessary, and nothing more. When he uses a drawknife, every stroke counts. You can tell that Dave enjoys his work. There is a sense

A Dave Sawyer continuous-arm Windsor finished with barn red milk paint. (Collection John and Joyce Alexander.)

of satisfaction as each piece is completed. When a tool is slightly dull, Dave stops to sharpen it. Above his workbench there's a clipping from an advertisement: "At Ford, quality is job number one."

I had seen Dave's "bending show" several times previously, but the demonstration was still a treat. After the hickory rail was drawknifed to specifications, it was steamed for 30 minutes. Dave's steamer is similar to the one described in chapter 9. (In fact, Dave built it when he was teaching at Country Workshops.) During the steaming, he had

just enough time to rive and shave a set of Windsor back spindles.

When the steaming was complete, Dave clamped the bending jig to the workbench. He also got out a selection of pegs and wedges and two small C-clamps. Dave put on clean cotton gloves for handling the hot wood, then centered the rail on the bending jig. A wedge was placed between the rail and a peg just above the apex of the curve. He limbered the back section of the rail by exercising it several times. Working quickly, one half was pegged and wedged, and the other half was done a few moments later. Each elbow bend was limbered, then clamped to the bending form. The performance took less than two minutes.

After the back rail was bent, Dave decided to do some lathe-work. His Windsor turnings are a precise and carefully proportioned version of the late-18th-century tapered baluster style. He uses cardboard patterns and adjustable calipers to insure uniformity within a set. Dave had finished three legs when Susan called us for supper. The quality of the turnings was first rate, but Dave is not a particularly fast turner. A production turner would have been finished. That evening, Dave returned to the shop to turn the fourth leg, three stretchers, and two arm stumps.

At 4:30 the next morning, the Sawyer household woke up in unison when one youngster began crying loudly. Eventually, the disturbance ebbed, but I didn't linger in bed long, because the Sawyers' unheated upstairs doesn't invite it. I quickly dressed and repaired to the workshop.

Dave and the boys had been in the shop "since about 5:00 so Susan could sleep." Dave was busy sharpening tools, getting ready to shape a chair seat, and the boys were quietly playing with their postcard collections. Dave said that these early mornings are common, and that once Susan gets up he often takes a pre-breakfast nap.

Dave Sawyer's formal education includes a degree from MIT in mechanical engineering. He worked for IBM for a while but "retired" when he was 28.

Sawyer dabbled with restoring old cars, then spent half a year in Bolivia with the Peace Corps Craft Program. He then worked for some Amish farmers in Pennsylvania. There in Lancaster County, he met Daniel O'Hagan, a craftsperson and homesteader who readily shared his philosophy of simple living and introduced Dave to working wood with hand tools. In 1969, Dave returned to his native New England and began working wood full time.

In the '70s, Dave Sawyer's main production item was a greenwood ladder-back chair with three slats and posts with a back bend at the middle rung under the seat. The design is a copy of a chair he once saw in a store. He also made "mule ear" chairs, which were a cross between a shaved stick chair and a Windsor. In addition, he made bentwood hayforks, using a design from Daniel O'Hagan, who learned how from a Mennonite neighbor. And Dave produced a firewood carrier which he designed. The firewood carrier is the project at the end of chapter 9.

Once Dave started making Windsor chairs, he lost interest in his earlier work. When I visited the Sawyers, there wasn't a ladder-back chair in the house. They did have an interesting selection of Windsors, including one or two old ones and several made by chairmaker friends. (Dave estimated that there were several dozen craftspeople making traditional Windsors.) My favorite was a child's Windsor, which Dave made. When he finished making this one, Susan Sawyer said that Dave had arrived as a Windsor chair maker. It is a masterpiece.

Dave's approach to craft and design is to carefully work out all the details on paper and then get to work. To figure the compound boring angles for his Windsors, he uses some "trickiometry" from his engineering background. Refinements are made as necessary; he's not particularly interested in new designs. But although Dave's Windsors are traditional, he doesn't make reproductions of a specific antique chair. His approach has been to combine outstanding features of different chairs within a particular style.

Sawyer makes a full line of Windsors, all on special order. Dave markets exclusively by direct sales to customers. He's generally booked with orders six months to a year in advance. When I visited, Dave was making a set of eight chairs, in three styles, for a customer in Colorado.

Dave's standard line of Windsor chairs includes side chairs (bowback and fan-back); arm chairs (continuous-arm, sack-back, comb-back); settees in any length; and high chairs for children. Options include two styles of turnings, carved knuckles, carved scroll ears, rockers, and a braced back. In 1985, Sawyer charged from $330 for a basic bowback to $715 for a settee for two. Most of Dave's Windsors are painted with milk paint, but he also makes oil finished chairs with butternut seats, cherry turnings, and oak backs.

Each chair comes with a lifetime guarantee to outlast either Dave or the original purchaser. The guarantee is simple: "If anything goes wrong, I'll fix it."

*   *   *

Making a Shaving Horse

Most of the classes at Country Workshops require a shaving horse for each student. Having built over a dozen, I've designed a shaving horse that works well and is fairly simple to make. This shaving horse holds up under heavy use, and it can be partially broken down for storage or transporting. The design is similar to one that I used at the shop of my Swiss cooperage teacher, Ruedi Kohler.

Before discussing the construction, I want to emphasize that you can easily make modifications to suit your needs and your physical size. The exact dimensions of most parts are not particularly important. You should be able to use locally available materials, including some I haven't suggested. Finally, if you want to make a different type of shaving horse—for instance, one using a rustic hewed beam, a three-legged version, or an English-style bodger's horse—go ahead. Fine woodworking can be done using any variation.

A shaving horse consists of two units, the swinging arm and the bench. The arm has a head at the upper end and a treadle at the lower end (I've made up these names; they're not official). The bench includes an angled bridge, supported by a riser. You'll need to make four legs, two large wedges (used to secure the head and treadle), and four small wedges (driven into the leg tenons). You'll also need six 2-inch wood screws, a bolt or rod for the pivot, and white or yellow glue.

Before building the bench, you should be familiar with boring and tenoning methods, covered in chapter 8, and wet/dry joinery, discussed in chapter 10.

In the plans, the plank used for the bench is 60 inches long. This is a bit short. I prefer a full 6-foot bench, because I occasionally sit near the end to work on long materials. Also, extra length at the seat end is useful for carpentry or as a support for a horizontal three-peg-and-wedge holding system used for boring or mortise work. You may want to make a shorter bench to fit in a small shop or for transporting. The practical minimum length is about 54 inches. Shorten the seat section, not the bridge.

The bench, bridge, and riser can be made of any strong, lightweight wood. Yellow pine, Douglas fir, and ash are excellent. Most lumberyards sell yellow pine for utility construction, such as basement stairways. A nominal 2×10 is actually 1-1/2 inches thick and 9-1/2 inches wide. Perfect.

I used to make the large mortises for the swinging arm by boring and chopping, but I now use an electric saber saw for this job. Here's how to do it the traditional way: Begin the large mortise for the swinging arm by lightly indenting the mortise outline with a 1- to 2-inch chisel. (This prevents grain tear-out when you begin boring.) Then bore two rows of 1-inch holes within the mortise area, staying 1/8 inch inside the outlines. The holes can overlap. To avoid grain tear-out as the auger exits, bore from both sides of the plank. Use a chisel and a hammer or mallet to clean up the mortise. Precise chisel-work isn't required since the mortise is oversized by 1/4 inch.

Use the 1-inch auger to bore the leg mortises. To prevent tear-out, bore from both sides of the plank or into a scrap board. The end splay angle and the side cant angle are both 13° from vertical. The bench is narrowed to 7 inches at the center so that you don't have to spread your legs around the full plank to reach the treadle. This detail is optional. The cutouts can be made with a bow saw, saber saw, or by hewing followed by shaving with a drawknife.

The bridge and riser are made from nominal 2×6 lumber. You may want to lengthen the riser by an inch or so—particularly if you're long bodied, or if the bench has a shortened seat.

One important dimension is the length of working surface on the bridge when the head is lowered. This should be at least 4 inches; otherwise, the piece being shaved tends to loosen by pushing upward against the head. (This happens because the front edge of the bridge acts as a fulcrum when pressure is put on the unsupported end of the wood being shaved.) Basket makers who work long, thin material should consider lengthening the bridge an additional 6 to 10 inches.

The pivot hole in the side of the bridge is 9/16 inch in diameter. To avoid tear-out, bore the hole from both sides of the plank before chopping out the arm

"Dumb head" shaving horse. On this one, the seat could be a little longer.

mortise. Saw a 15° wedge from the lower front edge of the bridge; the base of the wedge is 3/4 inch thick. The step and cutout at the working end of the bridge is an option for drawknife work using a breast bib.

The legs are made from a ring-porous hardwood, such as oak, ash, hickory, or locust. You can also turn the legs at a lathe, using just about any hardwood. With 20-inch legs, the bench will be 18 inches high. This is an average bench height. If you're taller than 6 feet, lengthen the legs about 2 inches. You can always cut the legs down. The leg taper shown in the plans is an aesthetic option. Legs can also be straight cylinders or octagonal in section.

If you shape the legs from green wood, oversize the tenons by 1/16 inch. The legs must be dry—5 to 10 percent m.c. when the tenons are fitted. The tenons are 2 inches long and 1 inch in diameter. Saw 1-1/2-inch-deep kerfs for the tenon wedges oriented tangentially to the growth rings.

The four 1-inch-wide wedges for the leg tenons can be shaved from dry rived stock or sawed from a 1-inch board. They are 2 inches long, tapering in thickness from 3/16 to 1/16 inch.

The swinging arm, head, and larger wedges are often oak, but any hard species is suitable. Where we live, wood of the specified thickness is available at local sawmills. If you can't find something this thick, you can laminate stock thicknesses planed to 3/4 to 7/8 inch. Use a double thickness for the arm and a triple thickness for the head. The thickness of your material may require altering the width of the mortises through the bench and bridge.

Use a sliding bevel and a square to lay out the tenons at each end of the arm. The tenons are made with a hand ripsaw and a crosscut saw. Use a 9/16-inch auger to bore the bolt pivot holes in the arm. The offset hole locations, 1-1/2 inches from the near edge, cause the arm to open automatically when the foot treadle is released.

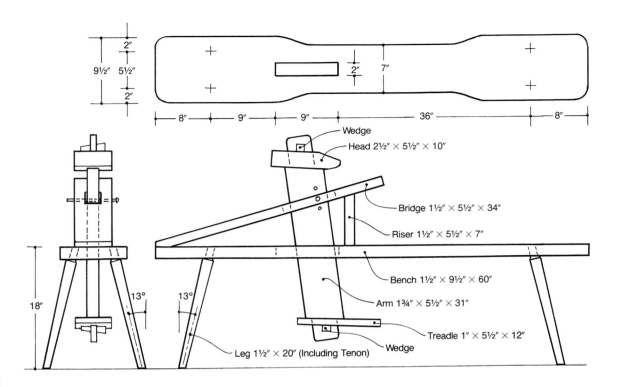

Plans for a dumb head shaving horse

Wedge

Head 2½″ × 5½″ × 10″

Bridge 1½″ × 5½″ × 34″

Riser 1½″ × 5½″ × 7″

Bench 1½″ × 9½″ × 60″

Arm 1¾″ × 5½″ × 31″

Treadle 1″ × 5½″ × 12″

Wedge

Leg 1½″ × 20″ (Including Tenon)

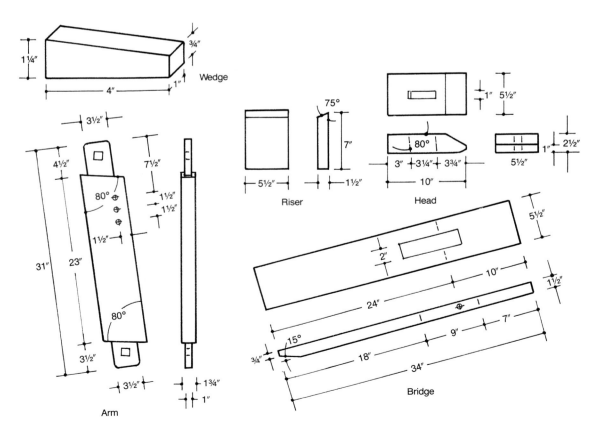

Wedge

Riser

Head

Arm

Bridge

*Off-center
pivot holes
cause the
head to open
automatically.*

The wedge mortises in the tenons are 1 inch wide. Make the mortises 1-1/8 inches high at the entrance, tapering to 1 inch at the exit. Locate the base of the mortises 1/16 inch under the outer plane of the head and treadle.

Bore and chop the mortise through the head before shaping it. The lower holding surface of the head is slightly rounded to increase the friction area when the head is closed. The wedges that secure the head and treadle are sawed from 1-inch-thick hardwood. Make them 4 inches long, with the height tapering from 1-1/4 inches to 3/4 inch.

For the pivot, I like a $1/2 \times 8$-inch bolt, with the threaded end hacksawed off.

Assembly is straightforward. The bridge and riser are attached to the bench plank with countersunk wood screws. Use two screws at each joint. The bridge and riser add considerable stiffness to the bench. The legs should be oriented so that the wedge slots are perpendicular to the length of the bench.

Put glue on the tenons, and hammer the legs home against the tenon shoulders. Glue the wedges and hammer them tightly into the slots. Use a chisel to remove extra wedge material and the protruding ends of the tenons. Leveling the bench is described at the end of chapter 10.

When assembling the arm, don't force the head or treadle over the tenons. If the fit is tight, locate the problem and fix it. Forcing will cause these parts to split. For the same reason, the wedges should be slightly loose at the sides of the tenons. I use an ordinary hammer to tighten or loosen these removable wedges.

Bark Seating

For the seating of a post-and-rung chair or stool, I prefer to use the inner bark (or *bast*) from hickory. It's a natural fiber from trees that grow in our woods. But more important, hickory bast is beautiful to look at and very strong. If it isn't abused, a hickory bast seat should last for decades.

Other natural seating materials that are attractive include white oak splits and ash splints, rush, and sea grass. Usable bark species that I haven't tried include pecan, sycamore, black willow, paper birch, linden, and tulip poplar. The Shakers' chairs used dyed cotton tapes—quite handsome. Basketry supply shops sell some of these materials—but never bark—as well as split reed and paper fibers. Leather and rawhide can also be used, in strips or as a single sheet.

Hickory bark peels most easily in late spring and the first month of summer. Bast can be peeled from any type of hickory, and a similar material can be taken from pecan. I prefer to work with a tree between 6 and 10 inches in diameter. Bark from larger trees can be used, but the tough outer bark is hard to remove. Try to find a hickory that's relatively free of knots below the major branches. Tall trees with minimal taper yield the most bast.

You can peel bark from a felled tree in the woods, but I prefer to drag poles home. Peeling hickory is time consuming; working a 30-foot pole can take most of a day. Twenty feet is an average length. Don't crosscut the sapling into shorter lengths. Weaving is much faster when you don't have to make many splices. The leftover wood is often good for chair parts; anything else becomes first-rate firewood.

It's best to work in a shady area, where intense sun won't dry out the bast too quickly. Your workshop will do if you don't mind getting the floor wet.

Dave Sawyer has convinced me that it's worth rigging up some props to support hickory poles horizontally at chest height before peeling them. You can use a pair of sawhorses, but leaning over a pole for hours at a time is hard on the back.

First shave off the hard outer bark with a drawknife. You'll be amazed at how tough this stuff is, especially toward the butt end. It comes off in chunks. When you begin to shave into the pulpy inner bark, you'll notice a netlike pattern of interlocking veins. As you shave deeper, the veins get thinner; if you take a knife and cut straight across the veins, you'll see that they form a "V" in cross section. The objective is to stop shaving just before the bottom of the V disappears. The remaining bast should be close to the right thickness for peeling and weaving into a chair seat.

When you shave the pulpy material, a residue tends to stick to the edge of your drawknife. To get this stuff off, dip the drawknife into a bucket of water as it accumulates. Be sure that your drawknife is sharp, or the bast will tear instead of cut.

If you have to leave a shaved pole—for lunch or overnight—first drench it with water. Use a hose or a dripping-wet scrub brush. Then cover the pole with wet burlap or tarps.

Once the outer bark is removed, rotate the sapling so that the nicest, clearest section faces up. Cut the strips using a sharp knife with a short blade. The pen blade in a good pocketknife works well. Make a knife cut the full length of the pole, and as straight as possible. Cut all the way down to the wood. Try to avoid making two passes. If you wander off the original cut, which is easy due to the crisscross pattern of the fibers, you'll get frazzled edges.

Make a second knife cut parallel to the first one and about 3/4 inch to one side. (If you want very narrow strips, cut them later from the original strip with scissors or small tin snips.) Start peeling from either end of the pole. To get started, slip your knife blade under the bark. You may discover that the bast is too thick because you didn't shave off enough pulpy material. If so, do some more shaving but, for now, confine it to the area where you're peeling the first strip.

To a certain extent, thin bast strips are actually stronger than thick ones, which tend to be brittle. Thin strips also tie and weave much more easily than thicker strips. A thickness of 1/16 inch is about right.

With some hickory bast, you can subdivide a strip into two layers for a double yield. The tech-

Peeling hickory bast. First, the outer bark is removed with a drawknife.

nique is the same as that used in making white oak basketry splits, described in chapter 6. Our hickory bast won't do this, but Dave Sawyer says he often subdivides hickory bast collected in New England. Try it.

After peeling a strip, coil it up with the inner side facing out and tie it with a bark scrap or string. If you're not going to use the bast immediately, prevent mold formation by hanging coils in a drafty shelter to dry. Dry coils can be kept indefinitely. Just soak the bark for about 30 minutes and it's ready to work with again.

Before peeling more strips, observe the exposed edge of the bark where the first strip was peeled. This is a good time to do some more shaving to the correct thickness.

As you continue peeling, some strips will run into knots. You can include knots less than 1/4 inch across in the strip. Small holes don't appreciably weaken the bast. Because a pole tapers, some strips will terminate before reaching the tip end. With foresight, it's often possible to end strips at a large knot or other defect.

Weaving

Weaving chair seating with hickory bast is basically the same as using other strip materials. One difference is that hickory bast can be tied with a sheet bend knot. (See illustration on page 170.) Less flexible seating is spliced by cutting two pairs of notches on the sides of the material, then tying the overlaps with strong thread. Cotton tape is spliced with an overlap tacked by a few stitches. The chair frame should be finished—with something like tung oil—before weaving the seat.

Hickory bark is used with the original inner surface facing down. Wrap a few loops of seating material around a back post. Then begin the **warp**, a series of parallel windings. Wrap the bark around the front and back rungs. Don't wrap the warp too tightly around the rungs; as the seat is woven, it will tighten up. Make any necessary splices on the seat bottom.

The warp is complete when you've filled in the back and the front rungs. If you're seating a chair with a trapezoid-shaped frame, there will be two narrow triangles left open at each side. These "ears" are woven later, as the last step.

Wrap the end of the warp under the back post and then up over the adjacent side rung. For a neat job, use a scissors to reduce the width of the material where it wraps around the post.

Continue by weaving the **weft** across the warp. Bark and similar materials are usually woven in a herringbone pattern. With Shaker tape, weave a checkerboard—a herringbone will come out too loose.

To begin a herringbone weave, cross over two warps, then go under two warps and repeat. When you start the second round, cross over one warp, then under two, over two, and so forth. For the third round, go under two, then over two. Round four begins under one, then over two. This process repeats beginning with round five.

The bottom side of the seat can be woven in a large checkerboard pattern. For the first two rounds, start over two, then under two. For rounds three and four, start under two, then over two.

As you weave, be sure to pull the weft tightly against previous rounds—it will tend to pooch outward in the middle, but this must be corrected. The last few rounds are a challenge to weave as the construction will be very tight. A kitchen butter knife is useful for guiding and tucking the bark under the warp.

Use small scraps of bast to fill in the side triangles. They will stiffen and stay in place after the bark dries.

When the weft is complete, weave the beginning of the warp—the end originally wrapped around the back post—into the bottom of the seat.

Hickory bark is dull gray brown when new and takes on a beautiful patina with use.

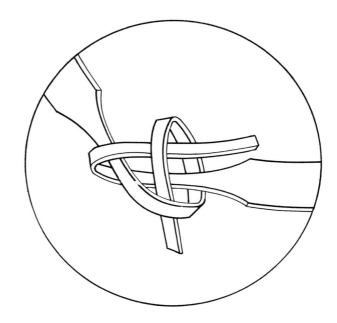

Sheet bend or weaver's knot, used to splice hickory bast seating

Beginning the warp. The tied-off end is woven into the bottom of the seat after the weft is complete. This stool is rectangular. On a chair, the seat is a trapezoid. The warp leaves two small open triangles at the sides. These are filled in after weaving the weft.

Weaving the weft with a herringbone pattern

The bottom side, which has all the splices, can be woven in a checkerboard pattern. This one is over three and under three.

My daughter, Ami, in a white oak hamper made by Darry Wood

A TOPICAL BIBLIOGRAPHY

Cultural Perspectives

Adney, Edward Tappan, and Howard I. Chapelle. *The Bark Canoes and Skin Boats of North America.* 1964. Reprint. Washington, D.C.: Smithsonian Institution Press, 1983.

Andrews, Edward Demming, and Faith Andrews. *Shaker Furniture.* 1937. Reprint. New York: Dover Publications, Inc., 1964.

Davidson, Susan J. "Kerf-Bent Boxes." *Fine Woodworking* (1980) May/ June. Reprinted in Fine *Woodworking on Bending Wood.* Newtown, Conn.: Taunton Press, 1985.

Eaton, Allen H. *Handicrafts of the Southern Highlands.* New York: Russel Sage Foundation, 1937.

Edlin, Herbert L. *Woodland Crafts in Britain.* 1949. Reprint. Devon, England: David & Charles, 1974.

Gilbertson, Donald E., and James F. Richards, Jr. *A Treasury of Norwegian Folk Art in America.* Callaway, Minn.: Maplelag, 1975.

Jenkins, J. Geraint. *Traditional Country Craftsmen.* London: Routledge and Kegan Paul, 1965.

Kilby, Kenneth. *The Cooper and His Trade.* London: John Baker, 1971.

Langsner, Drew, and Louise Langsner. *Handmade.* New York: Harmony Books,1974.

Sloane, Eric. *Diary of an Early American Boy.* New York: Funk & Wagnalls, 1965.

_____. *A Reverence for Wood.* New York: Funk & Wagnalls, 1965.

Sprigg, June. *Shaker Design.* New York: W. W. Norton & Company in association with the Whitney Museum of Art, 1986.

Stewart, Hillary. *Cedar.* Vancouver: Douglas & McIntyre, 1934.

Sturt, George. *The Wheelwright's Shop.* 1923. Reprint. Cambridge: Cambridge University Press, 1974.

Viires, A. *Woodworking in Estonia.* Jerusalem, Israel: Israel Program for Scientific Translations; Washington: Smithsonian Institution Press and the National Science Foundation, 1969.

Wetherbee, Martha, and Nathan Taylor. *Legend of the Bushwhacker Basket.* Sanbornton, N.H.: Martha Wetherbee Basket Shop, 1986.

Wigginton, Eliot, ed. *The Foxfire Book - Vol. 1.* New York: Doubleday & Company, 1972.

Williams, Christopher. *Craftsmen of Necessity.* New York: Random House, 1974.

Greenwood Crafts (How-To Books)

Abbott, Mike. *Green Woodwork.* East Sussex, England: The Guild of Master Craftsmen, 1989.

Alexander, John D., Jr. *Make a Chair From a Tree.* Newtown, Conn.: Taunton Press, 1978. Reprint: Mendham, New Jersey: The Astragal Press, 1994.

Brown, John. *Welsh Stick Chairs.* Fishguard, Wales: Abercastle Publications, 1990 (and) Fresno, California: Linden Publishing.

Dunbar, Michael. *Make a Windsor Chair with Michael Dunbar.* Newtown, Conn.: Taunton Press, 1984.

Hart, Carol, and Dan Hart. *Natural Basketry.* New York: Watson-Guptill Pùblications, 1978.

Langsner, Drew. *Country Woodcraft.* Emmaus, Pa.: Rodale Press, 1978.

_____. "Making Wooden Buckets." *Fine Woodworking* (1983) May/June. Reprinted in *Fine Woodworking on Bending Wood.* Newtown, Conn.: Taunton Press, 1985.

Law, Rachel Nash, and Cynthia W. Taylor. *Appalachian White Oak Basketry.* Knoxville, Tennessee: University of Tennessee Press, 1991.

Mastelli, Rick. "Green Woodworking." *Fine Woodworking* (1982) Mar./ Apr. Reprinted in *Fine Woodworking on Chairs and Beds.* Newtown, Conn.: Taunton Press, 1986.

Sundqvist, Wille. *Swedish Carving Techniques.* Newtown, Connecticut: The Taunton Press, 1990.

Underhill, Roy. *The Woodwright's Shop.* Chapel Hill, N.C.: University of North Carolina Press, 1981.

Vaillancourt, Henri. *Making the Attikamek Snowshoe.* Greenville, N.H.: The Trust for Native American Cultures and Crafts, 1987.

Wright, Dorothy. *Baskets and Basketry.* 1954. Devon, England: David & Charles, 1974.

Green Woodworking Materials

Brown, William H. *The Conversion and Seasoning of Wood.* Fresno: California: Linden Publishing, 1989.

Dent, D. Douglas. *Professional Timber Falling* Beaverton, Oreg.: D. Douglas Dent, 1974.

Gordon, J. E. *The New Science of Strong Materials.* New York: Walker and Company, 1968.

Hart, Carol. "Basket Willow." *Threads* (1986) Feb./Mar.

Hoadley, R. Bruce. *Understanding Wood.* Newtown, Conn.: Taunton Press, 1980.

_____. *Identifying Wood.* Newtown, Connecticut: The Taunton Press, 1990.

Little, Elbert L. *The Audubon Society Field Guide to North American Trees—Eastern Region.* New York: Alfred A. Knopf, 1980.

_____. *The Audubon Society Field Guide to North American Trees— Western Region.* New York: Alfred A. Knopf, 1980.

U.S. Department of Agriculture. *Properties, Selection, and Suitability of Woods for Woodworking.* Madison, Wis.: Forest Products Laboratory, n.d.

U.S. Department of Agriculture. *Silvics of Forest Trees of the United States.* Washington, D.C.: Government Printing Office, 1965. (Order Agriculture Handbook No. 271.)

Green Woodworking Tools

Goodman, W. L. *The History of Woodworking Tools.* London: G. Bell and Sons, 1962.

Hall, Walter. *Barnacle Parp's Chain Saw Guide.* Emmaus, Pa.: Rodale Press, 1977.

Lambert, F. *Tools and Devices for Coppice Crafts.* London: Evans Broth ers, 1957.

Miller, Warren. *Crosscut Saw Manual.* Washington, D.C.: U.S. Depart ment of Agriculture, 1977. (Available for $1 from Government Printing Office, Documents Department, Washington, D.C. 20402-9235; order stock no. 001-001-00434-1.)

Salaman, R. A. *Dictionary of Woodworking Tools.* Reprint—Newtown, Connecticut; The Taunton Press, 1990.

Sloane, Eric. *A Museum of Early American Tools.* New York: Funk & Wagnalls, 1964.

Weygers, Alexander G. *The Making of Tools.* New York: Van Nostrand Reinhold Company, 1973.

Green Woodworking Videos

Beaver Tail Snowshoes. Greenville, New Hampshire: The Trust for Native American Cultures and Crafts.

Building an Algonquin Birchbark Canoe. Greenville, New Hampshire: The Trust for Native American Cultures and Crafts.

Carving Swedish Woodenware. Newtown, Connecticut: The Taunton Press.

Chairmaker. Whitesburg, Kentucky: Appalshop.

Hand Carved. Whitesburg, Kentucky: Appalshop.

Swiss Cooperage: Two Days in the Workshop of Reudi Kohler. Marshall, North Carolina: Country Workshops.

The Cooper's Craft. Williamsburg, Virginia: Colonial Williamsburg.

Traditional New England Basketmaking. Brookfield, Connecticut: Brookfield Craft Center.

INDEX

Page numbers in *italic* indicate tables. Page numbers in **boldface** indicate illustrations and photographs.